Human Well-Being Research and Policy Making

Series Editor

M. Joseph Sirgy
Department of Marketing
Virginia Polytechnic Institute & State University
Blacksburg, USA

This series includes policy-focused books on the role of the public and private sectors in advancing quality of life and well-being. It creates a dialogue between well-being scholars and public policy makers. Well-being theory, research and practice are essentially interdisciplinary in nature and embrace contributions from all disciplines within the social sciences. With the exception of leading economists, the policy relevant contributions of social scientists are widely scattered and lack the coherence and integration needed to more effectively inform the actions of policy makers. Contributions in the series focus on one more of the following four aspects of well-being and public policy:

- Discussions of the public policy and well-being focused on particular nations and worldwide regions
- Discussions of the public policy and well-being in specialized sectors of policy making such as health, education, work, social welfare, housing, transportation, use of leisure time
- Discussions of public policy and well-being associated with particular population groups such as women, children and youth, the aged, persons with disabilities and vulnerable populations
- Special topics in well-being and public policy such as technology and well-being, terrorism and well-being, infrastructure and well-being.

This series was initiated, in part, through funds provided by the Halloran Philanthropies of West Conshohocken, Pennsylvania, USA. The commitment of the Halloran Philanthropies is to "inspire, innovate and accelerate sustainable social interventions that promote human well-being." The series editors and Springer acknowledge Harry Halloran, Tony Carr and Audrey Selian for their contributions in helping to make the series a reality.

Lorena Ronda • Garazi Azanza
Alazne Mujika-Alberdi
Editors

Leisure and Human Development

Navigating Socio-cultural Landscapes

Springer

Editors
Lorena Ronda
University of Deusto
Bilbao, Spain

Garazi Azanza
University of Deusto
Bilbao, Spain

Alazne Mujika-Alberdi
University of Deusto
Bilbao, Spain

ISSN 2522-5367 ISSN 2522-5375 (electronic)

ISBN 978-3-031-90777-7 ISBN 978-3-031-90778-4 (eBook)
https://doi.org/10.1007/978-3-031-90778-4

Human Well-Being Research and Policy Making

This Springer imprint is published by the registered company Springer Nature Switzerland AG
The registered company address is: Gewerbestrasse 11, 6330 Cham, Switzerland

Introduction

Leisure is a universal human experience, yet its meanings and implications can vary significantly across sociocultural contexts. In recent decades, researchers and scholars have increasingly turned their attention to leisure as more than just a temporary escape from daily routines. Leisure, in its multiple forms, holds the potential to enrich human lives, foster social connections, and contribute greatly to personal and collective development. The chapters compiled in this book build upon this growing body of knowledge, exploring the intersection of leisure and human development across different settings, cultures, and generations.

The idea of leisure as a mere pursuit of pleasure has evolved to include broader dimensions of well-being and social responsibility. This book, a collaborative effort of authors from various disciplines, reflects this shift, examining leisure not only as a time of rest or recreation but also as a vehicle for emotional, intellectual, and social growth. The chapters in this book reflect this evolving understanding of leisure, offering a comprehensive exploration of its influence on human development across diverse settings, cultures, and generations. While each chapter examines a distinct facet of leisure, several consistent themes emerge. These key narratives illustrate leisure's role in personal well-being, intergenerational connections, social engagement, and policy implications.

Leisure as a Pathway to Well-being and Personal Development

A central narrative throughout this book is the recognition of leisure as a vital contributor to overall well-being and personal growth. Far from being a simple break from the demands of daily life, leisure is an essential resource for emotional and intellectual fulfillment. The opening chapter, Chapter 1: Leisure in Prisons: Fostering Well-being, Social Reintegration, and Personal Development, explores the role of leisure in the prison environment, emphasizing its significance for well-being and social reintegration. It also addresses misconceptions about prison life, particularly regarding leisure opportunities. Chapter 2: Exploring Our Leisure Time: Youth

Participation and Participatory Action Research investigates leisure, free time, and work–life balance from the perspective of young people, focusing on their routines and the impact of leisure on their personal, social, and family development. This theme is further developed in Chapter 3: The Quest for Emotion in Leisure and Its Contributions to Human Development, where leisure is shown to offer opportunities for emotional release and self-reflection, particularly for higher education teachers. These educators share personal experiences, illustrating how leisure activities contribute to their emotional well-being beyond professional demands. Chapter 4: The Effectiveness of Leisure Education Programs for the Elderly examines how leisure activities promote successful aging, emphasizing leisure education programs that foster competence, satisfaction, and autonomy among older adults. Through these discussions, leisure emerges not as a luxury but as a crucial component of human life, contributing to individuals' overall well-being.

Leisure as a Bridge Between Generations

A second narrative centers on leisure's unique ability to bridge generational divides, fostering stronger intergenerational relationships. As societies face demographic shifts and the challenges of maintaining familial bonds, leisure emerges as a vital tool in connecting different age groups. Chapter 5: Shared Digital Leisure Between Grandparents and Grandchildren Before, During, and After the Pandemic offers a timely exploration of how digital leisure has been used to sustain relationships between grandparents and grandchildren, particularly during the isolation of the COVID-19 pandemic. Digital platforms, such as video games and social media, have provided an innovative way to maintain these connections, allowing families to bridge the physical distance imposed by the pandemic. In tandem with this, Chapter 6: Intergenerational Environmental Leisure Practices in Post-Pandemic Times highlights the role of nature-based leisure in bringing generations together. Shared outdoor activities, like hiking or environmental conservation, offer meaningful experiences that strengthen family ties and promote understanding across generations. These chapters underscore the potential of leisure to serve as a conduit for connection and mutual understanding in an increasingly fragmented world.

The Social and Cultural Dimensions of Leisure

Leisure's role in shaping social and cultural identities forms the third key narrative of this book. Cultural institutions and events serve as focal points for communal engagement, offering spaces for the exchange of ideas and the celebration of shared heritage. Chapter 7: The Role and Future of Art Fair Audiences: Visitors' Perspectives on the Hybrid Art Fair in Madrid explores the often-overlooked social impact of art fairs, focusing on audience perceptions and how these events, despite their commercial nature, can serve as vital spaces for education and cultural engagement. The chapter illustrates how these fairs serve as vibrant spaces for socialization and cultural enrichment, highlighting their role in fostering deeper community engagement. Similarly, Chapter 8: The Significance of Ethnographic Museums in the BizkaiKOA Network explores how museums work to engage local communities, using exhibitions and technology to enhance participation and collaboration. Chapter 9: The Impact of Platform Economy on Spanish Sun and Beach Destinations explores the growing influence of the platform economy on tourism, specifically focusing on the rise of free tours and their contribution to overcrowding in popular sun and beach destinations, offering valuable insights for sustainable tourism management and policy development. These chapters reinforce how leisure activities, rooted in cultural and social contexts, not only reflect but also shape collective identities and social dynamics.

Leisure, Policy, and Social Change

Finally, the book addresses the intersection of leisure, public policy, and social activism, highlighting how leisure practices are influenced by larger economic and political forces. Chapter 10: National Plans of Well Living (WLNP) and their Influence on the Ecuadorian Cultural Sector offers a critical examination of how Ecuador's National Plans for Good Living have shaped the country's cultural and leisure sectors. The chapter questions the effectiveness of these plans in fostering growth and promoting entrepreneurial opportunities, illustrating the crucial role that public policy plays in shaping leisure opportunities. Expanding on the theme of leisure as a tool for social change, Chapter 11: Restorative Leisure in Citizen Participation introduces the concept of restorative leisure in the context of community resistance movements in Colombia. Here, leisure is presented as a means of fostering community solidarity, empowering rural and urban collectives to resist socio-political marginalization. These chapters collectively highlight the broader societal impacts of leisure, positioning it not only as a personal or recreational pursuit but also as a vehicle for social resilience and political empowerment.

Taken together, the narratives woven throughout this volume demonstrate that leisure is far more than a superficial activity. It is a profound, multidimensional force that shapes individual well-being, bridges generational divides, fosters cultural engagement, and promotes social change. By examining these themes, this book offers a comprehensive understanding of leisure's role in human development, providing valuable insights for academics, practitioners, and policymakers alike. Leisure emerges not just as a luxury or a pastime but as an essential aspect of human life, with the potential to enrich individuals, build communities, and contribute to a more equitable and sustainable world. As you read through these chapters, we invite you to reflect on your own experiences with leisure and consider how they contribute to your well-being, relationships, and understanding of the world.

Universidad de Deusto, Bilbao, Spain
Lorena Ronda
Garazi Azanza
Alazne Mujika-Alberdi

Contents

1 **Leisure in Prisons: Fostering Well-Being, Social Reintegration, and Personal Development** ... 1
Marcos Javier Barriga Ávila and Diego Galán-Casado

2 **Exploring Our Leisure Time: Youth Participation and Participatory Action Research** ... 21
Victoria Pérez de Guzmán, Teresa Rebolledo-Gámez, and Rocío Rodríguez-Casado

3 **The Quest for Emotion in Leisure and Its Contributions to Human Development: Experiences of Higher Education Teachers** ... 37
Luz Angela Ardila Gutiérrez, Aurora Madariaga Ortuzar, and Tony Honorato

4 **The Effectiveness of Leisure Education Programs for the Elderly: A Systematic Review** ... 57
Luciana Pereira de Moura Carneiro, Aurora Madariaga Ortuzar, Maria Begoña Garcia Zapirain, and Ricardo Ricci Uvinha

5 **Shared Digital Leisure Between Grandparents and Grandchildren Before, During, and After the Pandemic** ... 73
María Ángeles Valdemoros San Emeterio, Rosa Ana Alonso Ruiz, Luis Corral Fernández, and Álvaro Eraña Martínez

6 **Intergenerational Environmental Leisure Practices in Post-Pandemic Times** ... 91
José Manuel Martínez-Villar, Rosa Ana Alonso Ruiz, María Ángeles Valdemoros San Emeterio, Cristina Medrano Pascual, and Magdalena Sáenz de Jubera

7 The Role and Future of Art Fair Audiences: Visitors' Perspectives on the Hybrid Art Fair in Madrid 111
Alexandra Zagrebelnaia

8 The Significance of Ethnographic Museums in the BizkaiKOA Network 131
Sofía Moreno-Domínguez

9 The Impact of Platform Economy on Spanish Sun and Beach Destinations: A Case Study of Free Tours 149
Asunción Fernández-Villarán, Jorge Rivera-García, and Ricardo Pastor-Ruiz

10 National Plans of Well Living (WLNP) and their Influence on the Ecuadorian Cultural Sector 169
Carlos Alberto Buitrón Mendizábal

11 Restorative Leisure in Citizen Participation: An Alternative for the Promotion of Social Demands 187
Santiago Forero-Lloreda, Johanna E. Zarate, and Camilo A. Angulo

Chapter 1
Leisure in Prisons: Fostering Well-Being, Social Reintegration, and Personal Development

Marcos Javier Barriga Ávila and Diego Galán-Casado

Abstract This chapter describes leisure as a social and human concept within the prison context. Research highlights that physical and psychological well-being, happiness, recognition of others, and companionship are values to be fostered through constructive time use during incarceration. Misconceptions often lead outsiders to assume that incarcerated individuals have abundant time for self-reflection or unlimited opportunities for activities such as studying, developing professional skills, working, attending workshops, or participating in socio-educational programs. However, time for recreation or rest—often enjoyed through voluntary sports, cultural, artistic, or social activities—differs from mandatory efforts aimed at accessing the labour market to cover expenses such as housing, childcare, food, or travel. Academic processes designed to improve educational levels for greater well-being and personal fulfilment, along with training programs linked to labour market skills, also play a crucial role. Within this framework, education and leisure are key tools for social reintegration, focusing on preventing recidivism and reducing returns to correctional facilities. Leisure activities, in particular, enable individuals to develop as competent and socially responsible citizens, capable of leading fulfilling lives both during and after incarceration. These efforts aim to promote resilience and ensure successful reintegration into society.

M. J. Barriga Ávila (✉)
Escuela Internacional de Doctorado de la UNED, (EIDUNED), Madrid, Spain
e-mail: mjbarriga@psi.uned.es

D. Galán-Casado
Universidad Nacional de Educación a Distancia (UNED), Madrid, Spain
e-mail: diegog@edu.uned.es

L. Ronda et al. (eds.), *Leisure and Human Development*, Human Well-Being Research and Policy Making, https://doi.org/10.1007/978-3-031-90778-4_1

1.1 Introduction

The Royal Spanish Academy defines *leisure* ("ocio") as "the cessation of work, inaction, or total omission of activity". However, it also encompasses other meanings that emphasize fun, relaxation, and free time. We will consider these leisure activities as a fundamental pillar of life, providing a time and space free from work or other obligations. Moreover, in today's world, personal and professional development is increasingly tied to our ability to navigate digital technologies. Research by organizations such as the University of Santiago de Compostela (2024) highlights the significance of leisure studies. The human right to internet access (Anzures Gurría, 2021) reflects our aspirations for a more equitable and just society. Yet, our daily lives are marked by a growing concern: excessive connectivity or hyper-connectivity (Puolakka & Suomela, 2023; Ryan & Bradshaw, 2019; SIPS, 2023). This phenomenon permeates our personal, familial, and social interactions.

In the context of prisons, leisure, cultural, recreational, artistic, or sports-related activities that constitute leisure time should be valued as a right and a fundamental need, rather than a privilege. Following Manuel Cuenca (2016) leisure occupies an undeniable space of influences and effects on human and economic development generating a market full of activities offered and demanded. Etymologically (p. 26) leisure comes from the word *otium* and *skholé*. The first term comes from Latin and the second from Greek. Both were intended for activities proper to "free citizens" who perform "specifically human functions". Already in antiquity, Aristotle differentiated two types of leisure: the one dedicated to rest and amusement and the other more focused on human fulfilment. The first has to do with play, so necessary that it frees and relieves us from the fatigue and effort of work. The leisure that focuses on human fulfilment is that in which pleasure is obtained through "knowledge or moral beauty". It has to do with intellectual activity and the enjoyment that comes from studying, science, philosophy, and art. Paul Lafargue in 1880, in his Marxist philosophical approach of repudiation towards the alienation produced by work as an enslaving phenomenon, resorted to the idea of the necessary emancipation from a work that oppresses and prevents people from ceasing to be slaves (Alvarado, 2013, p. 57). Today (Cuenca, 2016, p. 29) offers the idea of exercising healthy participatory citizenship and seeing subjects as emancipated citizens point to the reality of *ocio valioso* ("valuable leisure"). Leisure benefits should be considered from research developed in the last few years. Physical, emotional, social, behavioural, and cognitive benefits, among others (p. 31). Time management and motivation towards those activities that can enrich human development and welfare (Ryff, 1995) are the basis for participation in activities of different orders a priori, but whose purpose is the greater social reintegration of the person deprived of liberty as well as the acquisition of skills and knowledge (Baranger et al., 2018).

Our argument is grounded in the notion that acts of moral goodness evoke positive emotions. This principle underpins what McClelland (1989, p. 126) terms "normal behaviour", and leisure activities in prison are pivotal in fostering such conduct. As Julio Martínez (2023) observes in the editorial of issue eight of the magazine

Desde el Páramo, published by Villanubla Penitentiary (Valladolid), cultural and artistic pursuits within prison settings can mitigate feelings of sorrow, stimulate aspirations, and counteract vulgarity and scorn. This issue, dedicated to cultural and artistic leisure activities, includes a section exploring the multifaceted concept of *culture* and delving into its significance in five specific contexts (p. 2):"

- "Nurturing of human potential".
- "Body of scientific, literary and artistic knowledge of a person, people or era".
- "The result or effect of cultivating human knowledge and sharpening, through exercise, the intellectual faculties".
- "What man learns, as opposed to what is acquired by biological inheritance".
- "Set of technological and artistic traditions that characterize the first studies of mankind".

Osuna (2019, 2022) reminded us through her ethnographic studies of women deprived of liberty how the "prison stigma" is manifested and the space of second chances that prison represents. The issue of gender in prison contexts (Marcoux, 2020; Yuen et al., 2012) will be important in terms of the analysis of time management. Inmate stigma reduction and re-entry through education are researched by Galán-Casado et al. (2024a).

Aspects such as child rearing, receiving family visits, care work, continue to be very present in the cultural schemes of society. These realities are represented in Galán-Casado et al. (2024b). Añaños et al. (2021) highlight how women decide to invest time in studying to obtain a better stay in prison as a way of abstracting from an unsatisfactory environment. They are aware of the future benefits for a post-release life project. According to Callejo and Viedma (2008) cited in Ostiny and Farley (2022) having a life project planned for release is essential in motivating them to invest time and effort by conducting studies on the inmates participating in their research on the state of higher education in European Penitentiary Institutions. This goal is also integrated into leisure activities (Yuen et al., *Op. cit*). There are aspects related to life post incarceration. Evans et al. (2017) include in the "self-stigma" that each subject, due to deficient self-esteem, faces multiple barriers of different kinds that prevent adequate social reintegration. They allude to the term "empowerment". This is fundamental in human motivation towards the change to which leisure must contribute (Enjuanes et al., 2024, p. 91). Some actors share their views on the change that can occur while in prison from their experiences in the auditorium of the Faculty of Law of the UNED in a seminar held as a debate. The speakers are male prisoners from the *Educational Therapeutic Unit* (*UTE*) of the Madrid VII Penitentiary Centre (Estremera). Among the audience there are inmates of the speakers who intervene generating a very rich shared conversation (Canal UNED, 7 de mayo de 2024).

1.2 Leisure Time in Prison: Motivational Factors, Well-Being, and Learning Opportunities

Intrinsic motivation is considered a prototype of autonomous behaviours, which means that such behaviours are performed with a full sense of willingness, volition, and choice (e.g. Deci & Ryan, 2000; Ryan & Deci, 2000b). When intrinsically motivated, people experience an internal perceived locus of causality for their behaviour (de Charms, 1968)—that is, they feel initiative and ownership in acting (Deci & Ryan, 1991). As already noted, the play of children is a characteristic example of intrinsically motivated behaviour, and many leisure-time pursuits of adults also fall into that category (Deci & Ryan, 2016, p. 12).

Emotions could be "natural incentive indicators" that provide interest in activities that generate well-being and foster intrinsic motivation (Ryan & Deci, 2000a). Being imbued with the rewarding task could be considered a vital preliminary step for human transformation or at least for true social reintegration of inmates.

For Vuk and Doležal (2019), the uses of time from the point of view of "misconduct" or delinquent behaviour can be predicted according to certain personal factors and habits performed at leisure. They point to a relationship between inmate behaviour and time use from the point of view of criminology. Based on a literature review to document their research, which is not abundant, they suggest the following hypothesis: "Idleness has a negative impact on inmates' behaviour and well-being, while participation in structured, prosocial activities fosters positive behavioural and emotional outcomes" (p. 6). They conducted a study based on the Bureau of Justice Statistics' 2002 *Survey of Inmates in Local Jails* (2002 SILJ). From the results, interesting insights are gleaned regarding passivity in leisure time, as in the case of television viewing during certain hours and the avoidance of "misconduct" as the inmate escapes from the reality of confinement in which they find themselves. As a sanction for the infraction of rules, the penitentiary regime makes inmates spend a long time in isolation in their cells. The study uses "misconduct" as a dependent variable with seven categories of rule violations and dichotomous responses by inmates—"Yes" or "No"—stating whether they have been punished or blamed for these acts since their admission (Camp et al., 2003):

- *Any misconduct*: Having been disciplined or convicted of any rule violation.
- *Violent conduct*: Physical assault on another inmate, physical assault on staff/professionals, and possession of a weapon.
- *Property offenses*: Possession of stolen property; possession of unauthorized item, object or substance; and contraband.
- *Drugs*: Possession, consumption, and/or trafficking of drugs. Possession, consumption, or sale of alcohol.
- *Matters of responsibility*: Disobeying staff instructions; escape or attempted escape; and being in an unmarked place.
- *Security*: Serious infractions such as delays in work activity, hunger strikes, arson, riots, etc.; minor infractions such as disturbing the order and operation of

facilities, inappropriate language, jokes (*horseplay*), failure to comply with health regulations, etc.
- *Other infractions* not included above.

As independent variables to measure "inmate time use" operationalized as daily, weekly, or monthly activities:

- *Visits* (in the past month)
- *Phone calls* made in the past week
- Weekly activities:
  - *Work activity* (inside and outside the facility)
  - *Religious activities* ("prayer" or "meditation")
- Daily activities:
  - *Recreation* (arts, crafts, playing cards, etc.)
  - *Reading*
  - *Watching TV*
  - *Physical activity*
  - *Time in cell*

The study results highlight that, according to numerous studies in social psychology, spending time with others is a good way to counteract the negative effects of loneliness, such as low self-esteem, lack of self-control, and feelings of not belonging.

The underlying concept of programming designed by entities responsible for the educational management and individual treatment plans of inmates in penitentiary centres is to establish a connection between leisure activities and the promotion of inmate well-being (Chiclana et al., 2021; Chiclana, 2023).

Barriga et al. (2024) will establish an analysis around "time management, self-managed time, and emancipation" (p. 109). Specifically, self-management becomes more complex in contexts of risk and social exclusion. There are social realities that play a leading role in the process of living a "self-managed time": socio-labour difficulties, homelessness, and severe mental disorders. Other situations that affect psychological well-being are depressive episodes, anxiety, and low self-esteem.

In Enjuanes et al.'s (2024) study, the aim was to explore the benefits of "educational leisure" through an exploratory study conducted in a Catalan penitentiary. After selecting a sample of 243 inmates from a total of 700 who had leisure activities included in their individual treatment plans, 76 participants were excluded due to a lack of knowledge or potential mental health issues that could bias the results (p. 91). Finally, 60 inmates participated. One of the most significant findings relates to the motivations driving participation in workshops and activities (Table 1.1). Data was collected from a 2-month questionnaire designed specifically for this research project (p. 91).

Mansfield et al. (2020) conducted a comprehensive review of studies examining the link between effective well-being and purposeful leisure activities. Their analysis, drawing from various disciplines and perspectives, critically evaluates existing

Table 1.1 Motivations for participation in leisure activities

Motivations	Sport activities	Cultural activities	In general
"Occupying free time"	72.7%	65.9%	60.6%
"Adapt to the dynamics of the centre"	50%	50%	45.4%
"Spending time constructively"	63.6%	65.9%	58.3%
"Learning new ways of doing things"	52.3%	65.9%	50%
"Meet new people"	47.7%	45.5%	42.4%
"Other motivations"	18.2%	136%	12.8%

research. Notably, one study within their review (p. 6) delves into the impact of leisure practices in coastal environments on individuals' well-being. They highlight the significance of "multiculturalism, the intersection of place/space, ethnicity, and socioeconomic status" (Wheaton et al., 2019). Consequently, well-being, as a human concept and experience, is greatly influenced by its context, including geographical location, cultural practices, and experiences of exclusion. A leisure education program developed by the University of Oregon in the 1990s for young male offenders highlighted that "race, ethnicity, and religion significantly influence leisure attitudes, interests, limitations and learning styles" (Robertson, 2002, p. 146). Incarcerated individuals at Monterroso Penitentiary in Lugo, Spain, reported that their participation in a leisure project helped them develop both relational skills and self-control. While the project fostered a strong sense of identity and group cohesion, its primary goal of empowering participants to sustain their actions over time was not fully realized: *"participación proyectiva"* (Barba-Núñez et al., 2021, p. 93).

Emotional self-regulation and positive and negative effects are two of the seven levels that make up human motivation and personality functioning according to Kuhl et al. (2021). Berry and Hansen (1996) examined the relationship between positive and negative effects and social interaction, defining "High Positive Affect" (*High PA*) as a state characterized by enthusiasm, confidence, and a sense of excitement. "High Negative Affect" (*High NA*) on the other hand, is associated with fear, guilt, and nervousness.

Grounded in Self-Determination Theory (Deci & Ryan, 2000), Van der Kaap-Deeder et al. (2017) examined the construct of *perceived choice* among inmates in seven Flemish prisons. Their study revealed four distinct categories of perceived choice, highlighting the complex ways in which individuals experience agency within institutional environments. "Perceived afforded choice". "The degree to which participants experienced afforded choice was assessed in eight domains, categorized into four general types" (p. 571):

1. "Daytime activities": *education, work, and leisure.*
2. "Social networking": *visits, or making phone calls.*
3. "Physical needs": *eating, taking a shower.*
4. "Religious beliefs": *religion/spirituality.*

Their findings indicate a positive correlation between perceived choice, valuation of choice, satisfaction with autonomy, and quality of life.

Table 1.2 Levels of motivation

Level 1: Elementary perception and motor control	"Habits form based on connections between two elementary cognitive processes of object (stimulus) recognition and intuitive behaviour (response) control"
Level 2: Global arousal and activation	"One of the adaptive functions of global emotions may be seen in the increase of degrees of behavioural freedom (p. 6)"
Level 3: Specific affect (positive and negative affect/reward and punishment)	"This third level of motivation relates to specific emotions in terms of positive or negative affect that is reliably associated with an object (p. 7)"
Level 4: Stress-dependent regression	"Achievement motivation was replaced by competing incentives such as getting involved in favourite activities or well-established habits (playing computer games or soccer, or checking social media, etc.). Notably, this distraction by attractive incentives or habits frequently happened when children experienced school as very demanding and stressful"
Level 5: Motives (affiliation, achievement, power, autonomy)	"Motives belong to the three high-level (neocortical) processes that are to inhibit low-level habits and affective impulses unless they are compatible with one's current needs, goals, intentions and circumspect self-concerns"
Level 6: Complex cognition (concepts/constructs and associative semantic networks)	"The greater robustness of intuitive judgment compared to analytical judgment in dealing with missing information can be explained by a feature of parallel processing that has been called "graceful degradation"
Level 7: Self-management (self-control and self-regulation)	"Self-regulatory strategies include a variety of competencies, for example, the ability to plan ahead when and how to work for school, the ability to motivate oneself when faced with unpleasant tasks and calm oneself down when confronted with anxiety and stress"

As proposed by Kuhl et al. (2021), the seven levels of human motivation are as follows (Table 1.2):

Note. These seven levels of motivation arise from the work developed by Julius Kuhl during his stay as a tutor of German students in a secondary school ("high school"). His goal was to improve grades because parents considered their children to be "lazy and idle".

Enjuanes et al. (2024) label the activities undertaken by inmates as "educational leisure". The inclusion of educational components in leisure pursuits suggests the occurrence of learning. Aligned with the broader understanding of social learning (Andrews & Bonta, 2010; Firmansyah & Saepuloh, 2022), it can be inferred that all human activities, including leisure, foster social learning. However, self-determined learning driven by strong intrinsic or extrinsic incentives, coupled with self-efficacy beliefs, will be key factors (McClelland, 1989; Bandura, 1997; Ryan & Deci, 2000a). As highlighted by Nie (2016), Albert Bandura defined self-efficacy as "beliefs in one's capabilities to organize and execute the courses of action required to produce given attainments" (p. 261), a definition that has been widely adopted in the field.

It is essential to differentiate between programs and services promoting leisure activities in various forms (cultural, artistic, sports, tourism, etc.) and the formal nature of education offered at all levels and modalities (occupational workshops, employment services courses, basic or higher education) by regional educational administrations, the National Distance Education University, (*UNED*) which has an agreement with the General Secretariat of Penitentiary Institutions, and other entities such as employment services.

Leisure activities are not merely recreational but also pedagogical in nature. This realization has led to a demand for qualified professionals in the field of education to design and implement programs within penitentiary settings. Research, including the work of Morata et al. (2019), has highlighted the role of educational leisure in promoting civic values and social skills. For incarcerated individuals, participation in such programs has been associated with reduced recidivism and improved mental health (Galán-Casado, 2021, pp. 10–11; García-Bravo, 2023).

Ryff (1989) proposes the following dimensions of well-being (p. 1072). It is argued that leisure time activities within penitentiary institutions should prioritize the development and attainment of these dimensions. Ryff relied on various psychological well-being measurement instruments to correlate these six dimensions in a sample of "321 men and women" divided into three age groups: young, middle-aged, and older (Table 1.3). Young individuals were selected from educational institutions, while adults belonged to community and civic organizations.

1.3 Leisure and Incarceration: A Study of Prisoners' Experiences

Within the context of correctional facilities, Muth and Müller (2023) examined the impact of physical activity on the health and well-being of incarcerated individuals. Their study, involving 568 inmates across 12 German prisons, revealed a substantial decline in inmate's perceived "general health" ($d=0.52$) and "life satisfaction" ($d=0.84$), as well as an increase in reported health problems ($d=0.71$). However, inmates participating in sports activities demonstrated a significantly slower rate of health deterioration.

Martin-González et al. (2019) employed narrative techniques, including the "Life History" (Bolívar et al., 2001), in an ethnographic study to investigate the role of Physical and Sports Activities (AFD) as a deterrent against substance use among incarcerated women: "La drogadicción es un recurso recurrente en prisión, habida cuenta del hastío que provoca la rutina y la ansiedad de ver pasar los días y los años encerrada, lejos de la familia" (p. 154). In English: "Drug addiction is a recurring resource in prison, given the boredom caused by routine and the anxiety of seeing the days and years pass while being locked away, far from family" [author's translation]. The researchers utilized Creative Analytical Practices ("Prácticas Analíticas Creativas") (p. 151) to explore the potential of AFD in this context. The study highlighted the need to further investigate potential benefits of sports participation, such as improved interpersonal relationships (Martín-González et al., 2018). Within the context of correctional facilities, the construction of a healthy identity and the adoption of structured, healthy routines are crucial. However, it is important to acknowledge the unique challenges and barriers that may exist within these settings, which

Table 1.3 Ryff's dimensions of psychological well-being (1989, p. 1072)

Dimension	High scorer	Low scorer
Self-acceptance	A high score on this dimension will indicate a positive attitude towards oneself, acknowledging and accepting diverse aspects such as strengths and weaknesses, and having positive feelings about past experiences	A low score indicates feelings of self-dissatisfaction, disappointment with past experiences, concern about personal qualities, and a desire to be someone different
Positive relations with others	Maintaining warm, affectionate, and trusting relationships with others, caring about the well-being of others, the ability to feel empathy, affection, and intimacy, and understanding the reciprocity of human relationships	Conversely, a low score on this dimension will make it difficult to form close, trusting relationships, hinder the expression of affection and trust, and reduce concern for others. It is associated with feelings of isolation, frustration, and a reluctance to make personal sacrifices to maintain interpersonal relationships
Autonomy	The individual is self-determined and independent. They can resist social pressures, regulate their behaviour, and evaluate themselves according to their own criteria	Low scorer: "Is concerned about the expectations and evaluations of others; relies on judgments of others to make important decisions. Conforms to social pressures to think and act in certain ways"
Environmental mastery	To have a sense of mastery and competence in managing the environment; control a complex set of external activities; effectively take advantage of opportunities in the environment; choose or create contexts appropriate to his or her personal needs and values	To have difficulty managing day-to-day affairs; feels unable to change or improve the context around him; unaware of opportunities around him; lacks a sense of control over the outside world
Purpose in life	Experiences a sense of purpose, with clear goals and a sense of direction. They believe that their past and present experiences have meaning and establish goals and objectives to guide their future	Lacks a sense of direction in life; has few goals or objectives, does not see a purpose in past experiences; does not hold beliefs that give life meaning or significance
Personal growth	Has a feeling of continued development; sees self as growing and expanding; is open to new experiences; has sense of realizing his or her potential; sees improvement in self and behavior over time; is changing in ways that reflect more self-knowledge and effectiveness	Has a sense of personal stagnation; lacks sense of improvement or expansion over time; feels bored and uninterested with life; feels unable to develop new attitudes or behaviours

could hinder the implementation of physical activity programs (Martínez-Merino et al., 2018, p. 47). These barriers may be related to the difficulty of scheduling physical activities around daily routines, such as work. Family visits are another factor that must be considered. This means that "institutional" barriers can limit the amount of time available for physical activity. A variety of factors, including socioeconomic considerations and institutional barriers, can influence inmates' ability to participate in physical activities. Inmates may be hesitant to give up their prison jobs due to financial concerns, and physical limitations within the prison environment, such as the distance between housing units and security protocols, can restrict access to physical activity areas. Additionally, the potential for engaging in unhealthy behaviours during physical activity time must be considered.

A systematic review by De-Juanas et al. (2022) examined the link between time management and social outcomes: "Leisure-based strategies for substance use prevention". Experiences during childhood and adolescence play a crucial role in developing the skills necessary for "the creation of shared spaces and norms that allow for a certain degree of control over the social order" (Morata et al., 2019, p. 108).

Kuhl et al. (2021) posit a seven-level model of motivation that shapes human behaviour, decision-making, and emotionality. They argue that emotional development is significantly influenced by the fulfilment or deprivation of needs experienced in early life. Focus on immediate social environments and how negative emotions impact vulnerable youth. These "natural incentives" that are emotions can guide human behaviour (McClelland, 1989, p. 126).

Over time, the ways in which we interact socially evolve (Carstensen et al., 1999). Consequently, interpersonal relationships strengthened in prison leisure activities gain increased significance. As Granovetter (1973) and later Sandstrom and Dunn (2014) suggest, interpersonal relationships with acquaintances or so-called weak ties, beyond the more intimate circle of family, close friends, or spouses, are a catalyst for a better, more fulfilling, healthier life and for experiencing genuine well-being (Carstensen, 1992; Berkman, 1995; Berry & Hansen, 1996; Moreton et al., 2023).

> Thus, twice a year, the teaching team organized extracurricular outings that, as excursions, allowed their students to participate in various leisure activities: visits to museums, attendance at events in civic centres, outdoor trips, etc. One of the things that surprised me the most when I participated in the excursions was the absolute anonymity of the women, the total invisibility of the penitentiary stigma. They walked the streets, ate in restaurants, looked at shop windows... There was nothing about them that could suggest they were imprisoned. Nobody had any way of knowing we came from the prison, and they often joked about it. On the first outing, we passed a group of young police officers, and several of them greeted the officers very politely. A few meters later, they started laughing and said, "If only they knew!" Outside the prison, the deeply discrediting attribute of being incarcerated was suspended (Osuna, 2022, p. 106) [author's translation].

As explaine the author, "for providing categorization, the school director classified these activities within the framework of scheduled or therapeutic outings, as defined in Article 114 of the Penitentiary Regulations. These outings are designed to promote "reintegration into society":[1]

---

[1] *"Salidas programadas o terapéuticas"* are regarded in Penitenciary Regulations by *"Real Decreto 190/1996, de 9 de febrero, por el que se aprueba el Reglamento Penitenciario"* (BOE, de 15 de febrero de 1996).

> The regulations adopt a broad conception of treatment, which not only includes therapeutic and assistance activities but also formative, educational, labour, sociocultural, recreational, and sports activities, conceiving the reintegration of inmates as a process of comprehensive personal development, equipping them with effective tools for their own emancipation. (BOE, 1996, p. 6) [author's translation]

In an upcoming study by Martínez-García et al. (2020), Galician adolescents report a direct link between their emotional connection to nature and the amount of time they spend in natural settings. These findings suggest that exposure to natural environments, as opposed to urban settings characterized by screen time, is associated with improved emotional outcomes among the 683 Secondary and Baccalaureate students from Pontevedra who participated in the study. To assess these relationships, an ad hoc questionnaire was administered. Notably, two factors stood out: location and gender. First, residing in rural environments was associated with more leisure time spent in nature and a stronger emotional connection. Girls demonstrated a significantly higher level of this connection than boys. Notably, the study concludes that leisure time is not merely a passive activity but can be shaped through education and its "environmental and ecological dimensions" (Cuenca, 2014, p. 169) that can foster the development of interests, values, and hobbies that contribute to rewarding experiences in natural settings, promoting an emotional connection with the environment (p. 12). Consequently, it is reasonable to conclude that the physical settings in which leisure activities occur play a crucial role in promoting social development and human well-being by fostering deeper emotional connections.

The prison population is characterized by a broad age range, with individuals entering at a young age and potentially aging within the institution. While the maximum age is variable and dependent on factors beyond the scope of this research, it is clear that prison is an environment where individuals can spend a significant portion of their lives. There is a coexistence of individuals from different generational cohorts. Educational programs facilitate mutual support among peers of different ages in the development of their learning projects (Pérez Yuste, 2023). According to Carstensen (1992), as individuals evolve and develop throughout their lives, their valuation and experience of interpersonal relationships undergo significant changes. In a similar vein, leisure activities may also exhibit this phenomenon (Martín-González et al., 2018).

> As people move through life, they become increasingly aware that time is, in some sense "running out." More social contacts feel superficial—trivial—in contrast to the ever-deepening ties of existing close relationships. It becomes increasingly important to make the "right" choice, not to waste time on gradually diminishing future payoffs. Increasingly, emotionally meaningful goals are pursued (Carstensen et al., 1999, p. 165).

Leisure time spent with family is highly enriching, providing valuable educational experiences and strengthening familial bonds. Hernández-Prados and Álvarez-Muñoz (2022) argue that family leisure time, whether spent at home, travelling, or engaging in cultural activities, plays a significant role in the transmission of values such as respect, happiness, tolerance, empathy, and trust. Therefore, in the penitentiary context, it has been considered that furloughs and visits are crucial for the well-being of inmates.

Valdemoros et al. (2022) conducted a study, using questionnaires and focus groups, to explore how children aged 6–12 in northern Spain spend time with their grandparents. The study focused on primary school students. The study, conducted in the northern Spanish regions of Cantabria, Vizcaya, Guipúzcoa, Álava, La Rioja, Navarra, Burgos, and Palencia, involved a sample of 1080 participants and focused on the leisure and cultural dimensions of their experiences. The concept presented in this research, focusing on shared leisure activities between grandparents and grandchildren and their positive impacts, holds significant promise for application within penitentiary contexts, where incarcerated individuals with diverse age ranges maintain familial ties. The phenomenon of early childbearing can sometimes give rise to the unexpected circumstance of relatively young individuals serving prison sentences as grandparents (Paynter et al., 2023). In many instances, both foster homes within public child protection systems and grandparents have stepped in to provide care for children whose parents are incarcerated (Mapson, 2013). These variables warrant analysis utilizing official statistical datasets (Ministerio del Interior, 2024).

The temporal dimension of "successful aging" is a focal point of contemporary discourse, driven by prevailing demographic trends (Monteagudo, 2020). Galán-Casado and Del-Pozo-Serrano (2019) emphasize the centrality of *envejecimiento activo* ("active aging") within the objectives of their prison-based "respect module" programs.

To address the unique needs of its aging inmate population, Valencia Penitentiary has taken a significant step. A Memory Unit has been created within Valencia Penitentiary (Spain) specifically for inmates aged 65 and over. The Penitentiary Studies Journal (Revista de Estudios Penitenciarios), issue 258, provides an in-depth account of the development of this program, which was prompted by the requests and concerns of older inmates experiencing memory difficulties. This innovative initiative highlights the growing recognition of the specific needs of older adults within the correctional system.

> The regulations adopt a broad conception of treatment, which not only Elderly individuals have greater and more flexible learning capacities than previously assumed. This learning ability makes stimulation and the teaching of strategies to develop cognitive skills effective. Studies clearly show that people who engage more in intellectual activities during their leisure time suffer less cognitive decline. Furthermore, it is known that the higher the level of education received, the better memory is preserved, and being mentally active throughout life serves as a protective factor against cognitive deterioration (Fernández Orviz, 2015, p. 31) [author's translation].

In closing this chapter, it is intriguing and relevant to the integration of research on leisure and its role in fostering education and well-being within penitentiary settings to note its relatively limited presence[2] in theoretical examinations for certain professional positions. The July 28, 2021, Resolution of the Secretary of State for

[2] The term 'relatively' is used because the complete composition of the programs detailed in the annexes pertaining to each competitive process and specialization within different professional categories remains undetermined.

Table 1.4 Program contents according to speciality

Professional group M2 First exercise: 50 questions	Specialty: *Social education and educational sciences* 6 positions Destinations sites: Jaén, A Lama, Valencia, Archidona, Ocaña, Puerto de Santa María	Issue 3. Lifelong learning and leisure time. The interconnection of work, leisure, and education. Linkages among adult education, lifelong learning, and sociocultural animation Issue 5. Leisure and free time. the characteristics of leisure in contemporary society. Implications for social development. Social needs and demands. Pedagogical criteria for socio-educational and leisure activities. Attention to groups with special difficulties: technical aids, adjustment of programs, techniques, and activities
Professional group M1 First exercise: 80 questions	Specialty: Early childhood education 1 position Destination site: Palma de Mallorca	Issue 4. Current models of early childhood education and care in Spain: *Model* bases of early childhood education. Globalized teaching. Creative teaching. Individualized teaching. Socialized teaching. Standardized teaching. Assistance modalities. Leisure and free time. Possibilities of future development Issue 5. The material as a didactic resource. The organization of spaces as a didactic resource. The organization of time as a didactic resource. Growth and physical development of the child from 0 to 6 years: Phases and their characteristics. Significant disorders and implication in the teaching-learning process. Instruments for the follow-up of growth and physical development. b) Primary childhood needs Issue 11. Organization, programming, and implementation of extracurricular, leisure, and recreational activities for children: Application of programming to play-based activities. Management of material resources: organization, utilization, and maintenance of materials and toys. Space planning. Activity implementation: practical challenges

Public Function, which "calls for a competitive process for internal promotion to fixed-term labour personnel" (Ministerio de Hacienda y Función Pública), exemplifies this. The significance accorded to "leisure" is explicitly summarized in Table 1.4.

Childhood is a formative period for learning to structure one's time, with leisure pursuits playing a significant role in shaping lifelong habits and well-being (Moreno-Carmona et al., 2020). The focus on childhood development in the existing literature, while informative, is less applicable to the adult prison population, underscoring the need for theoretical frameworks that specifically address the unique challenges and opportunities presented by incarceration. This call seeks to fill a position for an early "Childhood Educator" in a penitentiary establishment, specifically in the Mothers' Unit, to provide educational care for young children. Additionally, it is essential to support the development of parenting skills among incarcerated mothers (Schultz et al., 2000).

The deontological framework of Social Education establishes professionalism as a fundamental value, emphasizing the importance of a consistent educational purpose throughout all professional endeavours (Pantoja et al., 2018, p. 164). It is a profession of an educational nature that constitutes a right of citizenship and "generates educational contexts and mediating and formative actions" (CGCCES, 2007, p. 12).

The "M2" professional exam in Social Work, administered on January 23, 2022, includes a question (number 22) that requires candidates to distinguish between the exclusive competences of the Spanish State, as stipulated in Article 149 of the Constitution, and other powers. *The promotion of sports and leisure activities*, as defined in option "a", falls under the 19th competence of Article 148.1, which can be transferred to the Autonomous Communities. Consequently, it cannot be classified as an exclusive competence of the central government.

The "M2" assessment for internal promotion in the field of "Social Education and Educational Sciences" places considerable emphasis on candidates' understanding of leisure, as evidenced by the multiple questions devoted to this topic:

- *Question 14: Identify the most appropriate term to describe a range of activities designed to facilitate the social participation of individuals with disabilities during their non-working hours. The options provided are* "integrated leisure", "inclusive leisure" (correct), and "adapted leisure".
- *Question 15: Identify the term that best defines leisure activities characterized by their intrinsic value, promoting both individual and collective well-being, and rooted in the principles of autonomy, satisfaction, and gratuity. The options are*: "casual leisure", "useful leisure", and "autotelic leisure". The correct answer is *autotelic leisure*.

References

Alvarado, J. (Trans.). (2013). *Paul Lafargue: el derecho a la pereza* [Original title: *Le droit á la paresse*, 1880]. Maia Ediciones.

Andrews, D. A., & Bonta, J. (2010). A general personality and cognitive social learning approach: The personal, interpersonal, and community-reinforcement (PIC-R) perspective. In D. A. Andrews & J. Bonta (Eds.), *The psychology of criminal conduct* (5th ed., pp. 131–156). Routledge. https://doi.org/10.1016/B978-1-4224-6329-1.50009-9

Anzures Gurría, J. J. (2021). Naturaleza jurídica y funciones del derecho humano a Internet. *Boletín Mexicano de Derecho Comparado, 1*(158), 521–552. https://doi.org/10.22201/iij.24484873e.2020.158.15628

Bandura, A. (1997). *Self-efficacy: The exercise of control.* W H Freeman/Times Books/Henry Holt & Co..

Baranger, J., Rousseau, D., Mastrorilli, M. E., & Matesanz, J. (2018). Doing time wisely: The social and personal benefits of Higher Education in prison. *The Prison Journal, 98*(4), 490–513. https://doi.org/10.1177/0032885518776380

Barba-Núñez, M., Expósito-Diéguez, A., & Morán de Castro, M. C. (2021). Ocio en prisión. Estudio de caso de una experiencia de participación proyectiva. *Educació Social. Revista d'Intervenció Socioeducativa, 79*, 77–99. https://doi.org/10.34810/EducacioSocialn79id386386

Barriga, M. J., Galán-Casado, D., Hossein-Mohand, H., & De Juanas Oliva, Á. (2024). Intervención en la autogestión del tiempo con colectivos vulnerables. In Á. de Juanas Oliva, F. J. García-Castilla, H. Hossein-Mohand, & H. Hossein-Mohand (Coords.), *Juventud y autorregulación del tiempo: Intervención socioeducativa para el bienestar integral* (pp. 109–120). Dykinson. ISBN 978-84-1070-274-5.

Berdychevsky, L., Stodolska, M., & Shinew, K. J. (2019). The roles of recreation in the prevention, intervention, and rehabilitation programs addressing youth gang involvement and violence. *Leisure Sciences, 44*(3), 343–365. https://doi.org/10.1080/01490400.2019.1571966

Berkman, L. F. (1995). The role of social relations in health promotion. *Psychosomatic Medicine, 57*(3), 245–254. https://doi.org/10.1097/00006842-199505000-00006

Berry, D. S., & Hansen, J. S. (1996). Positive affect, negative affect, and social interaction. *Journal of Personality and Social Psychology, 71*, 796–809. https://psycnet.apa.org/buy/1996-06401-014

Bolívar, A., Domingo, J., & Fernández, M. (2001). *La investigación biográfico-narrativa en educación. Enfoque y metodología.* La Muralla.

Callejo, J., y Viedma, A. (2008). *Eurodesip: Diagnosis os state of Higher Education in Penal Institutions in Europe. Programa Socrates.*

Camp, S. D., Gaes, G. G., Langan, N. P., & Saylor, W. G. (2003). The influence of prisons on inmate misconduct: A multilevel investigation. *Justice Quarterly, 20*(3), 501–533. https://doi.org/10.1080/07418820300095601

Carr, N. (2017). Re-thinking the relation between leisure and freedom. *Annals of Leisure Research, 20*(2), 137–151. https://doi.org/10.1080/11745398.2016.1206723

Carstensen, L. L., Isaacowitz, D. M., & Charles, S. T. (1999). Taking time seriously: A theory of socioemotional selectivity. *American Psychologist, 54*(3), 165–181. https://doi.org/10.1037/0003-066X.54.3.165

Carstensen, L. L. (1992). Social and emotional patterns in adulthood: Support for socioemotional selectivity theory. *Psychology and Aging, 7*(3), 331–338. https://doi.org/10.1037/0882-7974.7.3.331

CGCCES [Consejo General de Colegios de Educadoras y Educadores Sociales]. (2007). *Documentos profesionalizadores.* ASEDES.

Chiclana, S. (2023). Bienestar en prisión. Promoviendo un enfoque positivo en los programas de tratamiento. *Revista de Estudios Penitenciarios, 258*, 191–201. https://www.interior.gob.es/opencms/pdf/archivos-y-documentacion/documentacion-y-publicaciones/publicaciones-descargables/publicaciones-periodicas/revista-de-estudios-penitenciarios/Revista_de_estudios_penitenciarios_265_2023_126150491_web.pdf

Chiclana de la Fuente, S., Galán-Casado, D., García-Vita, M. M., & De Juanas, Á. (2021). Ocio y tiempo libre en prisión. Los módulos de respeto como espacios que generan bienestar en tiempos de pandemia. *Edetania. Estudios y Propuestas Socioeducativos, 60*, 165–186. https://doi.org/10.46583/edetania_2021.60.906

Collins, N. (2009). Motivation and self-regulated learning: Theory, research, and applications. *The Journal of Higher Education, 80*(4), 476–479. https://doi.org/10.1080/00221546.2009.11779027

Cuenca Cabeza, M. (2016). Ocio y recreación para el empoderamiento de la ciudadanía. In R. Lema & M. J. Monteagudo (Eds.), *Espacios de ocio y recreación para la construcción de ciudadanía* (pp. 25–41). Documentos de Estudios de Ocio, 58. Universidad de Deusto. ISBN: 978-84-16982-12-7.

Cuenca, M. (2014). *Ocio valioso.* Documentos de Estudios de Ocio, número 52. Universidad de Deusto. ISBN: 978-84-15759-48-5.

de Charms, R. (1968). *Personal causation: The internal affective determinants of behavior.* Routledge. https://doi.org/10.4324/9781315825632

De Juanas, A., Díaz-Esterri, J., & Goig, R. (2022). Ocio y prevención para el consumo de sustancias en jóvenes en riesgo social: revisión sistemática. In A. Madariaga & M. P. Rodríguez Moriche (Eds.), *Ocio saludable y construcción de ciudadanía* (pp. 147–161). Aranzadi. ISBN: 978-84-1125-783-1.

Deci, E., & Ryan, R. (2016). Chapter 2. Optimizing students' motivation in the era of testing and pressure: A self-determination theory perspective. In L. W. Chia, J. C. Keng Wang, &

R. M. Ryan (Eds.), *Building autonomous learners perspectives from research and practice using self-determination theory* (pp. 9–30). Springer. ISBN: 978-981-287-629-4.

Deci, E. L., & Ryan, R. M. (2000). The “what” and “why” of goal pursuits: Human needs and the self-determination of behavior. *Psychological Inquiry, 11*, 227–268. https://doi.org/10.1207/S15327965PLI1104_01

Deci, E. L., & Ryan, R. M. (1991). A motivational approach to self: Integration in personality. In R. Dienstbier (Ed.), *Nebraska Symposium on Motivation (Perspectives on Motivation)* (Vol. 38, pp. 237–288). University of Nebraska Press.

Enjuanes, J., Pérez Pollero, M., Palasí, E., Lema, R., & Morata, T. (2024). Ocio educativo en espacios penitenciarios: deporte, cultura y recreación en los procesos de reinserción social. *Cuadernos del Claeh, 43*(119), 85–101. https://doi.org/10.29192/claeh.43.1.8

Evans, D. N., Pelletier, E., & Szkola, J. (2017). Education in prison and the self-stigma: Empowerment continuum. *Crime & Delinquency, 64*(2), 255–280. https://www.webofscience.com/wos/alldb/full-record/WOS:000422890300005

Fernández Orviz, J. L. (2015). Personas mayores en prisión. Un programa de entrenamiento de la memoria. *Revista de Estudios Penitenciarios, 258*, 19–48. https://dialnet.unirioja.es/servlet/autor?codigo=4000625

Firmansyah, D., & Saepuloh, D. (2022). Social learning theory: Cognitive and behavioral approaches. *Jurnal Ilmiah Pendidikan Holistik (JIPH), 1*(3), 297–324. https://doi.org/10.55927/jiph.v1i3.2317

Fornons, D. (2008). La práctica deportiva en la prisión: rehabilitación o evasión. In L. Cantarero, F. X. Medina, & R. Sánchez (Eds.), *Actualidad en el deporte: investigación y aplicación* (pp. 215–227). Ankulegi Antropologia Elkartea.

Galán-Casado, D., García-Vita, M., Añaños, F. T., & Díaz-Esterri, J. (2023). Ocio y ocupación del tiempo libre en prisión. Los instrumentos socioeducativos para la inclusión social. In A. De-Juanas Oliva & F. J. García-Castilla (Eds.), *Ocio para la inclusión. Inspirando el cambio desde la transferencia social del conocimiento* (pp. 135–154). Peter Lang Publishing Group. ISBN: 9781636675169.

Galán-Casado, D. (2021). La Educación como alternativa al desconocimiento en salud mental. *Sin prejuicios, 1*, 10–11. file:///C:/Users/Usuario 03/Downloads/01%20sin%20 prejuicios-4.pdf.

Galán-Casado, D., & Del Pozo Serrano, F. J. (2019). La intervención educativa con personas mayores en el ámbito penitenciario: derecho y oportunidad para el envejecimiento activo. In A. De-Juanas & A. E. Rodríguez-Bravo (Eds.), *Educación de personas adultas y mayores* (pp. 185–218). UNED.

Galán-Casado, D., Moraleda-Ruano, A., Añaños, F., & De-Juanas, A. (2024a). Educación y prisión: reducción del estigma y reinserción social. In D. Galán Casado & Á. Moraleda Ruano (Coords.), *Estigma y educación. Un enfoque para la igualdad* (pp. 143–160). Narcea.

Galán-Casado, D., García-Vita, M., Raya-Miranda, R., & Añaños, F. T. (2024b). Prison and stigma. A study from a socio-educational and gender perspective. *Multidisciplinary Journal of Gender Studies, 13*(1), 22–42. https://doi.org/10.17583/generos.12508

García-Bravo, E. (2023). Salud mental en el ámbito penitenciario. Un cambio de perspectiva: la importancia del contexto. *Revista de Estudios Penitenciarios, 265*, 159–170. https://www.interior.gob.es/opencms/es/archivos-y-documentacion/documentacion-y-publicaciones/publicaciones/publicaciones-descargables/publicaciones-periodicas-anuarios-y-revistas/revista-de-estudios-penitenciarios/index.html

Gobierno de España. (2023). *Anuario estadístico 2023*. Ministerio del Interior. Secretaría General Técnica. https://www.interior.gob.es/opencms/pdf/archivos-y-documentacion/documentacion-y-publicaciones/anuarios-y-estadisticas/ultimo-anuario-estadistico/Anuario_estadistico_2023_126150729_Prov.pdf

Goffman, E. (1963). *Estigma. La identidad deteriorada*. Amorrortu.

Granovetter, M. S. (1973). The strength of weak ties. *American Journal of Sociology, 78*(6), 1360–1380. http://www.jstor.org/stable/2776392

Harmes, M. K., Hopkins, S., & Farley, H. (2019). Beyond incarcerated identities: Identity, bias and barriers to higher education in Australian prisons. *International Journal of Bias Identity and Diversities in Education (IJBIDE), 4*(1), 1–16. https://doi.org/10.4018/IJBIDE.20190101

Hernández-Prados, Mª., & Álvarez-Muñoz, J. (2022). El ocio como práctica educativa en las familias. Perspectivas de los expertos. *Edetania. Estudios Y Propuestas Socioeducativos*, 62, 17–38. https://doi.org/10.46583/edetania_2022.62.1051
Honty. (Editor in chief). (2023). Mucha tela la cultura. *Desde el páramo, 8*, 1–36. https://www.institucionpenitenciaria.es/es/web/home/fondo-documental/publicaciones?_com
Kuhl, J., Quirin, M., & Koole, S. L. (2021). The functional architecture of human motivation: Personality Systems Interactions theory. In A. J. Elliot (Ed.), *Advances in motivation science* (pp. 1–62). Elsevier Academic Press. https://doi.org/10.1016/bs.adms.2020.06.001
Mansfield, L., Daykin, N., & Kay, T. (2020). Leisure and wellbeing. *Leisure Studies, 39*(1), 1–10. https://doi.org/10.1080/02614367.2020.1713195
Mapson, A. (2013). From prison to parenting. *Journal of Human Behavior in the Social Environment, 23*(2), 171–177. https://doi.org/10.1080/10911359.2013.747402
Marcoux Rouleau, A. (2020). Rethinking Incarcerated Women's leisure as subjected to coercive and normative prison missions. *Frontiers in Sports and Active Living, 2*, 588775. https://doi.org/10.3389/fspor.2020.588775
Martin-González, N., Martínez-Merino, N., Usabiaga, O., & Martos, D. (2019). (Re)construcción de identidades sociales en entornos penitenciarios: las presas deportistas. *Revista de Psicología del Deporte, 28*(2), 59–66. https://archives.rpd-online.com/article/view/v28-n2-martin-martinez-usabiaga-etal.html
Martín-González, N., Martínez-Merino, N., García Martos, D., & Usabiaga Arruabarrena, O. (2019). Entering and leaving: A story of drugs and sports with inmate women. *Ágora para la Educación Física y el Deporte, 21*, 148–169. https://doi.org/10.24197/aefd.0.2019.148-169
Martín-González, N., Martínez-Merino, N., Usabiaga Arruabarrena, O., & García Martos, D. (2018). ≏Puede el fútbol favorecer relaciones interpersonales positivas entre mujeres encarceladas? *Revista Internacional de Deportes Colectivos, 35*, 17–30. https://dialnet.unirioja.es/servlet/articulo?codigo=6749916
Martínez-García, R., Caballo-Villar, M. B., Varela-Crespo, L. (2020). El ocio en el medio natural como promotor de la conexión emocional con la naturaleza. Un estudio en clave ambiental con adolescentes pontevedreses (Galicia-España). *Pensamiento educativo, 57(2), 1–16.* https://doi.org/10.7764/PEL.57.2.2020.6
Martínez, J. (Ed.). (2023). Editorial: ocio, arte y privación de libertad. *Desde el páramo, 8*, 1–36. https://www.institucionpenitenciaria.es/es/web/home/fondo-documental/publicaciones?_com
Martínez-Merino, N., Martín-González, N., Usabiaga, O., & Martos i García, D. (2018). Beneficios y barreras identificadas por las presas que practican actividad física: Una revisión cualitativa de la literatura. *Retos: nuevas tendencias en educación física, deporte y recreación, 34*, 44–50. https://recyt.fecyt.es/index.php/retos/article/view/57650
McClelland, D. C. (1989). *Estudio de la motivación humana*. Narcea.
Ministerio del Interior. (2024). *Anuario estadístico 2023*. Secretaría General Técnica.
Monteagudo Sánchez, M. J. (2020). Factores determinantes del ocio de las personas mayores y su contribución al envejecimiento satisfactorio. In J. A. Caride, M. B. Caballo, & R. Gradaílle (Eds.), *Tiempos, educación en una sociedad de redes* (pp. 153–169). Octaedro. ISBN: 978-84-18348-91-4.
Morata, T., Palasí, E., Alonso, H., & Fernández, F. (2019). Ocio, acción sociocultural y cohesión social. In I. Alonso Sáez & K. Artetxe Sánchez (Eds.), *Educación en el tiempo libre: la inclusión en el centro* (pp. 93–112). Octaedro. ISBN: 978-84-17667-62-7.
Moreno-Carmona, N. D., Tasamá-Rincón, M., Rojas-Cruz, C. A., & Soto-Soto, J. D. (2020). La dimensión positiva de las actividades extraescolares en la niñez y la adolescencia. *Revista Aletheia, 12*(1), 97–116.
Moreton, J., Kelly, C. S., & Sandstrom, G. M. (2023). Social support from weak ties: Insight from the literature on minimal social interactions. *Social and Personality Psychology Compass, 17*(3). https://doi.org/10.1111/spc3.12729
Müller, J. (2024). 'For those few minutes you are free': The meaning of sport from imprisoned men's perspective. *International Review for the Sociology of Sport, 59*(4), 598–616. https://doi.org/10.1177/10126902231217186

Mutz, M., & Müller, J. (2023). Health decline in prison and the effects of sporting activity: Results of the Hessian prison sports study. *Health Justice, 11*(34). https://doi.org/10.1186/s40352-023-00237-6

Nie, Y. (2016). Chapter 14. Focus on competing for performance or mastering new knowledge? Insights from discovering the relations between classroom goal structures and students' learning in Singapore secondary schools. In L. W. Chia, J. C. Keng Wang, & R. M. Ryan (Eds.), *Building autonomous learners: Perspectives from research and practice using self-determination theory* (pp. 259–276). Springer. ISBN 978-981-287-629-4.

Ostini, J., & Farley, H. (2022). Beyond idealism to the realities of incarcerated higher education: What we know about the provision of higher education in prisons. In M. K. Harmes, B. Harmes, & M. A. Harmes (Eds.), *Histories and philosophies of carceral education: Aims, contradictions, promises and problems* (pp. 11–30). Palgrave Macmillan.

Osuna, C. (2022). El estigma penitenciario y la escuela en la cárcel como estructura de mediación. *Perfiles Educativos, 44*(175), 95–111. https://perfileseducativos.unam.mx/iisue_pe/index.php/perfiles/article/view/60166/52809

Osuna, C. (2019). "Yo allí soy feliz, voy de lunes a viernes sin faltar": Reflexiones desde una etnografía escolar en una cárcel de mujeres. *AIBR, Revista de Antropología Iberoamericana, 14*(2), 277–298. https://doi.org/10.11156/aibr.140206

Pantoja, L. (Coord.), Alonso, M. J., Arandia, M., Remiro, A., Rodríguez, A., & Rubio, D. (2018). *El código deontológico de la Educación Social. Una visión desde la práctica profesional* Ediciones Beta III Milenio. ISBN: 978-84-16809-90-5.

Paynter, M., Martin-Misener, R., Iftene, A., & Tomblin-Murphy, G. (2023). A qualitative case study of pregnancy and early parenting in Canada's federal prisons for women. *PLoS ONE, 18*(12). https://doi.org/10.1371/journal.pone.0294961

Pérez-Yuste, J. A. (2023). La educación en los centros penitenciarios. In J. L. M. de Baena Simón & J. M. E. Sánchez (Eds.), *Vigilar y educar. Buenas prácticas formativas en centros penitenciarios* (pp. 73–93) Tirant humanidades. ISBN: 978-84-19471-48-2.

Puolakka, P., & Suomela, M. (2023). Article 4. Digitalization supports human rights in Finnish prisons. *Advancing Corrections Journal, 16*, 50–61. https://icpa.org/resources/advancing-corrections-journal.html

Real Decreto 190/1996, de 9 de febrero, por el que se aprueba el Reglamento Penitenciario. *Boletín Oficial del Estado, 40*, 15. https://www.boe.es/buscar/act.php?id=BOE-A-1996-3307&tn=1&p=20220413

Resolución de 28 de julio de 2021 de la Secretaría de Estado de Función Pública, por la que se convoca el proceso selectivo para el ingreso, por promoción interna, como personal laboral fijo, en los grupos profesionales M2 y M1 sujetos al IV Convenio Único, para el personal laboral de la Administración General del Estado, en el Ministerio de Interior, Secretaría General de Instituciones Penitenciarias y Entidad Estatal Trabajo Penitenciario y Formación para el Empleo, encomendando la gestión del proceso a la Secretaría General de Instituciones Penitenciarias. Boletín Oficial del Estado, 31 de julio de 2021, páginas 93065–93066.

Robertson, B. J. (2002). La educación del ocio como antídoto para los comportamientos negativos de la juventud. In C. de la Cruz Ayuso (Ed.), *Educación del ocio. Propuestas internacionales* (pp. 139–158). Documentos de Estudios de Ocio, número 23. Universidad de Deusto. ISBN: 978-84-9830-450-3.

Ryan, R. M., & Bradshaw, E. L. (2019). Chapter 28. Envisioning progress and perils. Musings on the future of motivation research in a rapidly evolving world. In R. M. Ryan (Ed.), *The Oxford handbook of human motivation* (2nd ed.). Oxford Library of Psychology. ISBN: 978-01-90666-45-3. https://doi.org/10.1093/oxfordhb/9780190666453.001.0001

Ryan, R. M., & Deci, E. L. (2000a). Intrinsic and extrinsic motivations: Classic definitions and new directions. *Contemporary Educational Psychology, 25*, 54–67. https://doi.org/10.1006/ceps.1999.1020

Ryan, R. M., & Deci, E. L. (2000b). Self-determination theory and the facilitation of intrinsic motivation, social development, and well-being. *American Psychologist, 55*, 68–78. https://psycnet.apa.org/doi/10.1037/0003-066X.55.1.68

Ryff, C. D. (1995). Psychological well-being in adult life. *Current Directions in Psychological Science, 4*(4), 99–104. https://doi.org/10.1111/1467-8721.ep10772395

Ryff, C. D. (1989). Happiness is everything, or is it? Explorations on the meaning of psychological well-being. *Journal of Personality and Social Psychology, 57*(6), 1069–1081. https://web-p-ebscohost-com.bibliotecauned.idm.oclc.org/ehost/pdfviewer/pdfviewer?vid=4&sid=efcbec09-e805-4b63-b041-748d1c36a284%40redis

Sandstrom, G. M., & Dunn, E. W. (2014). Social interactions and well-being: The surprising power of weak ties. *Personality and Social Psychology Bulletin, 40*(7), 910–922. https://doi.org/10.1177/0146167214529799

Schultz, D., Izard, C. E., & Ackerman, B. P. (2000). Children's anger attribution bias: Relations to family environment and social adjustment. *Social Development, 9*(3), 284–301. https://doi.org/10.1111/1467-9507.00126

Secretaría General de Instituciones Penitenciarias. (2022). *Informe General 2022*. Ministerio del Interior, Secretaría General Técnica.

Sentse, M., Kreager, D. A., Bosma, A. Q., Nieuwbeerta, P., & Palmen, H. (2019). Social organization in prison: A social network analysis of interpersonal relationships among Dutch prisoners. *Justice Quarterly, 38*(6), 1047–1069. https://doi.org/10.1080/07418825.2019.1700298

Sociedad Iberoamericana de Pedagogía Social, SIPS. (2023, October 4–6). *La pedagogía social en una sociedad digital e hiperconectada: desafíos y propuestas* [Libro de resúmenes del Congreso en Salamanca]. https://cisips.wordpress.com/wp-content/uploads/2023/10/libro_resumenes_sips-23.pdf

USC-SEPA. (2024, July 2). *Foro Internacional OcioGune Compostela 2024*. https://www.sepa.gal/noticias/285-foro-internacional-ociogune-santiago-2024.html

Valdemoros, M. Á., Sáenz de Jubera, M. S., Alonso, R. A., Medrano, C., & Santamaría, M. (2022). Ocio lúdico-cultural y relaciones intergeneracionales. *HUMAN REVIEW. International Humanities Review / Revista Internacional de Humanidades, 15*(7), Article 7. https://doi.org/10.37467/revhuman.v11.4378

Van der Kaap-Deeder, J., Audenaert, E., Vandevelde, S., Soenens, B., Van Mastrigt, S., Mabbe, E., & Vansteenkiste, M. (2017). Choosing when choices are limited: The role of perceived afforded choice and autonomy in prisoners' well-being. *Law and Human Behavior, 41*(6), 567–578. https://psycnet-apa-org.bibliotecauned.idm.oclc.org/doi/10.1037/lhb0000259

Vuk, M., & Doležal, D. (2019). Idleness and inmate misconduct: A new perspective on time use and behavior in local jails. *Deviant Behavior, 41*(11), 1347–1369. https://doi.org/10.1080/01639625.2019.1614141

Wheaton, B., Waiti, J., Cosgriff, M., & Burrows, L. (2019). Coastal blue space and wellbeing research: Looking beyond western tides. *Leisure Studies, 39*(1), 83–95. https://doi.org/10.1080/02614367.2019.1640774

Yuen, F., Arai, S., & Fortune, D. (2012). Community (dis)connection through leisure for women in Prison. *Leisure Sciences: An Interdisciplinary Journal, 34*(4), 281–297. https://doi.org/10.1080/01490400.2012.687613

Chapter 2
Exploring Our Leisure Time: Youth Participation and Participatory Action Research

Victoria Pérez de Guzmán, Teresa Rebolledo-Gámez, and Rocío Rodríguez-Casado

Abstract This chapter presents the results of the research project "CON_LecerSanJuan", led by the GIAS research group of the Universidad Pablo de Olavide, which aimed to study leisure, free time and work-life balance from the point of view of young people, using a Participatory-Action-Research and Service-Learning approach. As part of this research, the "CON_LecerSanJuan" initiative, carried out in collaboration with the Town Council of San Juan de Aznalfarache (Seville, Spain), focused on the young people of the municipality, involving them in the study of their daily routines, including school, family, leisure and free time, and exploring the impact of leisure on their personal, social and family development. The project involved students from two local high schools who designed research instruments, collected and analysed data and shared the results. Overall, the initiative aimed to understand the reality of young people from their own perspective, to make suggestions for local policies and to improve the quality of young people's leisure experiences by actively involving them in the process.

2.1 Introduction

Our current context is subject to continual change and brings with it vulnerable situations, problems, needs and individual, social and community interests to which we try to respond through education. There is an increasing perception of an uncertain future and the establishment of a "culture of immediacy" conceived within the framework of technology and digital connectivity that accelerate our pace of life, managing immediate alternatives to situations and problems that lose validity almost instantly and which place us within a tendency towards a banal and superficial society.

V. Pérez de Guzmán · T. Rebolledo-Gámez (✉) · R. Rodríguez-Casado
Universidad Pablo de Olavide, Seville, Spain
e-mail: mvperpuy@upo.es; tjrebgam@upo.es; mrrodcas@upo.es

L. Ronda et al. (eds.), *Leisure and Human Development*, Human Well-Being Research and Policy Making, https://doi.org/10.1007/978-3-031-90778-4_2

In the last Report on Youth in Spain 2020 (Simon et al., 2021), digital leisure is identified as one of the main ways in which young people use their free time, noting that "75% of young people are connected to the internet between two and three hours a day" (p.166) [author's translation]. The digital leisure of the young people surveyed in this study is characterised by the use of activities related to connectivity on social media, watching films and series and listening to music on different online platforms.

Thus, digital leisure, dependence on technology and a lack of ethics seem to increase with artificial intelligence, as digital media will continue to grow and become the focal point of people's social time, especially young people (Valdemoros-San-Emeterio et al., 2017).

We are in "a liquid society", a term coined by the sociologist Zygmunt Bauman, which is characterised not only by an economy of excess and waste, an overdose of unfiltered information, the perception of time, etc., but also by the lack of credibility given to educational models. But how do we educate people to develop a sense of serenity in a world full of immediacy and uncertainty? Caride Gómez (2004) warned us two decades ago that we are in:

> (…) a society that feels increasingly obliged to rethink education in its varied typologies and achievements, inside and outside education systems, both within the framework of political actions and in the practices promoted by various social actors (teachers, educators, academics, social media, associations, trade unions, etc.), directly or indirectly affected by the impacts caused by globalisation and its controversial socio-economic, moral and cultural manifestations (p. 57) [author's translation].

The role played by different institutions in the education of young people today is always under debate. Universities, schools and local councils, among other public and private institutions, have a public or governmental social responsibility in the comprehensive and inclusive formation of citizens in general and young people in particular. We must emphasise public administrations here, since we cannot forget that every public institution represents us and, therefore, we are all responsible for their actions as active and participatory citizens (Navarro et al., 2017).

Specifically, the reality of our educational institutions requires the organisation and construction of proposals that help us improve our education practices and, therefore, the quality of teaching and learning. Teachers and other professionals working in schools both from within and from outside (such as social educators) are fundamental pillars and must be the driving force behind proposed innovation and socio-educational transformation.

Schools are looking for models, strategies, ways of thinking and acting that respond to the formative and educational needs of their students in the context in which we live. During our childhood and adolescence, we spend a great deal of time in schools. Let us remember that "the school is a microsystem, within the social macrosystem. It is the reflection of the context in which it is immersed" (Pérez de Guzmán et al., 2024, p.22) [author's translation].

Schools in general and teachers in particular have been modifying their role within the teaching-learning process. Pedagogical models lead us to theoretical proposals and practical approaches that guide teachers in the training plans they implement and thereby promote meaningful and contextualised learning.

Throughout history, different models have emerged (behavioural, constructivist, projective, pedagogical route 2030, etc.) and have led education professionals to consider and design initiatives that respond to the dictates of education laws and the demands generated by schools themselves and their surrounding context.

Those of us who work in the field of education must be aware of the interdependence or correlation that exists between sociocultural and educational systems, as well as the importance of generating methods that allow students who learn within the classroom to look beyond it, and not only learn about the socio-educational, cultural, economic, political, etc. problems and phenomena that exist, through the different subjects studied, but also learn to solve them. We must generate learning situations, as contemplated by the current education law in Spain (LOMLOE, 2020). Create shared innovation projects through a networking approach, with other institutions or organisations, with common objectives, through which learning acquires meaning, by means of socio-pedagogical approaches that, as noted in the latest UNESCO report (2021), cultivate values and principles of interdependence and solidarity.

From our perspective to generate innovative processes focused on youth education we have launched the project "CON_LecerSanJuan: exploring our leisure times", led by researcher María Victoria Pérez de Guzmán Puya, within the Collaboration Agreement between the Universidad Pablo de Olavide Research Group on Socio-educational Action (GIAS) and the town council of San Juan de Aznalfarache, Seville (Spain). Work began on the project in 2021, but it was implemented during the 2022–2023 school year.[1] In this chapter, we present the participatory action research process carried out during the design and implementation of this project, as well as the most relevant findings.

2.2 Justification, Objectives and Pillars of the Project

The authors of this chapter are members of the GIAS research group at Universidad Pablo de Olavide in Seville, Spain. The experience presented here is located within one of its lines of research, specifically that of Social Pedagogy: participation, citizenship, social education, and youth. This line was being developed through involvement in different research projects, including those carried out with the towns of Mairena del Aljarafe and San Juan de Aznalfarache (Seville, Spain) referring to the development of their Comprehensive Youth Plans as a result of a diagnosis of the situation affecting young people in these towns, with the participation of

[1]This innovation and research project is linked to the participation of GIAS (HUM-929) as an observer group and since 2022 as a member of the OCIOGUNE Excellence Network, as well as in the R&D project "Education and balance for equity: analysis of its incidence in the school and social times of childhood (CON_TIEMPOs)" (RTI2018-094764-B-100 of the National R&D/Innovation Plan), funded by the Spanish Department of Science, Innovation and Universities.

all the agents involved (youth population, municipality, municipal services, and resources).[2]

We were motivated to tackle this issue through the work we have been doing around the issues of youth, leisure, and balancing family, school, and work times within families, as well as our interest in learning about the reality of how families achieve balance with school-age children within compulsory education or any other age considered within childhood and adolescence, in addition to the impact of the problems of balancing times on the well-being of children and adolescents and, specifically, their leisure time.

A multitude of reports and research, at national and international level, have explored the balance of family, school, and work time, as well as the importance of developing valuable leisure in childhood and youth.

The Innocenti report (UNICEF, 2020) ranks Spain 14th out of 31 countries (within the Organisation for Economic Co-operation and Development and the European Union) in terms of work-life balance policies. The UNAF report (2019) on work-life balance policies in the European Union, as well as that of UNAF (2021), have led us to reflect on co-responsibility and work-life balance in Spain. Although we do not intend in this chapter to delve into such issues, it is important to situate ourselves within them, since they influence the dynamics and life of childhood and youth. As noted by Pérez de Guzmán et al. (2023):

> Within the fields of Social Pedagogy and educational research, we are constantly searching for concrete strategies that help us respond to the challenge of achieving a harmonious balance between family, work and school life for families with younger children (p. 63) [Author's translation].

Knowing how young people spend their free time, as well as their leisure time, is key to be able, through education, to draw up roadmaps that help them develop in a more holistic way. As indicated by Doistua Nebreda et al. (2016), "it is in youth that the foundations on which adult life will be based are most profoundly staked out" (p.135) [Author's translation].

The innovation and research project presented here as emerged from these and other premises, focusing on the participation of young people in the town of San Juan de Aznalfarache (Seville, Spain), conducting a Participatory-Action-Research project that allowed young people to understand and influence the reality of their town through Service-Learning.

To do this, young people themselves were placed at the centre of the project, taking on the role of researcher to find out what children and teenagers think about their everyday times (school, family, leisure, and free time), in addition to reflecting on the consideration of leisure and the impact on its development. That way, young

[2]Contracts signed under art. 83 LOU: "Study and research on the reality of youth in Mairena del Aljarafe for the development of the I Youth Plan of Mairena" (2020/00259/001), developed from 01/12/2020 to 30/09/2021; and "Diagnosis of the situation of the youth population in the town of San Juan de Aznalfarache (Seville). Proposed action for the Comprehensive Youth Plan" (2021/00022/001), developed from 01/02/2021 to 30/11/2021.

people drive their own learning process and develop proposals to improve their own reality in their town, directly related to a significant Service-Learning process.

Several initial meetings were held with political leaders and officers from the town council to design the proposal, exploring the possibility of carrying out this initiative in the town's secondary schools. In this regard, a network began to emerge, involving the Universidad Pablo de Olavide GIAS research team, the Youth Worker from the Local Council and two teachers (one male, one female) from the two secondary schools in the town, Severo Ochoa and Mateo Alemán.

The core idea at these meetings was that this innovation experience should be carried out during class time so the students did not have to give up any time outside of school and ensure this would be sustainable over the school year.

After a joint review of the subjects that could be linked to this project, we agreed to select an elective subject on first year of *Bachillerato* (pre-university education), which was newly created following the latest Education Law passed in Spain (LOMLOE, 2020), and therefore it had not yet been designed. The subject was "Anthropology and Sociology", and it was to be taught in both secondary schools. This flexibility would allow the project and the subject to be constructed cooperatively at the same time, tying in objectives, competences, content and learning outcomes in accordance with the evaluation criteria established.

Within the framework of this subject and through this innovation experience, the aim was not only to work on the academic, psychological, social, ethical and professional dimensions in order to learn about human facts and phenomena, both past and present, and the transformations that may derive from their findings, as contemplated in the Education Law, but also, through the design and implementation of a research project, for students to understand the phenomenon of leisure and how young people can balance school and family time, to propose improvements in their most immediate environment, and thus contribute to culture and social inclusion in their town.

This way, the students are encouraged to look beyond their personal circumstances, to understand other ways of seeing, other perspectives; social and emotional skills are developed, so-called soft skills, derived from the knowledge generated by learning through a theoretical-practical process about social phenomena, research methods, team-group work, verbal and non-verbal communication, distributed leadership and digital skills. All of these are part of the key competences established by the current Education Law as fundamental skills for the education system, such as linguistic communication, digital and personal skills, social and learning to learn skills, and of course citizen competence, among others.

The proposal was that the two groups of students in the first year of *Bachillerato*, guided by the teachers of this subject in each school, by the Youth Worker from the council and by the members of the GIAS research group, would receive training in research, in order to design a study based on a Participatory-Action-Research methodology.

All this with the idea that their training should not only trigger cognitive learning but also procedural and attitudinal learning, in addition to helping them to reflect on a socio-educational phenomenon in their immediate environment and design proposals for improvements in their locality. Based on this approach, the specific objectives established were as follows:

- Establish a research steering group between the young people living in the town and the team from the university, its schools and the local council.
- Train young people about educational and family times, leisure, and free time and educational research.
- Design a Participatory-Action-Research process based on Service-Learning.
- Analyse the results obtained to detect the main aspects of the educational, family, and leisure times of young people in the town.
- Establish a dissemination plan for the proposal and the findings, providing a service to the community as a result of their learning.

This project encompasses five key pillars, as shown in the following figure (Fig. 2.1):

The "CON_LecerSanJuan" project is based on a Service-Learning methodology, so that participants learn by offering a service to their surrounding community. Participation is an opportunity for citizens to give voice, responses and alternatives to the situations and social challenges that concern them, giving quality to the democratic factor framed in the design and development of public policies for their training in rights, duties and obligations. Thus, we can involve people, from childhood and adolescence, in initiatives that are not only merely consultative, but based on action, in which they are fully fledged protagonists (Ochoa et al., 2024).

As a result, this Participatory-Action-Research experience, based on Service-Learning, has put young people at the helm of their own learning process,

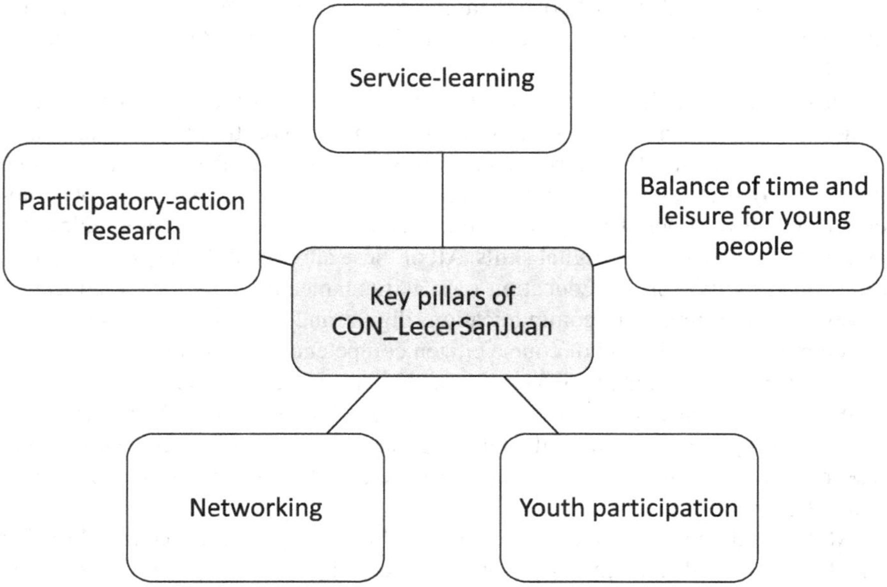

Fig. 2.1 Key pillars of CON_LecerSanJuan project

contributing to society and, above all, their nearest environment, in other words their town. At the same time, they can express their learning experiences about the importance of research in Social Sciences, reflect on its realities, investigate this reality and propose improvements for their locality.

In this regard, we would highlight a series of elements that we consider fundamental for the development of this project:

- The teaching-learning processes have been developed through a multilevel approach. Spaces have been created for reflection and individual learning (person), group learning (groups of students from each school, teaching staff, Youth Worker, GIAS team), in an interrelation way between the different parties and, of course, at the community level (at the level of town, with the fundamental involvement of the Council).
- One innovative aspect that has been of great assistance is the intertwining of the project with the competences that according to Spain's Education Law should be developed within the Secondary School subject that has been the context of this project development. For this purpose, it is essential to consider that, as a newly created subject with the latest Education Law, the possibilities of building these competences in collaboration between all parties has meant that the subject has been designed from a more integrated perspective.
- In addition to the skills that Secondary School students needed to acquire according to the curriculum, it has been very important to focus their attention on the learning of essential competences for a Service-Learning project, such as teamwork, collaboration and cooperation, distributed leadership and oral and written communication, among others.
- We must emphasise the value of a theoretical-practical approach in the students' teaching-learning processes. At all times, the calendar of theoretical knowledge that should be learned in the subject has been met, although usually combined with active and participatory methodologies that have linked knowledge to the praxis provided by the innovation project.

Furthermore, youth participation has been another central focus of the project. Youth participation is generally understood to refer to actions or processes that enable young people to influence their environment as active and responsible citizens, their personal and collective development, as well as their professional future. As noted by Lazcano Quintana and De Juanas Oliva (2020):

> Young people connect with each other like they had never done previously; they are real agents of social change and can contribute to the growth of the communities in which they live by transforming environments (p.3) [Author's translation].

Achieving a balance between school, family and leisure time has also become a central theme of the research process. Caballo Villar and Gradaille Pernas (2023) remind us that leisure is important in childhood and that it is conditioned by other social times, which define the rhythms of daily life and "directly affect their personal and social needs, as well as the ways of meeting them (p.9) [author's translation]. This area has been studied by means of Participatory-Action-Research, an active methodological process that has allowed students to be the subject or protagonist of the research. A participatory and collaborative process was carried out, which enabled the students to work with the intention of improving their own practices. They were responsible for designing the phases of the research process, and a self-critical community was created between students and teachers. As Pérez de Guzmán and Mendoza Ramírez (2020).

> The people involved are not only protagonists of the facts analysed; they also become the ones who investigate their own reality. They are not the object of the research, but rather the subjects of it (p.9.7) [Author's translation].

In this respect, the relationships created through a networking and co-construction approach as a way of working in a team and in a network have been fundamental. The entire project was constructed cooperatively and collaboratively between all the parties involved, continuously monitoring the actions to adapt the planning to the needs and interests that arose during the process. This socio-educational experience has been a transformational tool to enhance a teaching-learning process from within and outside the school. As Trujillo Herrera (2024) explains, we must "understand the school through a networked conception, taking advantage of the great variety of natural and institutional relationships that the school creates and generates in a regular, continuous and constant way" (p.150) [Author's translation].

2.3 Stages of the Project

To implement the project, a steering group was formed, made up of four members of GIAS, the Youth Worker from the Local Council of San Juan de Aznalfarache (social educator), as well as two teachers (one male, one female) from each of the two secondary schools involved in the project (Severo Ochoa and Mateo Alemán), who taught the elective subject "Anthropology and Sociology" in the first year of *Bachillerato*.

The initial meetings allowed us to focus on jointly defining the objectives of the project and tying them in with the subject, so that the execution of the project would allow us to work on the contents and competences established for the aforementioned elective subject by current regulations. The different stages of the project, set out in the figure below (Fig. 2.2), were as follows:

2.3.1 Stage One: Project Conceptualisation

The experience was designed collaboratively, mainly between the GIAS research team, the teachers from the secondary schools involved and the Youth Worker from the Local Council in San Juan de Aznalfarache.

During this first phase, regular meetings were held to agree on the content related to the project that was to be included in the subject taught in the first year of *Bachillerato*, where this teaching innovation project was framed. We agreed on the

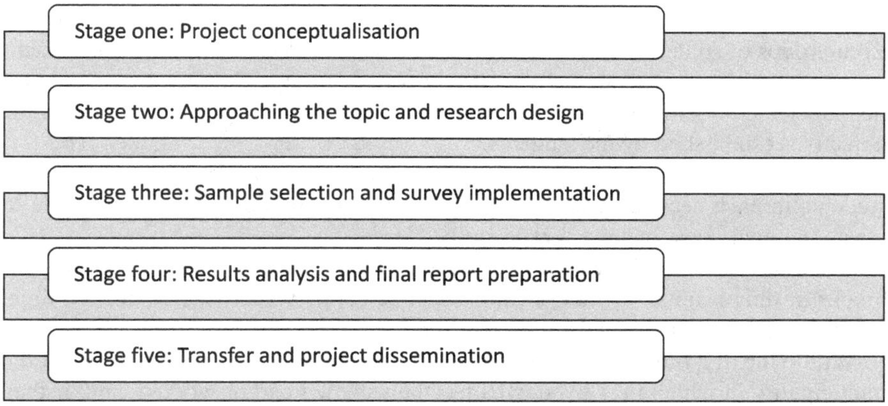

Fig. 2.2 Stages of CON_LecerSanJuan project

skills to develop and a basic outline of the contents covered in relation to leisure times and achieving a balance for young people, as a starting point for reflection on this area with the students enrolled on this subject who were going to participate in the project.

Likewise, the subject contents were devised, based on paradigms, theories and methodologies in social research, so that the participants were given guidance on how to design research about the reality they would be analysing.

2.3.2 Stage Two: Approaching the Topic and Research Design

The subject was taught within the regular school hours at each school, developing the learning in a theoretical and practical way. It was agreed that one day a week, the focus would be more on theoretical learning (with dynamic activities as well) and on another day, on applied and practical learning, aimed at designing the research project.

The subject introduced students to concepts, theories and practical applications around Anthropology and Sociology. Within the subject, an activity was established that was progressively structured through the acquired learning. The students, together with the teachers of the subject (with the support of the external team, GIAS, and the Local Council), designed the research, as part of the evaluation of the subject, focusing on the paradigmatic approach on which it was based. The study objectives, dimensions, and variables were defined, in order to design a questionnaire that would allow them to collect information to analyse the reality faced by young people in their town in terms of leisure time and striking a balance with their times, as well as their knowledge of the services and resources available in the village for youth engagement and leisure.

A questionnaire was created in each Secondary School. Once each group of students had designed their own questionnaire, two face-to-face meetings were held in the town's youth centre to jointly design the final instrument for data collection. Both groups of students participated in these sessions, along with the subject teachers, the Local Council team and the GIAS research group. Through group and participatory methodologies, a single research questionnaire was agreed, based on the objectives established by the students.

Subsequently, to validate the instrument, a pilot test was carried out with the students in each secondary school and the necessary modifications were made to create the final questionnaire for the study.

The final questionnaire was composed of 29 items, which were grouped into four blocks or dimensions: (1) identification details, (2) personal leisure and free time, (3) shared leisure, and (4) leisure in San Juan.

Within the first block, items were included in relation to: sex, age, the area of the municipality in which they lived, whether they studied and/or worked, and, if they studied, which level they were at, who they lived with, and their mother/father/guardian's level of education.

In the second block, they were asked to indicate: the time spent daily on tasks related to study, extracurricular activities or study support and household chores. They were also asked about the hours of personal leisure time they had daily and the weekly amount of money they usually spent on leisure. As well as whether they did a series of leisure activities and how often (watching TV, movies, series; playing with their video console, computer; connecting to social media; reading on print or electronic media; going shopping or to malls; going for walks, being out in the street or at the park; going on trips; doing sports; attending cultural or artistic events; engaging in artistic or cultural activities; board games or others).

They were also asked about the extent to which they agreed with a series of statements: (a) for me it is important to have free time, (b) I am satisfied with my leisure time to do the activities I like, (c) I like enjoying my leisure with others, (d) I usually choose my leisure activities, (e) I like participating in the leisure activities available in San Juan.

The last questions were meant to indicate whether the time they devoted to leisure was enough, what they were looking for in these activities (fun, joy, entertainment, satisfaction, disconnection, personal growth…), and, in general, how they found their leisure activities (boring, satisfying, interesting, exciting…), as well as what leisure activity they would like to spend more time on.

In the third block, they were asked who they mostly spend time with—if they spend time with others—and who they would prefer to spend time with (family, friends, classmates…). To indicate which leisure activities they usually did with others, they proposed: (a) watching television, films, series...; (b) playing with their video console, on the computer...; (c) social media (WhatsApp, Instagram, Facebook, TikTok, etc.); (d) reading in printed or electronic media (books, magazines...); (e) going shopping or to the mall; (f) going for walks, being out in the street or at the park; (g) going on trips (to the beach, hiking, etc.; (h) playing sports; (i) attending cultural or artistic events (concerts, theatre, exhibitions, etc.); (j) performing artistic or cultural activities (music, dance, painting, etc.); (k) participating in associations or volunteering; (l) board or role-playing games; (m) other.

They were also asked whether they felt it would be positive to share more leisure time with the people they lived with, to indicate the importance usually given to leisure in their families and the extent to which they agreed with statements such as: (a) the time I have to devote to school work eats into my leisure time; b) my parents' working day does not allow me to spend enough leisure time with them; c) do you sometimes feel that participating in extracurricular or study support activities becomes an chore?

Finally, the questions focused on answering whether their parents' working day allowed them to spend enough leisure time with them, if they felt that participating in extracurricular or study support activities became a chore, and if they regularly consumed alcohol, energy drinks, tobacco, other substances or consumed nothing in their leisure time.

In the last block, about leisure options in the town, they were asked if they knew about the leisure activities available in San Juan de Aznalfarache (sports activities in the sports centre, video games tournament, concerts and exhibitions in the municipal theatre, cultural fair, music or food workshops, charity market, astronomy workshops, etc.) and at what time of year they would like to use the leisure resources offered. Also if they used other leisure resources on offer at private institutions that were not part of the town council and which leisure activities they would organise.

This final questionnaire was changed to an online format, and it could be accessed through a QR code, although some groups answered in person on paper due to difficulties answering by means of an electronic device.

2.3.3 Stage Three: Sample Selection and Survey Implementation

The students, teachers, staff from the town council, and the university agreed who would make up the research sample, and a distribution of the target population was planned on which each group of students would focus. It was determined that the age of the sample would be between 12 and 20 years old. The sample population was accessed through the secondary schools themselves, disseminated through the information channels made available by the town council and also implemented in public spaces within the town. In total, 682 responses were collected.

2.3.4 Stage Four: Results Analysis and Final Report Preparation

In this part of the project, a meeting was held with students, teachers and members of the GIAS research group with the aim of explaining some important questions about data analysis in this type of social research. The research group carried out the task of analysing the results obtained, a process in which the students were also involved.

Once the data were analysed, between all the parties and, fundamentally, by students from both schools, a report was prepared with the conclusions of the research, around the four study blocks (Participant details, Personal leisure and free time, Shared leisure, and Leisure in San Juan de Aznalfarache), identifying proposals on how to improve leisure policies for young people at the local level based on the data collected. This report was addressed to the town council as a contribution to improving their own reality.

2.3.5 *Stage Five: Transfer and Project Dissemination*

Although this phase is explained as the last part of the project, it was actually present throughout the entire development of the project.

For the dissemination and transfer of the work carried out, different actions were planned in which the various agents involved in the project would participate. Therefore, the project has been disseminated on different occasions using local and university media.

In addition, representatives of the participating youth groups, together with the town council and the GIAS team have presented their experience at academic-professional forums, such as seminars on Service-Learning experiences or on youth and participation. Furthermore, the students, teachers, members of the town council (Councillor for Young People and Youth Worker) visited Universidad Pablo de Olavide, holding a meeting with students on the first year of the Degree in Social Education, studying the subject of Social Pedagogy, where the project was presented, and issues of interest to both parties were addressed.

Finally, at the end of the project, a radio programme was recorded for Radio Alma, a broadcaster in Brussels, involving representatives of all the parties involved, with the aim of spreading awareness about the project and recounting the experiences and learning achieved. This programme will be linked to the website of Civitas-Lab, the citizenship laboratory of the Universidad de Cádiz. Likewise, several academic papers have been published to spread awareness of the project among the scientific community.

2.4 Conclusions

We have described a project that has been co-constructed in a collaborative and cooperative way among the entire team composed of university faculty, the local Youth Worker for the town, and the teachers and students from the secondary schools, responding in this way to the needs and objectives of all the actors involved.

Based on the interests of young people, in addition to responding to the needs of other participating institutions, a series of actions have been carried out for the design, planning and execution of the participatory research proposal, through different activities and tasks such as participation in meetings, seminars and sessions planned to share spaces for reflection on the importance of co-construction in Participatory-Action-Research processes through a socio-critical approach. This has made it possible to motivate the secondary students involved to continue training in the future and to feel that they are active agents in the university.

We have learned about leisure time, free time, the balanced distribution of times, the use of those times within leisure activities, etc. The teachers and the students have learned about the different stages involved in carrying out a research project of this kind and the different paradigmatic and theoretical approaches, thereby designing a Participatory-Action-Research initiative from the classroom, to apply inside and outside the school. In addition, through the meetings that have taken place outside the school, the students have been able to find out about the youth centre in their town, its purpose, and to make proposals for its improvement.

The "CON_LecerSanJuan" project has been a valuable experience for all the parties that have made up this network of co-work and global commitment. Focusing on the people involved in this initiative, in general the high school students who participated said that they have learned a lot about the analysis of social and educational phenomena through different research methods. They have also acquired skills that have to do directly with finding and systematising information, critical thinking, etc., having had to train in research, design a concrete investigation, and put it into practice. They have clearly been excited to be able to do something that, in addition to generating cognitive, procedural, aptitudinal, and attitudinal learning, has allowed them to understand the importance of contributing to improving their hometown.

Getting out of the classroom to continue learning and becoming aware of how people can contribute to their most immediate environment through participation has been a fundamental aspect of this project. Likewise, being able to come to the university and get to know this setting and its students has also been valued very positively by the young people participating, because it has allowed them to reflect on possibilities in their future, as well as enrich the work they are doing through the perspectives of others.

In this sense, we should emphasise the need to use less traditional methodologies in education projects, such as Service-Learning and Participatory-Action-Research, since educational innovations that use such approaches motivate students and promote cross-cutting and democratic values that are acquired through practice, such as cooperation, altruism, social transformation, active, and responsible citizenship, and the common good, among others (Martin et al., 2021). In this case, being able to visualise throughout the whole process what they are contributing to improve their reality has been very positive, sharing spaces for participation together, and taking on responsibilities in research tasks.

To do this, the involvement once again of youth workers and members of the local council allowed the students to feel that participating in this initiative made sense because they were going to be able to make a real contribution to improving their immediate environment. Furthermore, the fact that the university proposes this type of initiative makes it easier to focus on the people who are the recipients of such research, involving them, giving them autonomy and decision-making power, as well as developing significant knowledge and promoting values of global citizenship.

When we talk about the young population, this aspect is fundamental. Giving prominence to young people and creating spaces for their engagement and involvement allows them to take power to decide on their future. Students look beyond their classroom and become aware of their contribution to the community, of their role as citizens, of the importance of developing leadership that improves and transforms their immediate surroundings and more removed environments. Thus, "participation is a process that impacts the personal dimension, which generates both personal and institutional identity, affecting the motivation to become involved in different school activities" (Ochoa et al., 2024, p.11) [Author's translation].

In this type of project, the promotion of networking and cooperation between different organisations working with young people is also relevant, as it provides an interdisciplinary and transdisciplinary perspective. To do this, all the parties must be present in the classroom with young people, although this type of initiative requires medium—to long-term processes and, therefore, more time, more resources (especially human), more commitment and a sense of responsibility within local institutions, as well as overcoming the resistance of the education system to change.

Finally, we must remember that the ultimate goal of Service-Learning should be the consolidation of the proposals in time and space, that is, that they are sustainable beyond the people or institutions that promote them initially. In this vein, from the experience presented here, we propose a series of elements that may favour the maintenance of the proposal in the future:

- Firstly, starting from the realities and interests of young people can awaken their motivation to continue participating in their environment once the project ends.
- In turn, projects that respond to the needs and interests of all parties involved (such as teachers, schools, universities, or public administration) can also encourage continued commitment to their implementation.
- A fundamental fact in this regard is that this project has been introduced as part of the curriculum of a subject studied in the first year of *Bachillerato*, which would facilitate its future maintenance and its subsequent extrapolation to other places and contexts of interest.
- Other actions that would promote the sustainability of this proposal over time have to do with the planning of joint activities among the members of the network, such as meetings, conferences, collaborative publications, etc. This would create spaces for shared reflection and analysis, but also for personal relationships that would further consolidate this network once the experience ends.
- Furthermore, spreading awareness of the project through institutional communication channels (of the university or the town council, for example), institutional social media, radio programmes, or academic publications would make it easier to reach out to other organisations or people interested in being part of this network.

In any case, we value the joint construction of the project between all of those involved from the moment of its inception, which has facilitated their personal and professional identification with the proposal that would not have been possible otherwise. All parties have been represented and driving forces throughout the process and that can make it easier for the project to be modified, updated or adapted to continue surviving in the future, thus generating quality based on a prosperous sustainability plan.

As future lines of socio-educational innovation and research, we would advocate further advancing the promotion of youth participation as a strategy in the development of public policies that directly affect future global citizens. That is, to renew joint policies immersed in current challenges facing today's society, as agreed in the Resolution of the Council of the European Union (2018), on the EU Youth Strategy 2019–2027. Within this regulatory framework, both the needs and interests of young people are considered, working on the issues of equality and non-discrimination, inclusion, participation, and tackling the global, European, national, regional, and local dimensions from a dual approach.

In short, on the one hand, we believe that we are responding to many of the objectives set out in the report drafted by the Youth Observatory in Spain (2012, p. 37), such as: improving the quality of learning; updating learning content in line with the knowledge society; open education and training for the local environment, Europe, and the world; and making the most of resources. And, on the other hand, by way of conclusion, we think that education is a fundamental element in the socio-educational transformation and development of people, even more so during childhood and adolescence. Education provides powerful tools to work on the sociocultural, educational, and political growth of a given context, laying the foundations to develop public management through the perceptions of citizens.

References

Caballo Villar, M. B., & Gradaílle Pernas, R. (2023). Educación y conciliación para la equidad. *Pedagogía Social. Revista Interuniversitaria, 43*, 9–12. https://doi.org/10.7179/PSRI_2023.43.00

Caride Gómez, J. A. (2004). ≃Qué añade lo "Social" al sustantivo "Pedagogía"? *Pedagogía Social. Revista Interuniversitaria, 11*, 55–85.

Doistua Nebreda, J., Pose Porto, H. M., & Ahedo González, R. (2016). Espacios, experiencias de ocio y participación de la juventud: contribución a los modelos de gestión e intervención a partir del análisis de buenas prácticas. *Revista Contextos Educativos, 19*, 133–145. https://doi.org/10.18172/con.2776

Lazcano Quintana, I., & De Juanas Oliva, A. (2020). *Ocio y juventud. sentido, potencial y participación comunitaria. UNED.*

LOMLOE. (2020, 30 December). Ley Orgánica 3/2020, de 29 de diciembre, por la que se modifica la Ley Orgánica 2/2006, de 3 de mayo, de Educación. *Boletín Oficial del Estado,* 340. https://www.boe.es/eli/es/lo/2020/12/29/3/con

Martín, X., Bär-Kwast, B., Gijón, M., Puig, J., & Rubio, L. (2021). El mapa de los valores del aprendizaje-servicio. *Alteridad. Revista Electrónica de Educación, 16*(1), 12–22. https://doi.org/10.17163/alt.v16n1.2021.01

Navarro Saldaña, G., Rubio Aguilar, V., Lavado Huarcaya, S., Minnicelli, A., & Acuña, J. (2017). Razones y propósitos para incorporar la responsabilidad social en la formación de personas y organizaciones de Latinoamérica. *Revista Latinoamericana de Educación Inclusiva, 11*(2), 51–72. https://doi.org/10.4067/S0718-73782017000200005

Observatorio de la Juventud en España. (2012). *Juventud y educación ante las nuevas sociedades tecnológicas del siglo XXI.* Instituto de la Juventud.

Ochoa, A., Solís, M. G., & Mayor, D. (2024). La participación del estudiantado en las prácticas de Aprendizaje-Servicio, percepciones de docentes universitarios españoles y mexicanos. *Revista de Investigación Educativa, 42*(2). https://doi.org/10.6018/rie.541661

Pérez de Guzmán Puya, M. V., & Mendoza Ramírez, C. B. (2020). El uso del método de investigación-acción en el estudio de las vejeces. In R. J. Guillén, C. B. M. Ramírez, & A. R. Abad (Eds.), *Introducción a la metodología cualitativa para el estudio de la vejez y el envejecimiento* (pp. 92–107). Universidad Autónoma de Tlaxcala.

Pérez de Guzmán, V., Vargas Vergara, M., & Rodríguez Díez, J. (2024). Cultura de paz, convivencia escolar y estrategias para la resolución de conflictos en los centros escolares. In M. V. P. de Guzmán Puya (Ed.), *Derechos humanos y convivencia escolar. Estrategias y propuestas para el éxito* (pp. 21–41). Peter Lang. https://doi.org/10.3726/b21460

Pérez de Guzmán, V., Vila-Merino, E., & Bas-Peña, E. (2023). Conciliación, educación y ocio en la infancia: Análisis mediante personas expertas. *Pedagogía Social. Revista Interuniversitaria, 43*, 61–73. https://doi.org/10.7179/PSRI_2023.43.04

Resolución del Consejo de la Unión Europea y los Representantes de los Gobiernos de los Estados miembros, reunidos en el Consejo, sobre un marco para la cooperación europea en el ámbito de la juventud: la Estrategia de la Unión Europea para la Juventud 2019-2027. *Diario Oficial de la Unión Europea,* 456, 18 December 2018. https://www.boe.es/doue/2018/456/Z00001-00022.pdf

Simon, P., Clavería, S., García Albacete, G., López Ortega, A., & Torre, M. (2021). *Informe juventud en España 2020.* Instituto de la Juventud.

Trujillo Herrera, J. F. (2024). Educar en participación comunitaria escolar. Derecho fundamental de la ciudadanía. In M. V. P. de Guzmán Puya (Ed.), *Derechos humanos y convivencia escolar. Estrategias y propuestas para el éxito* (pp. 137–156). Peter Lang. https://doi.org/10.3726/b21460

UNAF. (2019). *Políticas de conciliación de la vida laboral, personal y familiar en la Unión Europea.*

UNAF. (2021). *Corresponsabilidad y conciliación de la vida laboral, personal y familiar en España. Desigualdades y transformaciones después de la COVID-19.* Unión de Asociaciones Familiares.

UNESCO. (2021). *Reimagining our futures together: a new social contract for education*. UNESCO.

UNICEF-Innocenti. (2020). *Mundos de influencia ≃Cuáles son los determinantes del bienestar infantil en los países ricos?* Fondo de las Naciones Unidas para la Infancia (UNICEF).

Valdemoros-San-Emeterio, M., Sanz-Arazuri, E., & Ponce-de-León-Elizondo, A. (2017). Digital leisure and perceived family functioning in youth of upper Secondary Education [Ocio digital y ambiente familiar en estudiantes de postobligatoria]. *Comunicar, 50*, 99–108. https://doi.org/10.3916/C50-2017-09

Chapter 3
The Quest for Emotion in Leisure and Its Contributions to Human Development: Experiences of Higher Education Teachers

Luz Angela Ardila Gutiérrez, Aurora Madariaga Ortuzar, and Tony Honorato

Abstract This paper explores leisure imaginaries and their correlation with human development among faculty members in a Colombian higher education institution. The researchers gathered data through questionnaires and interviews using a qualitative approach alongside statistical techniques. The primary variables and analytical focal points included thoughts, emotions, and leisure practices. By triangulating the data, the researchers identified patterns and trends that elucidate the leisure imaginaries within this demographic. The findings suggest that leisure experiences serve as a means for teachers to navigate challenges, offering avenues for personal development and a sense of liberation from regulated environments. Emotions linked to leisure encompass happiness, tranquillity, joy motivation, sadness, and nostalgia. Professors express eagerness to explore their creativity and participate in activities that yield enduring happiness. However, concerns emerge about the absence of loved ones and a yearning for personal pursuits free from external impositions. This exploration underscores the significance of leisure beyond mere rest, emphasizing its potential for fostering human development.

3.1 Introduction

This research is based on the findings of a study on leisure imaginaries and their relationship with human development among teachers at a higher education institution in Colombia. The aim was to identify these leisure imaginaries and their correspondence with human development within a group of teachers. It is framed in the

---

L. A. Ardila Gutiérrez (✉) · T. Honorato
Universidad Estadual de Londrina, Londrina, Brasil
e-mail: angela.ardila@opendeusto.es; tony@uel.br

A. Madariaga Ortuzar
University of Deusto, Bilbao, Spain
e-mail: aurora.madariaga@deusto.es

L. Ronda et al. (eds.), *Leisure and Human Development*, Human Well-Being Research and Policy Making, https://doi.org/10.1007/978-3-031-90778-4_3

specific scenario of the experience of higher education teachers, so it is essential to justify and contextualize three fundamental aspects. First, to understand the general context in which the lives of teachers develop from a work and personal point of view; second, to delve into the relationship between leisure and human development from the perspective of social imaginaries, where emotions are relevant to understanding the phenomenon of leisure; and third, to provide an interpretation of the role of emotions in the leisure experiences of teachers from the perspective of Norbert Elías (1993). This third element constitutes a new way of interpreting the research findings by addressing the results based on this author's proposals for understanding emotions and their link with leisure experiences.

3.1.1 Teachers' Life Context: Professional and Personal Dimensions

In addressing the initial aspect, scholarly literature widely acknowledges the transformations that education has experienced in recent years due to globalization. These shifts, driven by neoliberal policies implemented in academia, have been termed "Academic Capitalism" by Slaughter and Leslie (1997).

Authors such as Gibbons et al. (1997), Ibarra (2003), Santos (2007), and Blanch and Cantera (2011) examine the concept of academic capitalism, defining it as universities' use of human capital to secure a position as a quality indicator. This transformation renders professors and researchers comparable to industrial workers, subject to stringent labour controls and a loss of autonomy. They shift from being skilled artisans of knowledge to becoming components within the larger machinery of knowledge production.

This scenario arises in part due to the influence of global organizations such as the UN (United Nations Organization), UNESCO (United Nations Educational, Scientific and Cultural Organization), the OECD (Organization for Economic Cooperation and Development), and the World Bank, which promote changes to improve the quality of higher education globally. These changes include better teacher training and qualifications, supporting "good teachers", and improving salary conditions. For example, the OECD reports on Colombia from 2013, 2015, 2018, and 2019 have highlighted problems such as low productivity in higher education, labour informality among teachers, low educational quality, and the need for investment in research and development. To address these challenges, governments have adjusted regulations concerning the quality of education at different times, raising standards in the training, selection, and dedication expected of teachers in their substantive roles.

This has had significant consequences on the working and personal conditions of teachers. Researchers such as Oliveira et al. (2004), Cornejo (2009), Restrepo and López (2011), Terán and Botero (2011), Castangna and Mufarrej (2015), González (2017), and Londoño et al. (2019) have identified various problematic conditions that affect teachers. These include high workloads, job insecurity, competition among colleagues, lack of camaraderie, job instability, and financial restrictions. Such factors negatively impact personal and family life, restricting free time, reducing opportunities to enjoy leisure spaces, and consequently disrupting their work-life balance.

The context above directly influences teachers' well-being and limits access to the potential benefits of leisure as a driver of human development, as identified in various investigations outlined below.

3.1.2 Leisure and Human Development Based on Social Imaginaries

The second topic, examined in detail, is the relationship between leisure and human development from the perspective of social imaginaries.

The link between leisure and human development has been widely addressed through theories such as humanistic leisure (Cuenca, 2000; San Salvador, 2000), which assert that studying leisure requires considering various areas and dimensions that shape people's leisure experiences. According to these theories, the areas in which leisure experiences can be analysed are culture, sports, recreation, and tourism.

Using this structure of areas and dimensions, a systematic review of research from Brazil and Colombia revealed multiple contributions of leisure to people's experiences, practices, emotions, as well as some negative effects.

From the cultural perspective, leisure facilitates adaptation to environments and the development of social skills. From the perspective of sports, leisure prevents diseases and enhances self-esteem. From the perspective of recreation, it contributes to family entertainment and helps address socio-emotional behaviours. In tourism, leisure provides privileged moments of connection. Lastly, leisure is reiterated as a fundamental social right. However, it was also identified that leisure can occasionally negatively impact people's quality of life and harm nature. The multifaceted nature of this phenomenon and the various ways leisure is understood and experienced prompted us to contemplate the significance of examining it through the lens of social imaginaries. This analytical approach has been employed to investigate numerous social phenomena. Nevertheless, the systematic review revealed a scarcity of studies specifically focusing on leisure as a social imaginary.

To confirm the above, a state-of-the-art review conducted by the Ibero-American Research Network on Social Imaginaries and Representations (Aliaga et al., 2018) was examined, which found only three theoretical studies linking leisure to social imaginaries. Additionally, 40 studies from the perspective of imaginaries were reviewed, but only one focused on imaginaries and representations of leisure in schools (Carreño et al., 2012).

These findings underscore the relevance of studying leisure from the perspective of social imaginaries, particularly from the approach proposed by Baeza (2003). This approach, among other features, asserts that social reality must be addressed in its complexity, considering four specific planes. The first is an ideational plane, which, in this research, relates to thoughts about leisure. The second is an underlying plane, connected to emotions about leisure. The third is an apparent plane, associated with leisure practices. Finally, a fourth, archetypal plane, emerges from analysing the first three planes to identify the constructed meanings and visions of leisure among research participants.

This text delves deeply into the results concerning the underlying level of emotions about leisure expressed by the participants. The analysis of these results is framed using Norbert Elias's approach to understanding the role of emotion in leisure.

3.1.3 Emotions from the Perspective of Norbert Elías

Norbert Elias (1897–1990) was an influential German sociologist of Jewish origin. In his most notable work, "The Civilization Process" (1993), he examines how social control impacts the regulation of human emotions and behaviours, arguing that as society becomes more complex, the forms of emotional expression and control evolve. His focus on the interdependence between society and individual psychology has significantly influenced the study of contemporary societies.

According to Elias (1993), emotions constitute an intrinsic aspect of human existence, intricately tied to socialization processes, social control, and civilization. He posits that as societies advance, changes emerge in the ways individuals regulate, express, and manage their emotions. These assertions are rooted in a body of theoretical and empirical research that has been further developed by various scholars over time.

Guarnieri et al. (2023) underscore the evidence Elias provides in his research on how transformations in social structure have profoundly influenced behavioural changes and the configuration of individual personality. His work demonstrates how people acquire and assimilate patterns of behaviour and ways of being, internalizing emotions, fears, and feelings through the civilizing process.

Other scholars, such as Pinheiro (2013), highlight the contribution of Norbert Elias to the sociology of emotions and its influence on the understanding of the social, considering that the latter is configured by extensive social networks and an emotional economy that governs interdependent relationships in contemporary Western societies. Additionally, he emphasizes analysis through research into etiquette manuals, codes of conduct, and behavioural treatises supported by empirical evidence. Based on these empirical and theoretical studies, Elias maintains that the civilizing process in the Western context differs from others by reducing physical violence, which is increasingly replaced by the internalization of emotions, especially shame, acting as a driving force of individual action in the cultural and social sphere.

In a similar vein, Urteaga (2013) asserts that Elias's framework primarily serves as an analytical model that requires engagement with empirical realities to render structural and interdependent processes more comprehensible. This approach enables the contemplation of social change, facilitating the apprehension and visibility of dynamic social processes and pivotal moments of disruption. Elias advocates for conceptualizing the individual and society in terms of relational and processual dynamics across time, emphasizing the essential role of empirical research at both micro and macro levels, spanning short and extended historical durations. This viewpoint is fundamental for the production and review of knowledge in sociology and history (Honorato, 2017).

Gebara and Wouters (2009), aligned with the concepts of Norbert Elias, scrutinized the evolution, up to the late nineteenth century, of a trend towards formalizing customs and imposing discipline on individual behaviour. This trajectory involved curtailing emotional expressions deemed perilous or likely to incite violence. The regime of customs expanded to include constraints on behaviours characterized as arrogant, humiliating, savage, violent, dirty, indecent, or lustful. Consequently, society grappled with feelings of shame and anxiety when confronting any emotion or impulse categorized as "dangerous".

Based on Elias, these authors point out that, in the twentieth century, a process of informalization of customs and a relaxation of personal discipline emerged. This change facilitated the loosening of previously imposed restrictions and enabled a greater diversity of emotional expressions in contemporary society. Nowadays, emotions occupy a central place in personal consciousness, and self-regulation and emotional regulation are highly valued. There has been a transition from external control to mechanisms of emotional self-control and an internalization of social norms, which influences the experience and expression of emotions. Within the framework of Elias's thought, this civilizing process recognizes the transition from social control to self-control as a fundamental condition for individuals to live in harmony (Negri, 2006).

In this type of society, adults must master the ability to restrain their strong emotions. Consequently, they have learned not to expose them to others, developing automatic control over themselves. Thus, emotional control has merged with the individual's personality structure (Elias & Dunning, 1992).

Aligned with the conceptual framework of emotions established by Norbert Elias and elaborated upon by other scholars, this study delves into the leisure phenomenon within contemporary societies. This exploration holds significant relevance, not solely as a reflection of historical preconceptions rooted in societies aiming to regulate behaviour, but also, as per the characteristics of present-day societies, as a domain fostering liberation and emotional relief for individuals. Within this context, individuals actively pursue distinct emotional experiences during their leisure time, contrasting with those encountered in their everyday lives, as evidenced by the study's outcomes involving teachers.

Leisure, Much More Than Free Time

According to Elias and Dunning (1992), in today's societies, the idea that recreational activities complement work is widely accepted, and the study of leisure is rarely raised as a research topic. This notion is rooted in the thinking of societies that have justified, as part of their myths and social beliefs, the polarization of work and leisure, and consequently the valuation of work as a moral duty and a purpose, while leisure has been degraded as a form of laziness and complacency.

In these societies, the pressure of relatively permanent internal and external control systems is observed, and satisfaction or dissatisfaction with leisure can considerably impact well-being at both the individual and social levels, even surpassing the importance assigned to leisure in the collective imagination. In part, this dichotomy between work and leisure is accentuated by confusion over the distinctions between what constitutes free time and leisure.

Elias and Dunning (1992) maintain that to establish a solid theoretical framework for the study of leisure that better fits the phenomenon's essence, it is imperative to differentiate and define the relationships between free time and leisure more precisely. This requires recognizing that only a fraction of free time is allocated to leisure activities, since, in these societies, most people dedicate a large part of their free time to various occupations.

Furthermore, the contemporary definition of leisure tends to link it with rest, directly relating it to work by arguing that leisure provides spaces of tranquillity to recharge energy for work. However, it is argued that the essence of this action lies in inducing people to states of immobility that do not necessarily involve the expression of emotions or the integral development of the individual.

The concept of recreational or leisure activities, which Elias and Dunning (1992) have called "mimetic", denotes that they are inherently imitative activities. From both a social and individual perspective, these activities serve a different function than the traditional understanding of leisure as rest and have a distinctive impact on people.

Regarding the crucial difference between leisure and free time, it is important to note that free time encompasses all the time not allocated to paid work. However, in contemporary societies, only some of this free time is dedicated to leisurely activities. To deepen this understanding, Elias and Dunning (1992) developed a typology of spheres that represent different uses of free time, which sheds light on the fact that allocating a substantial part of free time to leisure is not feasible. Table 3.1 summarizes each of these spheres and their respective meanings.

According to this categorization, only in activities classified as "mimetic" can people experience true leisure moments, seeking emotions different from those usual in their daily lives. These pleasant emotions share certain characteristics with those experienced in critical situations (Elias & Dunning, 1992).

Based on the above, the authors argue that the traditional polarization between leisure and work is inadequate. This perspective suggests that all free time, excluding time dedicated to paid work, can be used for recreational activities—a view questioned by the typology of time spheres presented.

Table 3.1 Use of time spheres

Spheres	Description
Private labour and family management	Domestic activities, including home provisions
Rest	Activities include sitting, smoking or knitting, daydreaming, wandering around the house, engaging in trifles, doing nothing in particular, and sleeping
Satisfaction of biological needs	Socially structured biological needs, e.g. eating, drinking, defecating, lovemaking, and sleeping
Sociability	His sphere of activities is neither work nor leisure. They involve considerable effort, ranging from highly formal to highly informal extremes, with many degrees in between
The kind of mimetic and play activities	Recreational activities such as going to the theatre, concerts, racing, movies, hunting, fishing, playing bridge, mountain climbing, gambling, dancing, and watching television. These are free-time activities with leisure characteristics. Participation as an actor or spectator, as long as they are not specialized occupations with which one earns a living

Note. Sphere descriptions have been adapted from Elias and Dunning (1992)

Delving deeper into the category of mimetic activities, it becomes clear that through this type of recreation or leisure, people seek not to release tension, but to experience a specific type of tension: a form of arousal often linked to fear, sadness, and other emotions they typically try to avoid. However, to adequately address these issues, it is necessary to overcome the reductionist view of leisure that focuses solely on "tension release" or "recovery from work", since these mimetic activities arouse emotions that stimulate the growth of individual capabilities and place people in situations of creativity that simple rest cannot achieve.

Following Elias's perspective, Honorato and Pires (2014) postulate that sport and leisure are specific and mutually dependent human manifestations in societies during their civilizational phase. Through sports and recreational practices, people internalize and spread the sense of civilization based on what are considered good habits—manifested in historically constructed behaviours—and transmitted to future generations. These practices distinguish a social group and differentiate an individual from others.

The author also specifies that the concept of modern leisure, according to Elias's (1993) studies, is based on three fundamental elements: (1) modern leisure does not correspond to the notion of freedom but is a specific historical product of balanced situations and restrictions in various emerging spheres of civilizational processes; (2) the reduction of violent, spontaneous, and intense emotions in contemporary society is attributed to the high degree of development of containment thresholds considered "civilized", compared to past times; (3) modern leisure is configured as an activity increasingly linked to forms of mimetic behaviour.

These approaches are framed within the humanistic leisure perspective, as described by Cuenca (2000). In this perspective, leisure is conceived as a source of personal experiences that enrich the quality of life and provide human enjoyment. This vision recognizes leisure's ability to provide meaning and create creative encounters that foster personal development. When considering leisure as a source of personal experiences, it is situated in the subjective realm, and the experiences vary depending on the personality of the person experiencing them, as Lazcano and Madariaga (2016) have pointed out.

Leisure offers people a different way to manage the tensions derived from stressful situations. They develop emotions and skills and discover people's potential for spontaneity. Ultimately, the humanistic approach to leisure highlights the importance of these personal experiences in enriching life and individual well-being. Aligned with leisure as a personal and subjective experience, Elias and Dunning (1992) argue that leisure becomes a space where, with social approval, people can publicly express a moderate level of emotion. This phenomenon directly impacts their well-being and, ultimately, affects individual quality of life, with consequences extending to society's collective spheres.

Leisure research has been scarce among teacher populations, possibly due to the expectations associated with their work. These expectations emphasize the relevance of topics such as effective teaching strategies or professional development, underscoring the need for total dedication to one's vocation and strict adherence to professional standards. Furthermore, society places its expectations on the teacher as an impeccable, all-knowing, and multifunctional role model (Abacín et al., 2022), mostly playing objective roles. This approach diminishes the relevance assigned to understanding their subjective and personal experiences.

In the following sections, the methodology used will be explained, and the results concerning the emotions that leisure experiences provoke in teachers will be analysed, based on the information collected during this research.

3.2 Methodology

Based on the contextual and theoretical elements of leisure and human development, an empirical study was designed from a phenomenological perspective, adopting a mixed-methods approach to explore the leisure experiences of the participating teachers. Both qualitative and quantitative techniques were used. A questionnaire with open and closed questions was administered to 160 participants, and the data were subjected to exploratory analysis. Additionally, interviews were conducted with 12 participants, and their stories were interpreted through hermeneutic analysis. This process identified patterns and recurring themes using both deductive and inductive techniques. A phase of result integration or triangulation of the two methods helped decode, identify, and generate an interpretative proposal for the leisure imaginaries according to the study's objectives.

As indicated in previous sections, the approach to leisure imaginaries was based on Baeza's (2000) proposal. This chapter presents the findings related to the underlying plane, which concerns the emerging emotions in leisure experiences. These findings are analysed in light of Elias's ideas on leisure and emotions.

3.3 Findings: Educators' Leisure and Emotions

The data presented below are part of a study that aimed to identify the leisure imaginaries of a group of educators in Colombia. The data were collected through questionnaires and, secondly, through semi-structured interviews.

The questionnaire sought to explore the perceptions of a sample of 160 teachers regarding their practices, emotions, and thoughts related to leisure, free time, and their impact on human development. The goal was to gain an overview of shared perspectives and experiences. The analysis used Exploratory Data Analysis (EDA) techniques following the approach of Huber and Gento (2018). The findings concerning participants' emotions when reflecting on leisure are presented below.

As the first aspect, we inquired about the emotions generated when thinking about leisure and free time. A list of related emotions was provided. Figure 3.1 presents the results.

These data reveal that 88% of teachers associate leisure and free time with the emotion of joy, followed by 85% who associate it with freedom. Furthermore, 78% of participants link leisure and free time with pleasure, while 74% relate it to gratitude. A minority of teachers report experiencing negative emotions in relation to leisure and free time. Only 3% mention feeling remorse, followed by 1.8% who report feeling fear, 1% who experience shame, and 0.6% who report feeling hate.

The findings highlight the predominance of positive emotions associated with leisure and free time, although some negative experiences are also evident among a minority of participants. Additionally, those who selected the "other" option were asked to specify the emotion that thinking about leisure and free time generated for them. Figure 3.2 shows positive emotions and words such as tranquillity, rest,

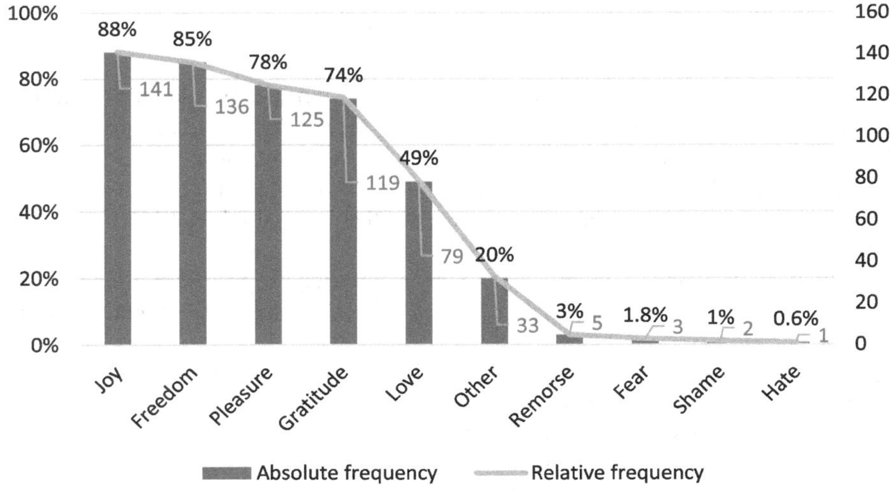

Fig. 3.1 Emotions generated by leisure and free time

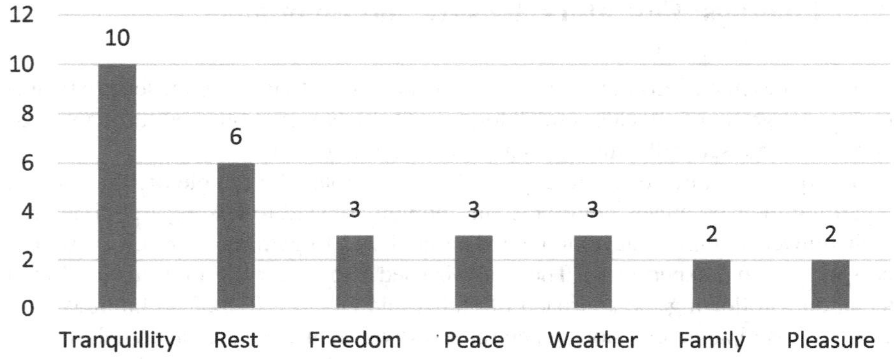

Fig. 3.2 Other emotions generated by leisure and free time (number of teachers)

Fig. 3.3 People who believe leisure develops emotions (%)

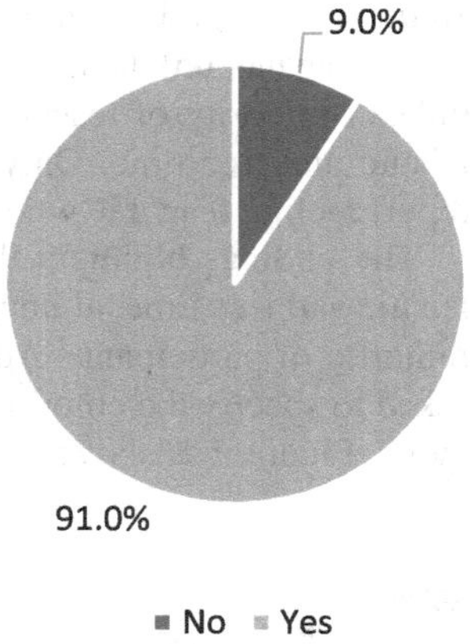

freedom, peace, family, and pleasure. Negative emotions, such as laziness and sadness, were mentioned less frequently—so they do not appear in the graph—and were mainly associated with the lack of time to enjoy leisure spaces.

Regarding whether people believe that leisure and free time allow them to develop emotions they cannot experience in other areas of life, 91% responded "yes", while 14% responded "no" (see Fig. 3.3).

Moreover, Table 3.2 categorizes the reasons provided to justify that leisure and free time allow the development of emotions that cannot be experienced in other areas.

Classifying the motives behind the idea that leisure allows one to develop emotions led to the identification of three main categories: sharing with others, personal development and freedom, and spaces for disconnection. Among these, the theme of freedom stands out, as teachers express that leisure spaces enable them to be more spontaneous and act without pressure. Additionally, the themes of connection and

Table 3.2 Reasons for leisure's role in emotional development

Motives	Leisure allows…
Sharing with others	Sharing with friends and family, engaging in activities with others, and discussing topics unrelated to work
Personal development and freedom	Engaging in physical and mental self-care activities. Developing personal aspects, emotions, and self-confidence. Exploring new interests and enhancing creativity. Acting freely, being more spontaneous, and without pressure
Spaces for disconnection	Breaking out of routine brings creativity, tranquillity, and relaxation. Becoming distracted and entertained with activities. Connecting with oneself. Releasing stress and rejuvenating the mind and body. Disconnecting, recovering, and resting. It is a personal and subjective time

disconnection are particularly relevant to their context, especially in light of the recent dynamics of teleworking.

These results from the questionnaire, which focus on emotions, reveal the diverse range of sensations that educators report experiencing in relation to leisure. The emotions most commonly mentioned are positive ones, such as joy, freedom, pleasure, gratitude, love, peace, and tranquillity. However, some negative emotions, such as sadness, were also noted. The findings emphasize that leisure provides an opportunity for spontaneity and the freedom to act without pressure, offering a stark contrast to the roles and expectations they must fulfil in their professional lives.

3.3.1 Emotions Manifested in the Interview Reports

To complement and contrast the findings from the questionnaire, an interview script was developed with the aim of exploring personal aspects in more depth, providing a comprehensive understanding of teachers' practices, emotions, and thoughts related to leisure, free time, and its impact on human development. Twelve interviews were conducted, with six female and six male participants, following a thematic life history approach (Tinoco, 2004). The analysis was hermeneutical, considering the emotions expressed in the narration of leisure experiences from the past, present, and future. This approach allowed for a broader analysis of the leisure phenomenon, extending beyond the confines of the teachers' work environment.

The emotions experienced at various stages of their lives became evident through the interviewees' narratives. Table 3.3 presents the key emotions identified, along with a series of testimonies that illustrate these emotions in the shared stories.

Regarding positive emotions, the participants expressed joy related to experiences from their childhood and youth, connections with family and friends, and the fulfilment derived from sharing knowledge and intellectual abilities with others.

When discussing their emotions, they reflect on the present, where they are working towards creating opportunities to enjoy moments of leisure in the future.

Table 3.3 Emotions about leisure

	Positive	Negative	Neutral
Childhood and youth	Joy—freedom—happiness—fun Serenity—tranquillity Gratitude—growth—satisfaction	Anxiety—sadness—fear	Longing
Present	Joy Trust—peace—security Enthusiasm Gratitude—satisfaction—pleasure Pride Serenity—tranquillity	Anxiety—worry Disillusion Frustration—bitterness—discomfort Sadness	Nostalgia
Future	Joy Hope—illusion—optimism Serenity—tranquillity—quiet	Nostalgia—loss	

This suggests that their current satisfaction with leisure is not optimal, which aligns with the well-being discomforts stemming from precarious working conditions.

> I experience joy because I like to learn from others and share my experiences so that others also learn from me. (Participant 5)
>
> I feel joy, and I think it is a motivation. Really, I don't think it is a utopia, although I know that there are many things that can oppose it, I think it is possible that, by doing serious and careful work, in the long term, I will be able to dedicate more time to the things that make my life happy […] It is a dream that helps me move forward. (Participant 3)

They express joy for the pleasant sensations they have experienced, such as winning sports tournaments and the freedom of being outdoors or on the street. However, this situation has change, for example, for their children, who now face insecurity and violence, leading to fear and uncertainty about moving freely. Additionally, the tensions of an unstable, competitive environment and power dynamics at work contribute to this shift in experiences.

> I remember, for example, that, in my childhood, whenever I was not studying at school, I was playing soccer in the street. The memories I have about that time are great and now that I have a son, I can compare, since unlike me, he cannot play in the street with the freedom with which I did. (Participant 3)

They mention feeling tranquillity, security, and satisfaction due to their intellectual abilities, especially when engaging in leisure practices such as reflection and prayer. These activities can be viewed as coping strategies that protect them from feelings of instability.

> It also means a sense of security because you feel like your hand is held by someone more able than you. And we are also doing it as a family. That means there is a sense of protection. It's like I'm filling myself, I'm wrapping myself in the bubble, which generates more power in me, not from Superman, but from the power to see, to know that there is hope, and it takes away the feeling of instability. (Participant 9)

Additionally, they express gratitude and satisfaction with their ability to manage their time effectively. They appreciate how their work enables them to advance projects and explore new environments. However, their stories also reveal issues such as work addiction, which has resulted from the demanding academic dynamics and reflects the precarious nature of their work.

> I have managed to be less addicted to work because I think I was addicted for a while. At this moment, I am trying to compensate a little more, although I have two jobs. But before, I had only one job, and I dedicated more time than I do now to both jobs combined. I have learned to manage those times. (Participant 6)

Regarding negative emotions, they express frustration about situations that they believe could have empowered them more in the past:

> When I think about that, I think I needed support to develop many capacities and skills. I like it a lot; I thought I was bad at crafts, and with my daughter, I have learned that I like it; it gives me feelings of pleasure and well-being. (Participant 8)

They express feelings of worry and sadness in moments of work overload, commitments, and stressful demands of studies and health issues resulting from these pressures. As highlighted in the literature, these perceptions and feelings have become increasingly common in recent years within higher education environments, with significant consequences for teachers.

> I try to keep the weekends free too, and sometimes even at night, I work late hours to try to have a free weekend since that happened before with another study I had where I didn't even have weekends for the family. (Participant 10)
>
> I used to work all day on Saturday, but thanks to my efforts, I have more free time. Excessive work caused me sleep apnoea problems, and I understood then the importance of leisure activities and free time to share with the family. (Participant 5)
>
> There are some moments of poetic outbursts when I can't find the space to develop that impulse. That makes me bitter; it rots me—the literal word for me is rot. I stay rotten for a while. (Participant 1)

In terms of neutral emotions, they express longing and nostalgia for the moments of leisure spent with family and friends during their childhood and youth.

> Well, the truth is I long for those times, the happiness. Because not only did we share time with friends, but also with our parents. My parents worked during the week; it was the time we were with them too. (Participant 10)
>
> I had a childhood of play and complicity because I was not a lonely child, I had someone to play with. And I remember that fondly with nostalgia but, above all, with gratitude because I know that not all people have that fortune. For example, my daughter did not have that possibility. (Participant 6)

This set of positive, negative, and neutral emotions accounts for the diverse experiences of educators regarding leisure. Positive emotions emerge when they refer to moments of sharing knowledge, enhancing their intellectual abilities, and interacting with family and other people. Negative emotions arise when they feel they could have better enhanced their abilities because they lack free time to express themselves and develop leisure practices of interest, and when they feel the pressure and overload of work. Emotions such as nostalgia and longing are related to leisure experiences in the past.

3.4 Discussion

This section critically examines the outcomes concerning teachers' emotional experiences in leisure, delves into the implications of these findings, and establishes connections with existing literature. In line with Urteaga's (2013) emphasis on aligning literature with empirical realities, this analysis seeks to enhance the comprehensibility of Elias's structural and interdependent processes. Four key issues derived from the results are scrutinized: firstly, the contextual factors influencing the development of teachers' emotions; secondly, their mechanisms of self-regulation and internalization of norms for emotional control; thirdly, the interplay between individual and societal dimensions; and fourthly, the distinction between free time and leisure.

3.4.1 About the Current Conditions in Which Emotions Develop

The results are related to previous findings by other authors (Oliveira et al., 2004; Cornejo, 2009; Terán & Botero, 2011) on the working conditions of teachers, which include lack of time, job insecurity, and their impacts on physical and emotional health. When the participants mention their emotions, they speak from a present in which they are building the ability to enjoy moments of leisure in the future. This suggests that their current satisfaction with leisure is not optimal, and they resort to emotions such as hope and optimism as euphemizing or mitigation strategies to tolerate current working conditions.

3.4.2 On Self-Regulation and Internalization of Norms for Coexistence with Others

Manifestations related to the feeling of freedom they experience in leisure, which allows them to be more spontaneous and act without pressure, are present both in the results of the questionnaire and in the interviews. As a synonym for freedom, they express the idea of connection and disconnection, which is particularly relevant in the context of teachers, given the recently implemented teleworking.

These findings align with the observations made by Elias and Dunning (1992), who contend that in contemporary societies, adults are expected to manage their intense emotions adeptly. This expectation is linked to the appraisal of self-regulation, emotional control, and the internalization of societal norms that shape emotional experience and expression (Gebara & Wouters, 2009). As articulated by Cuenca (2000) and Elias and Dunning (1992), study participants express the potential for personal development and the prospect of experiencing freedom and authenticity beyond regulated environments regarding their emotions and experiences.

When they mention feeling tranquillity, security, and satisfaction with their intellectual abilities, and when they develop their leisure practices such as reflection and prayer, these are associated with coping strategies that protect them from feelings of instability. From the perspective of authors such as Gebara and Wouters (2009) and Negri (2006), this can be understood as ways in which people seek leisure that allows them to act and feel in accordance with social norms, and, on the other hand, as how those who have managed to internalize norms experience emotions and self-control as a fundamental condition for living in harmony with others.

Emotional forms such as anxiety are evident and associated with behaviours such as work addiction. However, some of the participants express emotions such as gratitude for having managed this addiction, which clearly shows the assessment of self-control over emotions generated by dynamics external to their actions. Social control impacts the regulation of human emotions and behaviours, arguing that as society becomes more complex, the forms of expression and control of emotions change.

Furthermore, it becomes clear that they find ways to control and release their emotions in their leisure time despite social and work pressures. This process is related to the pressure of internal and external control systems, which impacts both individually and collectively.

3.4.3 On the Interdependence Between the Social and the Individual

The confirmation of social and individual interdependence emerges through the discovery of comparable emotions in both individual interviews and the collective responses from the group of teachers involved in the questionnaire application (Elias, 1993). Observable social networks contribute to the identification of shared expressions that have been amalgamated and standardized. This phenomenon aligns with what Pinheiro (2013) terms as emotional economy, wherein interaction is facilitated, and interdependent relationships are regulated within contemporary Western societies.

3.4.4 On the Difference Between Free Time and Leisure

While this segment of the research focused on emotions does not explicitly unveil a distinct differentiation in the participants' understanding between free time and leisure, upon reflecting on their leisure practices, educators independently discovered that not all their free time is dedicated to leisure. They acknowledge that the activities they predominantly engage in outside work are linked to private work and family management. Consequently, they discerned the disparity between leisure and free time, recognizing that although theoretically perceptible, as underscored by Elias and Dunning in the temporal domains, there exists a prevalent misconception in everyday experience wherein free time is erroneously equated with leisure.

Conversely, the findings of this research underscore the mimetic quality of teachers' leisure activities, aligning with Elias and Dunning's (1992) observations. Teachers actively seek to encounter emotions and experiences during leisure that they aspire to have in their daily lives but find constrained by their professional responsibilities and ethical-moral expectations. Leisure, in this context, serves as a space for alleviating pressures and tensions, providing an avenue for enjoying moments of spontaneity and emotional relief. Furthermore, it is evident that the working conditions of teachers, particularly those related to teaching and learning, have been so deeply internalized by the participants that they desire to replicate these experiences even in their leisure moments.

The above is related to Elias and Dunning (1992) when they express that leisure becomes a refuge for people to release burdens and pressures imposed on them. What they experience in leisure experiences serves as moments of liberation, emotional relief, and spontaneity, which is why they look for experiences in leisure that take them away from their daily lives.

3.5 Conclusions

In summary, this study confirms that working conditions affect teachers' leisure experiences. It also demonstrates how individuals must regulate their emotions to be part of today's society and facilitate coexistence. This is evident in forms of self-control that highlight the interdependence between the social and individual spheres, thus generating social imaginaries.

On the other hand, while the idea of free time as leisure is often presented, individual reflections reveal that not all time outside of work is linked to mimetic or leisure activities.

The participants express the value of leisure moments because they allow them to develop emotions that are not possible in other spaces and to act in ways that are not feasible at work.

The emotions reported by participants were classified into three main categories: positive, negative, and neutral. In most cases, both positive and negative emotions were related to family. As positive emotions, they are associated with the company and satisfaction of sharing, while as negative emotions, family dynamics sometimes impede the enjoyment of personal leisure moments.

This approach to the emotions teachers experience in their leisure activities highlights the potential and value they find in leisure, relieving it from the limitations of being just a space for rest based on work. Furthermore, the perspective of leisure time across the past, present, and future enabled the identification of different emotions at various life stages, offering an alternative to understanding leisure outside the leisure—work dichotomy that is so prominent today.

Clearly, the concept of leisure is not primarily associated with negative prejudices, as some Latin American authors have pointed out. Instead, the study reveals particular and reflective perspectives on leisure, emphasizing the importance of education in this field.

Among the research limitations, we can mention the restricted sample, which does not allow for the generalization of results to other populations. However, extrapolation of results was not the aim of the study. Additionally, although the data collection instruments were validated by experts, they have inherent limitations. Result interpretation may have been influenced by researcher bias. These limitations do not invalidate the results and conclusions but recognizing them provides a more complete and transparent view, opening opportunities for more robust future research.

For all that has been said, an interdisciplinary approach, mixed methods, longitudinal studies, and cross-cultural comparisons are suggested to better understand leisure imaginaries and, especially, the emotions that arise from these experiences. It is also recommended to explore how these emotions manifest in different profiles, urban and rural environments, public and private institutions, and how social and cultural constructions of gender influence emotions and leisure imaginaries.

References

Aliaga, F., Maric, M., & Uribe, C. (2018). Imaginarios y Representaciones sociales. Estado de la investigación en Iberoamérica. Ediciones USTA.

Abacín, R., Salazar, A., Castillo, Z., & Pérez, L. (2022). Enigmas en torno a la profesión docente: esclareciendo los mitos. *Revista EDUCARE-UPEL-IPB-Segunda Nueva Etapa 2.0, 26*(3), 4–29. https://doi.org/10.46498/reduipb.v26i3.1800

Baeza, M. (2000). *Los Caminos Invisibles de la Realidad Social. Ensayo de Sociología Profunda sobre los Imaginarios Sociales*. RIL Editores.

Baeza, M. (2003). *Imaginarios Sociales. Apuntes para la Discusión Teórica y Metodológica*. Editorial Universidad de Concepción.

Blanch, J., & Cantera, L. (2011). La nueva gestión pública de universidades y hospitales. Aplicaciones e implicaciones. In T. Agulló (Ed.), *Nuevas Formas de Organización del Trabajo y la Empleabilidad* (pp. 515–534). Universidad de Oviedo.

Castangna, M., & Mufarrej, S. (2015). Política de formação de educadores do campo no contexto da expansão da educação superior. *Revista Educação em Questão, 51*(37), 121–146. https://doi.org/10.21680/1981-1802.2015v51n37ID7174

Carreño, J., Rodríguez, A., & Gutiérrez, P. (2012). Representaciones sociales e imaginarios en torno a la escuela, la recreación, el tiempo libre y el ocio en tres escuelas de la ciudad de Bogotá. *Lúdica Pedagógica, 2*(17), 114–119. https://doi.org/10.17227/ludica.num17-1787

Cornejo, R. (2009). Condiciones de trabajo y bienestar/malestar docente en profesores de enseñanza media de Santiago de Chile. *Educação & Sociedade, 30*(107), 409–426. https://doi.org/10.1590/S0101-73302009000200006

Cuenca, M. (2000). *Ocio Humanista*. Documentos de Estudios de Ocio, (16). Universidad de Deusto.
Elias, N. (1993). *O Processo Civilizador 2: Formação do Estado e Civilização*. .
Elías, N., & Dunning, E. (1992). *Deporte y Ocio en el Proceso de la Civilización*. Fondo de Cultura Económica.
Gebara, A., & Wouters, C. (2009). *O Controle das Emoções*. Editora.
Gibbons, M., Limoges, C., Nowotny, H., Schwartzman, S., Scott, P., & Trow, M. (1997). *La Nueva Producción del Conocimiento. La Dinámica de la Ciencia y la Investigación en las Sociedades Contemporáneas*. Pomares-Corredor S.A.
González, G. (2017). La senda del perdedor; las políticas de cambio en la educación superior de México. *Diálogos sobre Educación. Temas actuales en investigación educativa, 8*(14), 1–21. https://doi.org/10.32870/dse.vi14.203
Guarnieri, D., De Almeida, E., Montagnini, M., & Honorato, T. (2023). Apontamentos para pensar os processos educativos. In A. De Jesús & G. De Araujo Tiroli (Eds.), *Teorías da Educação: Pensadores, Caminhos para a Educação Básica* (pp. 172–187). Universidade Estadual de Londrina.
Honorato, T. (2017). Pesquisas com Norbert Elias em história da educação. *Comunicações, 24*(3), 107–127.
Honorato, T., & Pires, A. G. M. (2014). Prácticas y representaciones del deporte y del ocio según el periódico 'Paraná Norte' (1934-1937). *Educación Física y Deporte, 33*(1), 15–30. https://doi.org/10.17533/udea.efyd.v33n1a02
Huber, G., & Gento, S. (2018). La aportación de la estadística exploratoria al análisis de datos cualitativos. *Perspectiva Educacional, 57*(1), 50–69. https://doi.org/10.4151/07189729
Ibarra, E. (2003). Capitalismo académico y globalización: la universidad reinventada. *Revista Educação & Sociedade, 24*(84), 1059–1067. https://doi.org/10.1590/S0101-73302003000300017
Lazcano, I., & Madariaga, A. (2016). El valor del ocio en la sociedad actual. In *La Marcha Nocturna: ≃Un Rito Exclusivamente Español?* (pp. 15–33). Centro Reina Sofía sobre Adolescencia y Juventud. Fundación de Ayuda contra la Drogadicción (FAD).
Londoño, S., Gómez, G., & González, V. (2019). Percepción de los docentes frente a la carga laboral de instituciones educativas colombianas sector público. *Revista Espacios, 40*(2), 26–34.
Negri, R. (2006). Tecnização e Civilização. *Revista Gestão Industrial, 2*(2).
OECD. (2013). *Estudios económicos de la OCDE. Colombia 2013: evaluación económica*. OECD.
OECD. (2015). *Colombia políticas prioritarias para un desarrollo inclusivo*. Serie: Mejoras Políticas. OECD.
OECD. (2018). *Revisión de Recursos Escolares*. Ministerio de Educación Nacional de Colombia. OECD.
OECD. (2019). *Estudios Económicos de la OCDE. Colombia 2019: Visión General*. OECD.
Oliveira, D., Gonçalves, G., & Melo, S. (2004). Cambios en la organización del trabajo docente. Consecuencias para los profesores. *Revista Mexicana de Investigación Educativa, 9*(20), 183–197.
Pinheiro, M. (2013). Emoções e Sociedade: Um passeio na obra de Norbert Elias. *História: Questões & Debates, 59*(2).
Restrepo, F., & López, A. (2011). La calidad de vida laboral del personal docente de la Universidad de Antioquia (Colombia). *XVI Congreso Internacional de Contaduría, Administración e Informática*.
Santos, B. (2007). La universidad en el siglo XXI. Para una reforma democrática y emancipadora de la universidad. *Umbrales. Revista del Postgrado en Ciencias del Desarrollo, 15*, 13–70.
San Salvador del Valle, R. (2000). Políticas de ocio: cultura, turismo, deporte y recreación. In *Documentos de estudios de ocio* (p. núm. 17). Universidad de Deusto.
Slaughter, S., & Leslie, L. (1997). *Academic capitalism: Politics, policies, and the entrepreneurial university*. Johns Hopkins University.

Terán, A., & Botero, C. (2011). El capitalismo organizacional: una mirada a la calidad de vida laboral en la docencia universitaria. *Cuadernos de Administración, 27*(46), 9–21.

Tinoco, R. (2004). Histórias de vida: um método qualitativo de investigação. *Psicología. com, 15*, 1–9.

Urteaga, E. (2013). El pensamiento de Norbert Elías: proceso de civilización y configuración social. *Barataria: Revista Castellano-Manchega de Ciencias Sociales, 16*, 15–31. https://doi.org/10.20932/barataria.v0i16.3

Chapter 4
The Effectiveness of Leisure Education Programs for the Elderly: A Systematic Review

Luciana Pereira de Moura Carneiro, Aurora Madariaga Ortuzar, Maria Begoña García Zapirain, and Ricardo Ricci Uvinha

Abstract The world is rapidly aging, raising the critical question of how to add life to years. Participation in meaningful leisure activities is a key predictor of successful aging and well-being, yet many older adults lack leisure literacy, limiting their ability to engage with existing opportunities. While Leisure Education Programs (LEP) have been developed to address this gap, their effectiveness remains underexplored. This systematic review (SR) assesses evidence on the effectiveness of LEP for adults aged 55 and older. A search of four databases—EBSCOhost, Web of Science, Scopus, and ProQuest—yielded 305 articles, of which 21 met inclusion criteria. Most studies were from North America, with a focus on "Therapeutic Recreation" and "Leisure and Recreation," and 53% addressing these themes. Limited international collaboration was noted. The review identified eight themes showing benefits for participants: Leisure Competence, Leisure Knowledge, Perceived Leisure Control, Leisure Satisfaction, Leisure Autonomy, Leisure Boredom, Stress, and Life Satisfaction. Limitations include the small sample sizes and a focus on high-income countries. Despite these constraints, strong evidence supports the effectiveness of LEP for older adults. The findings offer both theoretical and practical insights into advancing leisure education for this population.

L. Pereira de Moura Carneiro (✉)
Instituto Federal de São Paulo (Campus Avaré), São Paulo, Brasil
e-mail: lucianapmoura@ifsp.edu.br

A. Madariaga Ortuzar · M. B. García Zapirain
University of Deusto, Bilbao, Spain
e-mail: aurora.madariaga@deusto.es; mbgarciazapi@deusto.es

R. Ricci Uvinha
Universidade de São Paulo (EACH/USP), São Paulo, Brasil
e-mail: uvinha@usp.br

L. Ronda et al. (eds.), *Leisure and Human Development*, Human Well-Being Research and Policy Making, https://doi.org/10.1007/978-3-031-90778-4_4

4.1 Introduction

A 2015 comedy starring Robert De Niro and Anne Hathaway, written and directed by Nancy Meyers (*The Intern*), recounts a phenomenon commonly seen in Western society: A 70-year-old man who, after working for an entire lifetime and raising his family, feels as if he is useless after retirement, the death of his partner, and the cold relationship with his children and grandchildren. In the plot, the protagonist incorporates leisure into his new lifestyle, dedicating himself to traveling, physical activities, reading, gardening, cooking, learning new languages, and more. However, this does not satisfy him, which prompts him to look for a job to feel useful again.

For Ayyildiz-Durhan (2020, p. 381) "many people who can take advantage of leisure or recreation opportunities in their communities lack leisure literacy. Leisure literacy refers to the knowledge, skills and confidence to participate in leisure time, which is personally motivating and promotes health." Stebbins (2017, p. 8) considers that "to be leisure literate is essential to a complete experience of human life, referring to the capacities and desires of an individual (as a human being) to realize a wider range of his or her potential, through leisure, and thus enhance that person's quality of life." Nevertheless, Cuenca Cabeza (2013) states that this awareness does not come spontaneously but requires a special kind of training, known as Leisure Education (LE).

This article aims to assess the evidence regarding the effectiveness of Leisure Education Programs (LEP) for older adults. Our goal is to identify studies that describe the implementation and evaluation of LEP for this target audience.

4.2 Literature Review

The Universal Declaration of Human Rights of United Nations (1948) states that everyone has the right to leisure. Dattilo (2017) contended that having the right to leisure means having access to leisure opportunities and to LE. LE is a process that involves three aspects: an understanding of leisure, an understanding of oneself concerning leisure, and an understanding of the relationship among leisure, one's own lifestyle, and society (Mundy, 1998). However, since the mid-1970s of the last century, LE has received relatively little attention (Mobley, 1975; Sivan & Stebbins, 2011).

LEP are organized actions designed to improve various factors. The main objective is to enable people to use their leisure time more effectively and satisfactorily such as Sivan and Stebbins (2011), Dattilo and Williams (2012) and Kao and Chang (2017). Since 1975, this type of intervention has been understood as "a process for the enrichment of the quality of life" (Mundy & Cannon, 1975).

Although there are several LEP available, the gap in this field of research is "how to get these programmes into these settings where they can be delivered [...] and the need to educate not only individuals but those who could support and guide individuals as they navigate their lives, such as family members, educators, and recreation leaders" Hutchinson (2012, pp. 137–138).

Little is known about the effectiveness of LEP for older adults. Thus, the review authors provided feedback on the development of the question. The purpose of this SR is to present the LEP applied to the elderly around the world, highlighting what they entail, why they were implemented and what they improved in the lives of the elderly. A systematic literature search identified publications exploring the effectiveness of LEP applied to older adults.

4.3 Methods

An SR was conducted to identify studies that examined the implementation and evaluation of LEP for the elderly. The Preferred Reporting Items for Systematic Review and Meta-Analysis Protocols (PRISMA-P) guidelines were followed and applied for this review. It was conducted through academic partnerships, with the review team from Spain and Brazil. Original quantitative and qualitative research published in English was reviewed between February and March 2023. No restrictions were put on the publication date.

On February 16, 2023, four databases databases—EBSCOhost, Web of Science (WoS), Scopus, and ProQuest—were systematically searched for eligible studies. Search terms were developed by the methodology consultant following the Campbell Methods Series: Method Guide 1 of Kugley et al. (2017) in consultation with the review authors. In addition, we checked the reference lists of our records to find additional studies on this theme. Figure 4.1 presents the databases searched, the search strategy, and the search terms used.

All results from the searches were imported into Zotero, where duplicate records were identified and removed before screening. Out of 305 records screened, 107

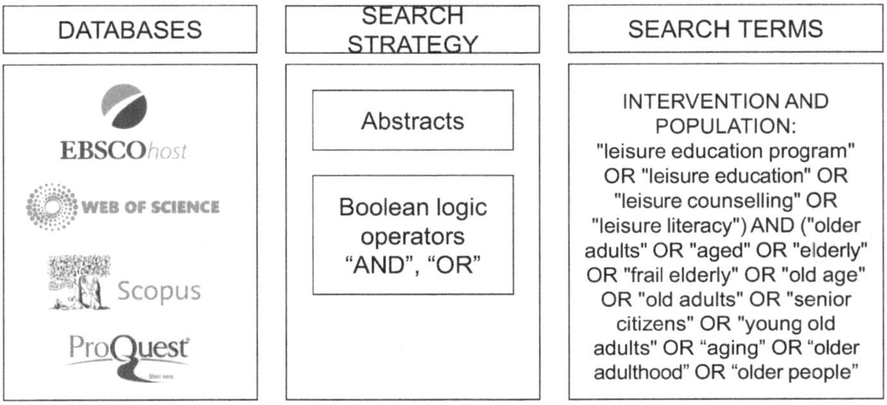

Fig. 4.1 Databases searched, search strategy, and search terms used

were duplicates across the four databases, leaving 198 unique records. A file in CSV (.csv) format containing data about the articles was used in VOSviewer software to create bibliometric maps illustrating co-occurrence between terms and co-authorship between researchers. All unique records were transferred to Covidence and screened in title and abstracts according to the eligibility criteria. The inclusion and exclusion criteria for screening records are presented in Table 4.1.

This process was conducted to find academic works that included the implementation and evaluation of LEP for older adults. Therefore, at this point, the text selection process was carried out in two stages. First, a title and abstract review was conducted to exclude studies that met specific criteria. Following this step, 167 records were discarded, leaving 31 records remaining. Records that could not be excluded based on title or abstract were full-text screened. At this step, reasons for exclusion were registered. Both a first and a second rater independently completed the process. Disagreements between them were discussed at each step.

Following the aforementioned, a complete reading of the 31 remaining documents was done, and 19 were selected for inclusion in the study. Of the 12 publications excluded, 4 of them were excluded due to the unavailability of the full text. Backman and Mannell (1986); Chiang et al. (2008); Mahon and Goatcher (1999); and Searle and Mahon (1993). We only had access to the title and summary of these four texts. Therefore, they were considered in some analyses, with information that was possible to infer. In others, in which it was necessary to read the full text, they were excluded.

In the case of Janssen's research, in addition to his dissertation, the article produced by this work, published in the Therapeutic Recreation Journal (Janssen, 2004), was located. In this case, we chose to include only the article in the analysis to avoid duplication. On the other hand, in the case of Hsieh (2009), we did not get access to the full text of the article by Hsieh and Janssen (2009) published as a result of his dissertation, so we included only the dissertation in the analysis by Hsieh (2009).

In addition, two other studies, although they do not appear in the databases, were identified in the reference lists of the selected articles and then included in the final analysis as they met the inclusion criteria such as Dunn and Wilhite (1997) and

Table 4.1 Inclusion and exclusion criteria

Criteria	
Inclusion	Exclusion
Full-text records that describe the implementation and evaluation of LEPs applied to the elderly	Studies not written in English
	Editorials or opinion papers
	LEP applied to other target audiences (not the elderly)
	Therapeutic recreation interventions that do not focus specifically on LE
	Interventions that address specific issues (e.g., retirement) or activities (e.g., walking or gardening)

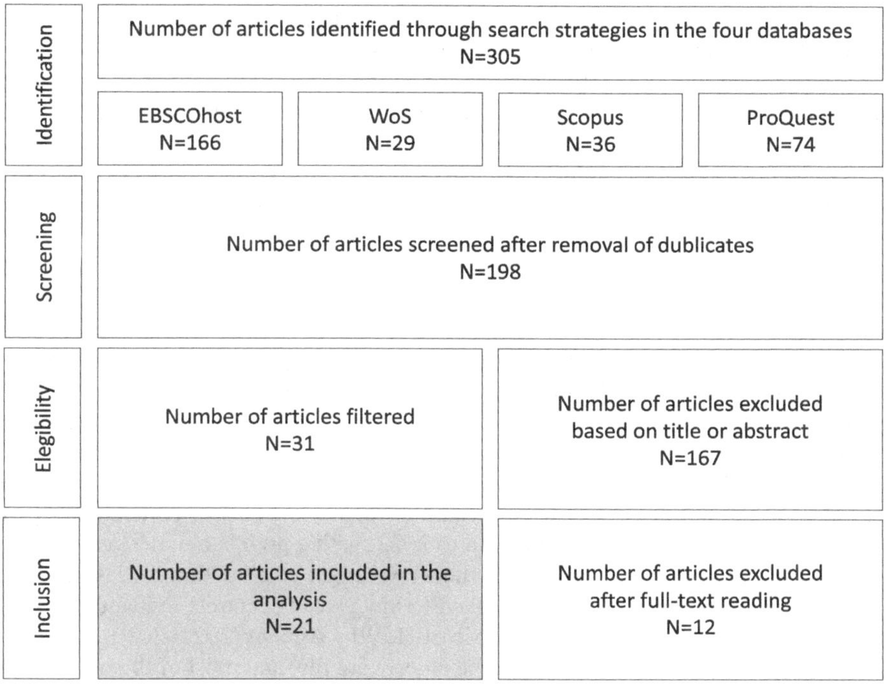

Fig. 4.2 Flow chart of SR for LEP with elderly. Source: Adapted from Moher et al. (2009). Note: The inconsistency in the total number of articles included and excluded in the inclusion phase is due to some articles being unavailable in full text. However, their abstracts were accessible and included in certain analyses

Hsieh (2009). Upon completing our search, 21 studies were identified for inclusion in the review. The flow diagram of studies is provided in Fig. 4.2. Here, we can note the different phases suggested by the PRISMA methodology.

4.4 Results and Discussion

Two types of maps were generated in VOSviewer based on Zotero file. One of them for the co-occurrence of terms and the other for co-authorship. When generating the co-occurrence map, it was found that 64 terms met the criterion of being cited at least five times in the information about the record (abstracts, keywords, titles, journal, etc.). Of these, 5 were discarded because they were not relevant to the study, leaving a final total of 59 terms. We can visualize the importance of terms such as "Leisure Education" and "older adults" in the 1990s and 2000s, represented on the map by the larger circles. In more recent years, words like "leisure" and "females" have gained more prominence. While the older studies have stronger links to the

United States, the more recent ones (in yellow) have stronger links to Taiwan. Figure 4.3 presents the co-occurrence map of terms.

It was found that of the 369 authors, 5 met the criterion of having at least three documents. Only two of them were grouped into a cluster (Searle & Mahon, 1993). The others appear with no connection to the remainder, such as John Dattilo, Hélène Carbonneau and Liang-Chich Chang. This suggests little collaboration between the principal investigators in this area when carrying out studies on LEP for older adults, mainly in recent studies.

A total of 21 full-text records were included in our analysis, most of which employed a quantitative research approach, encompassing a sample of 686 participants. The reference analysis of these studies provided insights into the decade and countries where the Leisure Education Programs (LEP) for the elderly were implemented, as well as the academic fields of the journals in which they were published. Although we were unable to access the full texts of articles by Backman and Mannell (1986), Searle and Mahon (1993), Mahon and Goatcher (1999), and Chiang et al. (2008), we included them in our analysis based on their reference data. From these references, bar and pie charts were created to facilitate a clearer understanding of the results. The studies span from 1986 to 2022, with a noticeable increase in publications in recent years—32% of the studies were published within the last decade. This uptick in publications may be linked to the growing interest in healthy aging, particularly with the onset of the Decade of Healthy Ageing (2021–2030).

Our results indicated that LEP for the elderly are few and most of them replicate (with few changes, if any) LEP proposed in the last century. Of the 21 studies that reported the implementation and evaluation of LEP applied to the elderly, 85% were based on interventions created up to the 2000s. Of the LEP identified as interventions applied to the elderly, only four are recent (less than 5 years): Chang and Kao

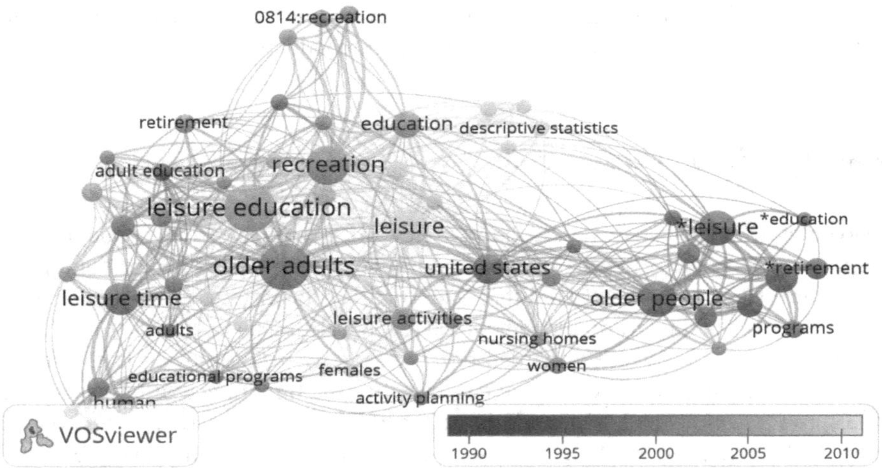

Fig. 4.3 Co-occurrence map of terms

(2019), Curtis (2021), and Dattilo et al. (2021, 2022). That is, this research shows that the LEP are mostly not recent, which demonstrates the need for current studies on the subject.

In addition to being old, they are very concentrated in North America. These findings are in accordance with Hutchinson (2012) who stated that the existing LEP still come predominantly from this region. However, Figs. 4.2 and 4.3 (VOSviewer) show that, in recent decades, the participation of authors from the Eastern world, led by Chang, has grown. All the 25 studies identified as a LEP applied for the elderly were published in English. Most of them were conducted in Western developed countries. We identified few studies published in other languages, such as Turkish or Chinese, that were not analyzed. The countries with publications about this theme in English were Canada (12 studies), USA (8) and Taiwan (5).

Indeed, Canada and the United States were responsible for the first articles describing the implementation and evaluation of LEP for the elderly, publishing ten studies even in the twentieth century. However, it is worth mentioning that, in the last 10 years, the participation of the East in the theme in question has grown. Of the eight studies published in this period, four are from Taiwan by Chang (2014), Chang et al. (2015), Kao and Chang (2017), and Chang and Kao (2019).

Therefore, we can state that policymakers and researchers should pay attention to the implementation and evaluation of LEP for the elderly from different countries, especially from developing countries, where most older people will live in 2050. It is urgent to think about strategies that impact the quality of life of older adults in developed countries, but especially in developing countries. Despite the barriers to digital literacy of the elderly in these countries, there is a window of opportunity if we think about the development of simple, self-teaching, and playful solutions to educate older adults for leisure in these territories.

Just over 16% of the LEP applied to the elderly are only published in dissertation format. Research published in journals is the majority (more than 80%). "Therapeutic Recreation" (29%) and "Leisure and Recreation" (24%) are the main journals about this theme. In third place is the area of "Aging," with 19% of the studies. Both with 14% of the studies, are "Mental Health" and "Gerontology." The distribution of works among different areas of knowledge is due to the multidisciplinary nature of LE for the elderly. Despite the remarkable predominance of this theme in the "Therapeutic Recreation" and "Leisure and Recreation," it is understandable that it should also be discussed in the areas of health, gerontology, and education, for example.

In order to evaluate the full-text of the LEP applied for older adults around the world, we determined a LEP Evaluation Protocol based on some Question Words: Which? To whom? What and Why? Where? How? In Table 4.2, these classifications used for LEP for the elderly are shown and described.

In Table 4.3, we present the components of our main research question.

Table 4.2 Research questions and purposes

Q	Question words	LEP's evaluation protocol
Q1	What?	Specific factor analyzed
Q2	To whom?	LEP's participants number and profile
Q3	Where?	LEP's implementation place
Q4	How?	Applied by whom?
		For how long?
		In what period?
		What was the methodology used?

Table 4.3 Research questions' components (PICOS)

Description	Abbreviation	Questions' components
Population	P	Older adults
Intervention	I	LEP
Comparison	C	Without comparison
Outcome	O	Effectiveness
Study type	S	Clinical trial, observational studies

Source: Adapted from Galvão and Pereira (2014)

4.4.1 Q1: What?

For what effects the LEP for the elderly, studies highlighted some factors, such as *total quality of life* (Nour et al., 2002; Janssen, 2004; Curtis, 2021), *physical quality of life* (Nour et al., 2002), *psychological quality of life* (Nour et al., 2002), *social support* (Chang & Kao, 2019), *subjective vitality* (Chang & Kao, 2019), *mental health* (Curtis, 2021), *depression* (Dunn & Wilhite, 1997; Nour et al., 2002), *leisure attitude* (Hsieh, 2009), *perceived leisure control/locus of control* (Lovell et al., 1996; Searle & Mahon, 1991; Searle et al., 1995, 1998; Hsieh, 2009), *barriers to leisure experiences* (Lovell et al., 1996; Hsieh, 2009), *leisure satisfaction* (Shimura, 1993; Mahon & Searle, 1994; Nour et al., 2002; Ritcey et al., 2016; Mcmahan, 2007; Dattilo et al., 2021, 2022), *loneliness* (Dunn & Wilhite, 1997; Dattilo et al., 2022), *affect* (Dattilo et al., 2022), *leisure frequency* (Dattilo et al., 2021), *leisure competence* (Searle & Mahon, 1991; Searle et al., 1995; Ritcey et al., 2016; Chang, 2014; Kao & Chang, 2017), *self-rated health* (Chang et al., 2015), *leisure boredom* (Searle et al., 1995; Dattilo et al., 2022), *leisure engagement/leisure participation/development of personal goals for future leisure participation* (Mahon & Searle, 1994; Lovell et al., 1996; Dunn & Wilhite, 1997; Stewart, 2000; Dattilo et al., 2021), *leisure knowledge* (Charters & Murray, 2006; Dattilo et al., 2021, 2022), *leisure motivation* (Ritcey et al., 2016), *leisure autonomy* (Chang et al., 2015; Kao & Chang, 2017), *stress* (Chang, 2014; Mcmahan, 2007; Kao & Chang, 2017), *physical functioning* (Curtis, 2021), *life satisfaction* (Shimura, 1993; Searle & Mahon, 1991; Mahon & Searle, 1994; Searle et al., 1995; Curtis, 2021), and *leisure interests* (Curtis, 2021).

The factors that presented improvement for the elderly that participated in these LEP (proven by two or more studies) were: (1) Leisure Competence, (2) Leisure Knowledge, (3) Perceived Leisure Control, (4) Leisure Satisfaction, (5) Leisure Autonomy, (6) Leisure Boredom, (7) Stress, and (8) Life Satisfaction.

4.4.2 *Q2: To Whom?*

Table 4.4 shows the target audience of each LEP analyzed. Of the 21 studies analyzed, in one case it was not possible to identify the profile of the participants in

Table 4.4 Target audience of each LEP analyzed

Reference	N°	Age	% of female	Specific group?
Chang (2014)	60	67–79	51	No
Chang et al. (2015)	60	67–79	51	No
Chang and Kao (2019)	42	65–79	Most (–)	No
Charters and Murray (2006)	4	50–80	100	No
Curtis (2021)	10	65 or over	Information not clear	People residing in a community living center with disabilities
Dattilo et al. (2021)	89	58–94	86	No
Dattilo et al. (2022)	52	71–98	79	People residing in three continuing care retirement communities (CCRC)
Dunn and Wilhite (1997)	2	77/97	100	Women
Hsieh (2009)	18	55 or over	78	Chinese older adult immigrants
Janssen (2004)	47	62–99	79	People residing in a residential-style retirement facilities
Kao and Chang (2017)	40	65–79	52.5	No
Lovell et al. (1996)	12	65 or over	100	Women with disabilities
Mahon and Searle (1994)	44	55 or over	68	No
Mcmahan (2007)	23	55 or over	78	Informal caregivers
Nour et al. (2002)	14	55 or over	28.5	People retired who had had a stroke
Ritcey et al. (2016)	42	65 or over	52.3	People that have multiple physical/ psychosocial difficulties
Searle and Mahon (1991)	53	55 or over	68	No
Searle et al. (1995)	30	65 or over	Most (–)	No
Searle et al. (1998)	22	65 or over	91	No
Shimura (1994)	30	55 or over	83.3	People residing in a Japanese retirement home
Stewart (2000)	2	65 or over	100	Women experiencing social isolation and living alone in the community

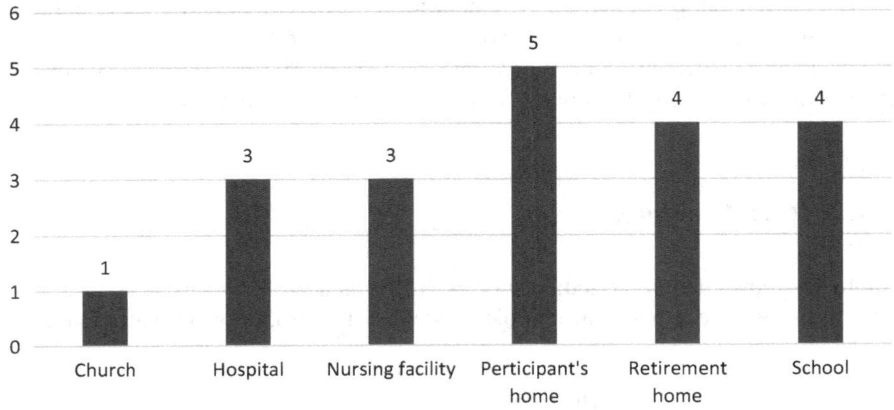

Fig. 4.4 Settings where the LEP were delivered (frequency)

terms of gender. All others (except one) had most female participants. All LEP target the elderly, however, there are some specificities, such as the exact age group and the existence of some characteristic of the group, such as diseases or limitations, origin, place of residence, among others.

4.4.3 Q3: Where?

The LEP analyzed on this SR was applied for older adults mainly in their own home, followed by the Retirement Home. Then, public places such as schools and hospitals are used. Nursing facilities are also mentioned. Finally, one study applied a LEP in a church. Figure 4.4 illustrates the distribution of the settings where the LEP were implemented.

4.4.4 Q4: How?

The facilitators of the LEP were primarily Therapeutic Recreation Specialists (TRS), with others referred to only as "facilitators." In some studies, the authors themselves implemented the program, alongside Research Assistants and Master's students hired specifically for this purpose. In one case, the facilitator was an insider familiar with the participants (a senior group leader). Figure 4.5 illustrates the deliverers of the LEP.

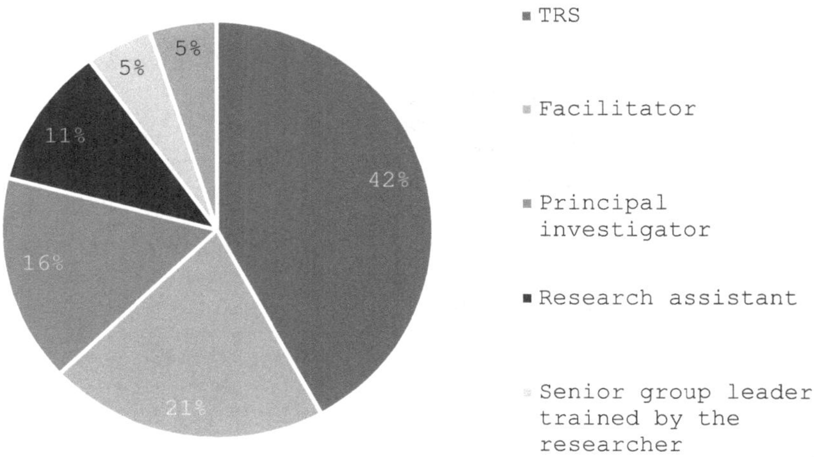

Fig. 4.5 Deliverers of the LEP (%)

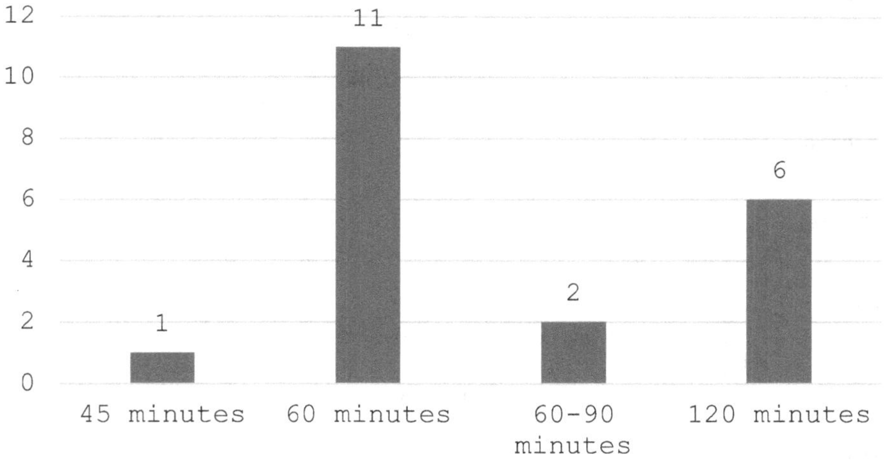

Fig. 4.6 Duration of the LEP in minutes (frequency)

In general, the LEP was applied for 1 h/week. Figure 4.6 presents the hours per week for the LEP.

Figure 4.7 illustrates the duration of the LEP in weeks, with the majority spanning between 6 and 12 weeks.

To conclude, the methodologies used by the authors in their LEP are presented in Table 4.5.

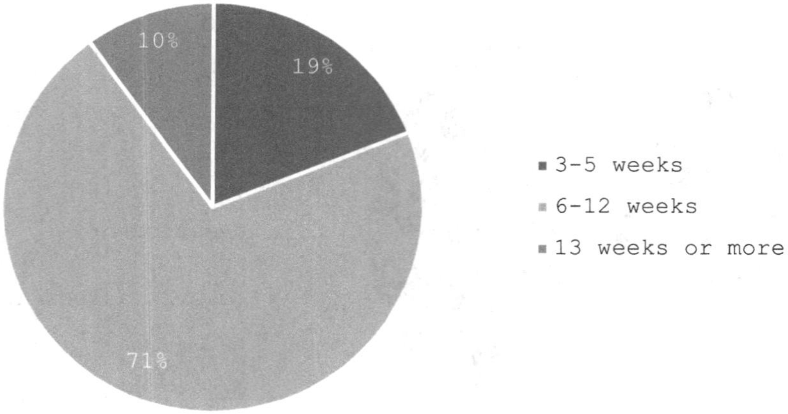

Fig. 4.7 Duration of the LEP in weeks (%)

Table 4.5 Methodologies used by the authors in their LEP

Reference	Methodology
Chang (2014)	Discussion exercises, role-playing, and participation in leisure activities
Chang et al. (2015)	
Kao and Chang (2017)	
Chang and Kao (2019)	
Searle et al. (1995)	
Curtis (2021)	Indoor activities and field trip(s) in places proximately located and the appropriateness
Dattilo et al. (2021)	Instructional videos, discussion, and workbook activities
Dattilo et al. (2022)	
Dunn and Wilhite (1997)	(a) Review of the previous session's topic, (b) formal introduction to the topic, (c) presentation of information, (d) learning activity to practice information learned, (e) questions designed to facilitate reflection on and expansion of ideas presented, and (f) conclusion and overview of the topic. Various paper and pencil, oral, and visual activities. Homework assignments were designed to facilitate the concepts discussed in each session
Hsieh (2009)	Learning activities, discussion questions, and debriefing. Activities such as music, art and crafts, exercise, and board games
Janssen (2004)	Information not clear

(continued)

Table 4.5 (continued)

Reference	Methodology
Charters and Murray (2006)	Guided discussion through paper and pencil completion of predesigned worksheets or projects (i.e., completing a leisure collage). The following sequence occurred: (a) at the beginning of each session, caregivers shared small talk; (b) review of the previous week's topic with reflection on what they learned in the previous week's experience; (c) sharing and review of tasks given the previous week, such as completed journal exercises applying knowledge and skill in leisure; (d) introduction of the new session topic; (e) teaching of new session content; (f) discussion of content with the intent to apply new knowledge to each participant's current situation; (g) assignment of journaling homework; (h) evaluation of learning outcomes by reporting how they felt via paper and pencil questionnaires; (i) collection of each participant's folder, which included their name tag, completed session activities, and completed journal entries; and (k) an opportunity to meet with the facilitator individually if a participant wanted to expand on her journal or share with the facilitator
Lovell et al. (1996)	Seated in a circular grouping. (a) orientation activity; (b) formal introduction of the topic; (c) presentation and discussion of information; (d) learning activity incorporating the information learned; (e) debriefing on activity for reflection on the topic; and (f) conclusions
Mahon and Searle (1994)	Written, oral, and audio-visual activities
Mcmahan (2007)	Introductory activity, a debriefing period (participant answers specific questions regarding the activity and their feeling toward the activity), paper and pencil exercises, written and verbal discussions, small group and large group discussions, relaxation activities, and leisure related activities. Verbal feedback and a formal written program evaluation at the end of the intervention period
Nour et al. (2002)	Homework. Work and reflection on leisure issues
Ritcey et al. (2016)	Daily journals produced by the research assistant, related to the leisure education sessions
Searle and Mahon (1991)	Paper and pencil, oral, and audio-visual activities
Searle et al. (1998)	Discussion exercises, paper and pencil exercises, role-playing, and recreation activity participation
Shimura (1994)	Personal achievement, activity preferences, individual activity, group activity, dream activity, possible dream activity
Stewart (2000)	Forms, manual with instructions and exercises, daily telephone checklists, recording their activities daily

4.5 Conclusion

This SR examined the effectiveness of LEP for older adults. We were interested in assessing the specific factors related to the effectiveness of these LEP. It is believed that, in general, LEP improved several aspects of older adults' lives, as evidenced by the findings of Searle and Mahon (1991), Shimura (1993), Mahon and Searle (1994), Searle et al. (1995, 1998, Lovell et al. (1996), Dunn and Wilhite (1997),

Nour et al. (2002), Janssen (2004), Charters and Murray (2006), Hsieh (2009), Chang (2014), Chang et al. (2015), Ritcey et al. (2016), Kao and Chang (2017), Chang and Kao (2019), and Dattilo et al. (2021, 2022), confirming the benefits of these interventions. This aligns with the findings of Fukushima and Schwartz (2021). In the literature, eight specific factors showed improvement in the samples analyzed in terms of LEP for older adults (proven by two or more studies): Leisure Competence, Leisure Knowledge, Perceived Leisure Control, Leisure Satisfaction, Leisure Autonomy, Leisure Boredom, Stress, and Life Satisfaction.

However, it is necessary to deepen the follow-up studies in order to verify whether the benefits generated are maintained over time. Mahon and Searle (1994), for example, identified that there were no significant differences between groups on life or leisure satisfaction and leisure participation at the 3-month follow-up. In other words, the LEP had a short-term effect for this sample. This demonstrates the need for leisure education that is continuously present in the lives of the elderly. Technological solutions can also contribute to making this topic part of their daily lives. These cheap, accessible and simple solutions can incorporate short videos, with Digital Storytelling, to talk about Leisure Education for elderly, a tool that is emerging as the most relevant way to deliver content in the digital age by Paolini and Di Blas (2014).

Our proposal reinforces what Dattilo et al. (2021) state about the need to develop relatively portable inexpensive effective interventions, which are easy to administer, designed to meet needs of older adults with limited education, cognition challenges, and few financial resources. These authors developed a video assisted LEP to literacy in leisure older adults. We believe that a next step could be taken in this field of knowledge, by reaching the elderly with an LEP through a mobile application, for example. This proposal goes beyond this traditional method by employing a more multidisciplinary and technologically innovative approach. In addition, from this SR, what we propose is the development of a technological solution that uses Artificial Intelligence to meet the elderly's needs and interests, within the context of their life and the community in which they reside (Stewart, 2000).

Further research about the theme is necessary to identify if these new delivery methods are as effective as traditional methods. In addition, we suggest future studies analyze other databases, using new keywords and Boolean operators, and extend approaches beyond examining LEP for the elderly, but considering other specific audiences, such as people with different disabilities, caregivers, women, young people, and so on. We especially, recommend that the studies be developed in low- and middle-income countries, where four out of five older people in the world will live by 2050 (World Health Organization [WHO], 2022).

Some limitations of the present review should be outlined, like the number and scope of studies that address LEP for elderly. Despite extensive systematic searches, the review included 21 full-text records only. Four studies were identified, but they could not be analyzed because we did not have access to the full text. In addition, some of the newer studies did not report on all the quality criteria. Most of the records on LE interventions were limited to high-income countries. Further, all of them were limited by small sample sizes.

References

Ayyildiz-Durhan, T. (2020). The effect of leisure literacy on leisure exercise in university students. *International Journal of Educational Methodology, 6*(2), 381–392.

Backman, S. J., & Mannell, R. C. (1986). Removing attitudinal barriers to leisure behavior and satisfaction: A field experiment among the institutionalized elderly. *Therapeutic Recreation Journal, 20*(3), 46–53.

Chang, L.-C. (2014). Leisure education reduces stress among older adults. *Aging & Mental Health, 18*(6), 754–758.

Chang, L.-C., Yu, P., & Jeng, M.-Y. (2015). Effects of leisure education on self-rated health among older adults. *Psychology, Health & Medicine, 20*(1), 34–40.

Chang, L.-C., & Kao, I.-C. (2019). Enhancing social support and subjective vitality among older adults through leisure education. *International Psychogeriatrics, 31*(12), 1839–1840.

Charters, J., & Murray, S. (2006). "Boon." Design and evaluation of a leisure education program for caregivers of institutionalized care recipients. *Topics in Geriatric Rehabilitation, 22*(4), 334–347.

Chiang, I., Kao, M., Chou, Y., & Chen, S. (2008). Impacts of leisure education interventions on promoting leisure and recreational sports participation competence for the elderly. *Journal of Aging & Physical Activity Supplement, 16.*

Cuenca Cabeza, M. (2013). Ocio valioso en tiempos de crisis. In S. Torío et al. (Eds.), *La crisis social y el Estado del Bienestar: las respuestas de la Pedagogía Social*. Universidad de Oviedo.

Curtis, L. G. (2021). *A nature-based leisure education program for older veterans residing in a community living center (CLC)*. M.S., California State University, Sacramento.

Dattilo, J., & Williams, R. (2012). Some thoughts about leisure education, therapeutic recreation, and the philosophy of Spiderman. *Therapeutic Recreation Journal, 46*(1), 1–8.

Dattilo, J. (2017). Inclusion and education: Creating a path to leisure and human development. In M. J. Monteagudo Sánchez (Ed.), *Leisure experiences, opportunities and contributions to human development*. Universidad de Deusto.

Dattilo, J., Lorek, A. E., & Sliwinski, M. (2022). Effects of video-assisted leisure education on leisure, loneliness, and affect of older adults. *Leisure Sciences*, 1–21.

Dattilo, J., Lorek, A., Sliwinski, M., Chen, S.-T., & Hill, N. (2021). An examination of video assisted leisure education in middle-aged and older adults. *Journal of Leisure Research, 52*(2), 227–246.

Dunn, N., & Wilhite, B. (1997). The effects of a leisure education program on leisure participation and psychosocial well-being of two older women who are home-centered. *Therapeutic Recreation, 31*, 53–71.

Fukushima, R. L. M., & Schwartz, G. M. (2021). Design, evaluation and outcomes of leisure education programs: A systematic review. *Licere – Revista do Programa de Pós-graduação Interdisciplinar em Estudos do Lazer, 24*(1), 106–129. https://doi.org/10.35699/2447-6218.2021.29498

Hsieh, C. Y., & Janssen, M. A. (2009). The effects of leisure education on leisure attitudes, perceived leisure control, and barriers to leisure in Chinese older adult immigrants in the United States. *American Journal of Recreation Therapy, 8*(4), 21–28.

Hsieh, C. Y. (2009). *The effects of leisure education on Chinese older adult immigrants*. California State University, Long Beach ProQuest Dissertations Publishing.

Hutchinson, S. L., & Robertson, B. (2012). Leisure education: A new goal for an old idea whose time has come. *Pedagogía Social. Revista Interuniversitaria, 20*, 71–95. https://doi.org/10.7179/PSRI_2012.20.06

Janssen, M. A. (2004). The effects of leisure education on quality of life in older adults. *Therapeutic Recreation Journal, 38*(3), 275–288.

Kao, I., & Chang, L. (2017). Long-term effects of leisure education on leisure needs and stress in older adults. *Educational Gerontology, 43*(7), 356–364.

Kugley, S., Wade, A., Thomas, J., Mahood, Q., Jørgensen, A. M. K., Hammerstrøm, K., & Sathe, N. (2017). *Searching for studies: A guide to information retrieval for Campbell systematic reviews*. The Campbell Collaboration.

Lovell, T. A., Dattilo, J., & Jekubovich, N. J. (1996). Effects of leisure education on women aging with disabilities. *Activities, Adaptation & Aging, 21*(2), 37–58.

McMahan, C. M. (2007). The psychosocial effects of a leisure education program on caregivers of aging adults with dementia [Ph.D., University of Arkansas]. In *ProQuest Dissertations and Theses*.

Mahon, M. J., & Searle, M. S. (1994). Leisure education: Its effect on older adults. *Journal of Physical Education, Recreation and Dance, 64*(4), 36–41.

Mahon, M. J., & Goatcher, S. (1999). Later-life planning for older adults with mental retardation: A field experiment. *Mental Retardation, 37*(5), 371–373.

Mobley, T. A. (1975). Leisure education and the quality of life. In J. Mundy (Ed.), *Leisure education and the quality of life*. Florida State University.

Moher, D., Liberati, A., Tetzlaff, J., Altman, D. G., & PRISMA Group. (2009). Preferred reporting items for systematic reviews and meta-analyses: The PRISMA statement. *PLoS Medicine, 6*(7), e1000097.

Mundy, J., & Cannon, F. C. (Eds.). (1975). *Leisure education and the quality of life*. Florida State University.

Mundy, J. (1998). *Leisure education: Theory and practice* (2nd ed.). Sagamore.

Nour, K., Desrosiers, J., Gauthier, P., & Carbonneau, H. (2002). Impact of a home leisure educational program for older adults who have had a stroke (Home Leisure Educational Program). *Therapeutic Recreation Journal, 36*(1), 48–64.

Paolini, P., & Di Blas, N. (2014). Storytelling for cultural heritage. In A. Contin, P. Paolini, & R. Salerno (Eds.), *Innovative technologies in urban mapping* (Vol. 10). Springer for Innovation.

Ritcey, A., Singleton, J., Webber, K., King, A., Cook, J., & Hopper, T. (2016). An exploratory study as to the effect of a leisure education program on a geriatric day hospital patient population. *Activities, Adaptation and Aging, 40*(2), 150–163.

Searle, M. S., & Mahon, M. J. (1991). Leisure education in a day hospital: The effects on selected social-psychological variables among older adults. *Canadian Journal of Community Mental Health, 10*(2), 95–109.

Searle, M. S., & Mahon, M. (1993). The effects of a leisure education program on selected social-psychological variables: A three-month follow-up investigation. *Therapeutic Recreation Journal, 27*(1), 9–21.

Searle, M. S., Mahon, M. J., & Iso-Ahola, S. E. (1995). Enhancing a sense of independence and psychological well-being among the elderly: A field experiment. *Journal of Leisure Research, 27*(2), 107–124.

Searle, M. S., Mahon, M. J., & Iso-Ahola, S. E. (1998). Examining the long-term effects of leisure education on a sense of independence and psychological well-being among the elderly. *Journal of Leisure Research, 30*(3), 331–340.

Shimura, K. (1993). The effects of leisure education on life satisfaction and leisure satisfaction among Japanese American older adults [Dissertação de mestrado, University of Wisconsin–La Crosse]. Microform Publications, University of Oregon.

Shimura, K. (1994). *The effects of leisure education on life satisfaction and leisure satisfaction among Japanese American older adults*. Thesis in Therapeutic Recreation. http://digital.library.wisc.edu/1793/48955

Sivan, A., & Stebbins, R. A. (2011). Leisure education: Definition, aims, advocacy, and practices – are we talking about the same thing(s)? *World Leisure Journal, 53*(1), 27–41.

Stebbins, R. A. (2017). Self-directed learning as a basis for complex leisure. *Loisir et Société/Society and Leisure, 40*(3), 377–387.

Stewart, W. R. (2000). Leisure education and older women's participation in leisure activities [M.Sc., University of Manitoba (Canada)]. In *ProQuest Dissertations and Theses*.

United Nations. (1948). *Universal Declaration of Human Rights*.

World Health Organization [WHO]. (2022). *Ageing and health*. Accessed March 22, 2023, from https://www.who.int/news-room/fact-sheets/detail/ageing-and-health

Chapter 5
Shared Digital Leisure Between Grandparents and Grandchildren Before, During, and After the Pandemic

María Ángeles Valdemoros San Emeterio, Rosa Ana Alonso Ruiz, Luis Corral Fernández, and Álvaro Eraña Martínez

Abstract The humanitarian and health crisis caused by the coronavirus pandemic (COVID-19) has changed family relationships, particularly the way grandparents interact with their grandchildren. Lockdowns, together with the restrictions imposed to prevent the spread of the virus, have limited intergenerational contact, primarily because of the vulnerability of the elderly. This has resulted in feelings of insecurity and unease for both generations, even causing emotional consequences due to the longing for shared time together. New technological dynamics are proof that the world is moving fast—a scenario that points to the need to continue developing intergenerational digital leisure activities involving grandparents and grandchildren and enhancing human development through valuable experiences. Technology became particularly important, enabling the apparent continuation of intergenerational social relations during lockdowns. Information and communication technologies (ICTs) allow constant contact between grandchildren and grandparents, fostering autonomy and promoting learning on both sides, as well as intergenerational understanding and solidarity. ICTs make it possible to overcome the obstacle of distance by providing a space for social bonding in a context of isolation. This has led to exponential growth in the digital environment.

The text we are presenting here is linked to the R+D+I project "Intergenerational leisure in the framework of the new normality. Education, opportunities and challenges" (PID2020-119438RB-I00) [years 2021–2024] funded by the Ministry of Science and Innovation.

M. Á. Valdemoros San Emeterio (✉) · R. A. Alonso Ruiz · L. Corral Fernández · Á. Eraña Martínez
University of La Rioja, Logroño, Spain
e-mail: maria-de-los-angeles.valdemoros@unirioja.es; rosa-ana.alonso@unirioja.es; luis.corral@alum.unirioja.es; alvaro.erana@alum.unirioja.es

L. Ronda et al. (eds.), *Leisure and Human Development*, Human Well-Being Research and Policy Making, https://doi.org/10.1007/978-3-031-90778-4_5

5.1 Introduction

The COVID-19 pandemic was unprecedented in recent history, triggering a humanitarian and health crisis that profoundly impacted all aspects of social, economic, and family life. Lockdown restrictions, as well as those imposed to control the spread of the virus, had a disruptive effect on daily interactions, particularly on intergenerational family relationships such as those between grandparents and grandchildren.

These relationships, fundamental to the emotional and social well-being of both generations, were disrupted by the need to protect the most vulnerable, namely older adults, who were identified as one of the groups most at risk from COVID-19 (Alonso et al., 2020; Brooks et al., 2020).

Lockdown not only limited physical contact between grandparents and grandchildren but also generated feelings of insecurity and emotional distress on both sides. This forced estrangement led many grandparents to experience a deep longing for time shared with their grandchildren, and this has had significant emotional consequences. Indeed, the lack of direct interaction not only deprived grandparents of a crucial source of emotional and social support, but also harmed the emotional development of grandchildren, who often depend on their grandparents for love, care, security, and guidance (Dalton et al., 2020). These changes in family dynamics highlighted the importance of finding new ways to maintain and strengthen these connections, even in adverse circumstances.

This is argued by Fuchsberger et al. (2021), who assert that ICTs are a very useful tool when grandparents are geographically distant from their grandchildren, as audio visual communication allows them to maintain an online relationship. In this context, information, and communication technologies (ICTs) have emerged as essential tools for mitigating the effects of social isolation. The rapid adoption and expansion of ICTs during the pandemic allowed intergenerational relationships to remain active through virtual channels, such as video calls, social media, and other digital platforms.

One example is the use of *Tik-tok* during the pandemic, where grandparents and grandchildren spent time designing and interacting with social networks, which was also a learning opportunity for the elderly (Nouwen & Hermine, 2021). In a similar vein, several authors (Galiano et al., 2020; Fernández & Sánchez, 2020; Valdemoros et al., 2020) have sought ways to strengthen relationships between grandparents and grandchildren through the use of digital tools, such as the creation of a blog with educational and playful resources that teach how to manage negative emotions and foster intergenerational relationships, or the development of an "intergenerational cinema" website, which provides both generations with resources that encourage the expression of opinions and emotions, and education in values. These technologies provided an alternative way for grandparents and grandchildren to continue interacting, sharing experiences, and maintaining a sense of normality during the crisis (Ayuso et al., 2020).

The importance of ICTs during this period lies not only in their ability to facilitate communication, but also in their potential to promote mutual learning and intergenerational solidarity, underlining their value as tools for intergenerational learning, and human and social development in times of crisis (Nimrod et al., 2019). In short, the use of ICTs during the pandemic proved to be an effective way to overcome the barriers imposed by social distancing, creating virtual spaces where social relations can flourish despite physical distance. This phenomenon was particularly evident in the interactions between grandparents and grandchildren, where digital platforms enabled the continuation of shared activities, such as games, conversations, and participation in social networks, which was crucial for maintaining intergenerational bonds during lockdown (Lago & Rivoir, 2021).

The experience of the pandemic highlighted not only the resilience of family relationships but also their capacity to adapt to new technological dynamics, suggesting the need to further develop and integrate intergenerational digital leisure strategies that strengthen human development and social cohesion in the long term. As the world moves into an increasingly digitised era, the pandemic accelerated the transition to the widespread use of ICTs in family interactions. However, it also revealed disparities in terms of access and digital skills, particularly among older adults, who often face significant challenges in adapting to these new technologies.

In a similar vein, recent studies such as those of, Jimena (2020), Martín (2020), and Chen et al. (2021) confirm that older adults, and more specifically those living in rural areas, suffer from the so-called digital divide, for example, due to difficulties in access and lack of knowledge and understanding of how these new technologies can be used. Therefore, it is essential to establish programmes and policies that not only promote digital literacy among older adults but also facilitate access to ICTs to ensure that all family members can benefit from the opportunities that these technologies offer (Calzado et al., 2021).

In short, the crisis caused by the COVID-19 pandemic radically transformed family relationships, especially intergenerational ones, prompting a shift towards the use of ICTs as a way of maintaining family contact and cohesion in a context of isolation. This change not only proved effective in the short term but has also opened the door to new possibilities for the development of stronger and more resilient intergenerational relationships through digital entertainment.

In the future, it will be essential to continue to support and promote the use of ICTs in family relationships, ensuring that these tools continue to play a key role in strengthening intergenerational ties, even outside crises (Alonso et al., 2020).

Intergenerational digital leisure between grandparents and grandchildren has become a topic of growing interest, especially in the context of the COVID-19 pandemic, which significantly changed family and social dynamics. This theoretical framework explores the main dimensions of this phenomenon, considering the existing literature and the changes brought about by lockdown and social distancing measures.

Based on these premises, the aim of this study is to examine the digital leisure activities shared by grandparents and grandchildren in the north of Spain at different times, corresponding to before, during, and after the COVID-19 pandemic.

5.2 Theoretical Framework

5.2.1 Digital Entertainment: Conceptualisation and Evolution

Digital leisure refers to recreational activities carried out using technological devices such as computers, smartphones, video game consoles, and tablets. These activities include the use of social networks, online games, video streaming, video calls, and other forms of digital entertainment (Cuenca, 2020). With the evolution of technology, digital entertainment has experienced a significant boom, becoming an essential part of everyday life for different generations (Alonso et al., 2022).

During the pandemic, digital entertainment gained unprecedented importance due to lockdown and restrictions on mobility. According to García-Peñalvo et al. (2021), digital tools became the main means of socialisation and entertainment, bringing people together despite physical distance.

5.2.2 Intergenerational Relations in the Digital Context

Intergenerational relationships, especially those between grandparents and grandchildren, have traditionally been built through face-to-face interaction, shared activities, and the transfer of knowledge. However, digitalisation has transformed those interactions, introducing new forms of connection that, although virtual, can be equally meaningful.

During the pandemic, video calls and online games became key tools for maintaining contact between grandparents and grandchildren. Esteban-Guitart and Chamarro (2021) note that these activities not only allowed family ties to be maintained but also promoted mutual learning, with grandchildren often acting as guides in the use of digital technologies.

5.2.3 Impact of the Pandemic on Intergenerational Digital Entertainment

The pandemic accelerated the adoption of digital technologies by older adults, a demographic that had traditionally shown reluctance or had difficulty integrating these tools into their daily lives (Hunsaker & Hargittai, 2020). This uptake was largely motivated by a desire to stay connected to loved ones, especially grandchildren.

Digital entertainment during the pandemic not only facilitated communication, but it also provided a shared source of entertainment and learning. Activities such as online video games, video call applications such as Zoom and Skype, and social networking platforms became the primary means for grandparents and grandchildren to share time together, overcoming the barriers imposed by physical distance (Seifert et al., 2021).

5.2.4 Challenges and Opportunities Presented by Intergenerational Digital Leisure

Intergenerational digital entertainment presents both challenges and opportunities. Challenges include generational gaps in the use of technology, and the frustration that can potentially arise due to differences in digital skills (Barnard et al., 2013). Furthermore, the risk of digital exclusion for older adults who lack access, or do not have the skills needed to be able to use these technologies is an important issue.

On the other hand, the opportunities are many. Digital leisure can strengthen intergenerational ties, foster mutual learning, and reduce loneliness, especially in situations of prolonged isolation such as those experienced during the pandemic (Aveiga et al., 2018; Concepción et al., 2020; Gatto & Tak, 2020; Hess & Schönfeld, 2020). Moreover, engaging in shared digital activities can improve the emotional well-being of older adults, and provide grandchildren with a sense of family connection and support.

5.3 Method

5.3.1 Participants

In this study, a quantitative methodology was used, with an ad hoc questionnaire with grandparents in the northern part of Spain, which comprises eight provinces distributed over five autonomous communities: Cantabria, Castilla y León, Navarra, Basque Country, and La Rioja (Fig. 5.1).

Information was collected on the role of intergenerational digital leisure among the different types of leisure, as well as the type of digital leisure activities most often engaged in. Specifically, the activities that included digital leisure were surfing the internet and using social networks. Data was collected at different times, corresponding to before, during, and after lockdown, in order to permit comparison and to assess the impact of this phenomenon. A sample of 357 grandparents before lockdown, 272 during lockdown, and 137 after lockdown was obtained.

5.3.2 Instrument

For the quantitative study, an ad hoc questionnaire was used, validated through a pilot test carried out in six educational centres in the different autonomous communities and assessed by ten experts from seven Spanish universities, who gave their approval for the final application.

The questionnaire made it possible to record fundamental information for this study based on six variables, which are defined below:

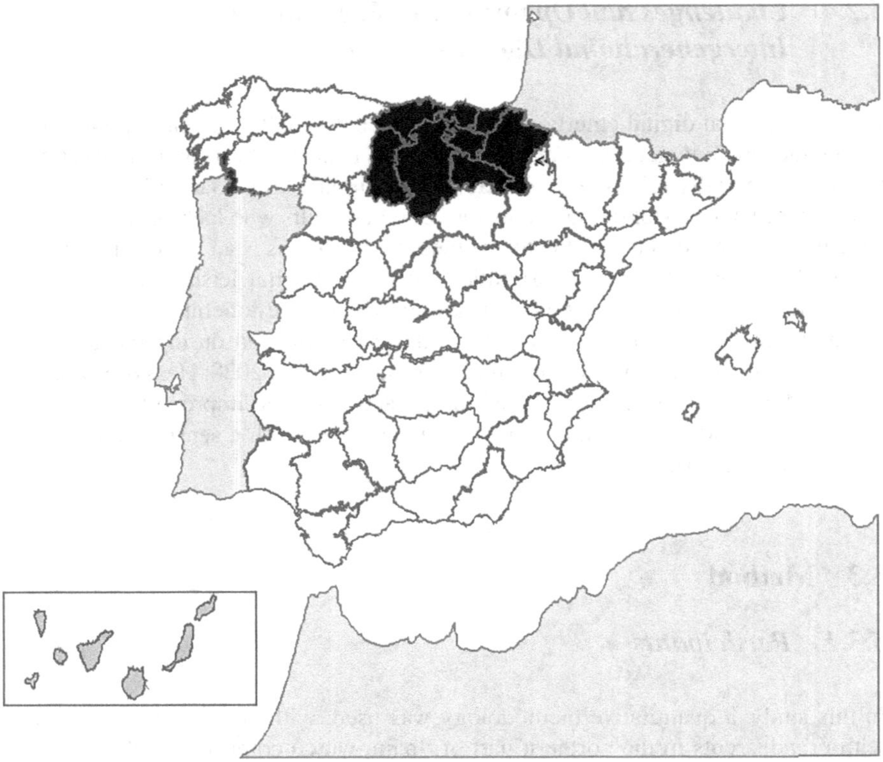

Fig. 5.1 Provinces of Northern Spain (according to Nielsen areas): Cantabria, Vizcaya, Guipúzcoa, Álava, La Rioja, Navarra, Burgos, and Palencia (shaded in black)

- Leisure shared with grandchildren before, during, and after the pandemic. This is a dichotomous variable that records whether participants share some form of leisure activity with their grandchildren (cultural activities, leisure activities, digital activities, environmental-ecological activities). The categories established were yes/no.
- Digital leisure shared with grandchildren before, during, and after the pandemic. This is a dichotomous variable that records whether participants share some form of digital leisure activity with their grandchildren. The categories established were yes/no.
- Typology of digital leisure activities shared with grandchildren before, during, and after the pandemic. This is a dichotomous variable that records whether participants share digital leisure activities with their grandchildren: video calls and social networking. The categories established were yes/no.
- Who grandparents share digital leisure time with. This is a categorical variable that records the person(s) with whom they share digital leisure: granddaughter(s), grandson(s).
- Where grandparents share digital leisure with their grandchildren. A categorical variable that captures the scenarios of shared digital leisure practices: at home, in

associations, in municipal spaces, in open public spaces, in leisure spaces, out in the countryside, in school facilities.
- Frequency with which grandparents share digital leisure with their grandchildren. A categorical variable that considers periods of shared digital leisure: only during holiday periods, only 1 or 2 days per month, weekends (1 day), weekends (2 days), weekdays (1 or 2 days), weekdays (3 and 4 days), weekdays (5 days).

5.3.3 *Procedure*

In the quantitative study, the questionnaire was used with the grandparents of the pupils of the different schools in each of the eight provinces that make up the northern part of Spain. The students were asked to give their parents and/or legal guardians a consent form regarding the research, which contained information about the study and where they needed to provide contact details for the grandparents wishing to participate in the study, to be subsequently handed in at the educational centre.

Five trained researchers contacted the grandparents by telephone and completed the questionnaire using the responses obtained. The recording time for the questions was around 30–45 min.

The University of La Rioja Ethics Committee approved this procedure on 17 December 2019. The positive report of the Ethics Committee was registered under code CE_02_2019.

5.3.4 *Data Analysis*

Data analysis was carried out using SPSS 23.0 statistical software and was carried out in two phases. Firstly, a descriptive study was done, which by using frequency statistics, provided information on the role of digital leisure, the type of leisure activities shared by grandparents with grandchildren aged between 6 and 12, intergenerational digital leisure activities, as well as the company, place, and frequency of shared digital activity.

In the second phase, an inferential analysis was performed using the Chi-square test (χ^2) to analyse digital leisure shared with grandchildren at different times. The level of significance considered throughout the study was set at $p < 0.05$.

5.4 Results

During the COVID-19 pandemic, digital leisure shared between grandparents and grandchildren showed a singular distribution when compared to other activities. The high proportion of grandparents who shared some digital leisure activity with their grandchildren during lockdown contrasts with the periods when there was no isolation. This trend can largely be explained by the increasing popularity of social networks and video calls via online platforms during the pandemic; these became the only way to communicate and support family members.

Prior to lockdown, 10.9% of respondents shared this type of leisure time; this increased to 96.3% during lockdown and fell to 6.6% in the post-lockdown period (Fig. 5.2).

The analysis of shared digital entertainment activity during the pandemic shows how much of an impact social media had. These became the principal means of communication for interaction between grandparents and grandchildren, allowing virtual connections to be shared through video calls, interactive games, etc. In contrast, face-to-face internet browsing, which would have taken place in the absence of the pandemic, was virtually non-existent (Fig. 5.3).

If data during lockdown is excluded from the analysis, the reduction in the percentage of social network use before and after lockdown becomes obvious and significant,[1] it falls from 7% to 1.5%, a reduction of more than 5%. The evidence shows that digital leisure played a distinct role during the pandemic, with more grandparents in northern Spain sharing digital leisure with their grandchildren during lockdown than any other type of activity.

This is a significant jump from the penultimate position, occupied before the pandemic, in terms of the percentage of people who engaged in these activities. However, since lockdown ended, digital entertainment has fallen back to almost marginal levels (Fig. 5.4).

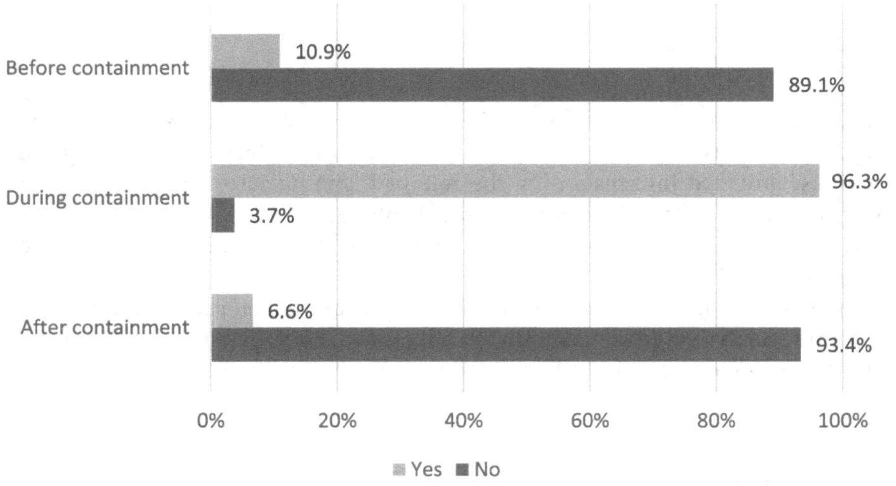

Fig. 5.2 Grandparents who share digital leisure with their grandchildren, depending on the time of year (%)

[1] χ^2=4.737/Sig.=0.030.

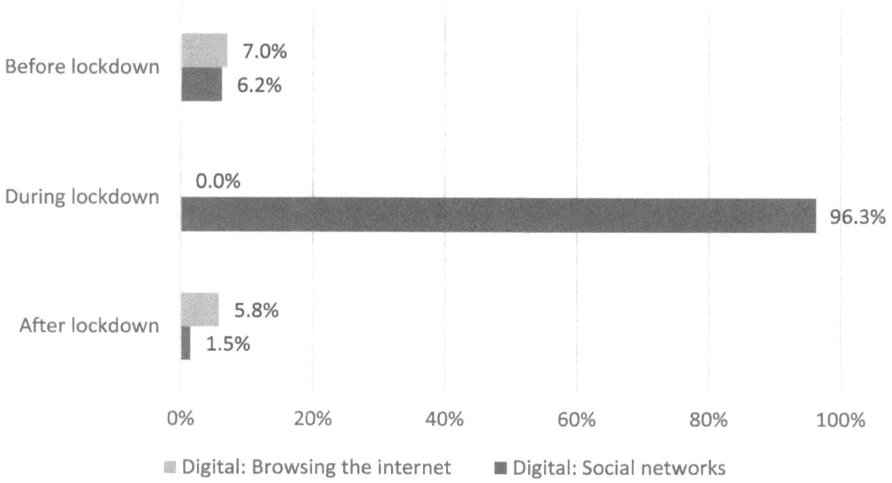

Fig. 5.3 Typology of shared digital leisure, by time (%)

5.4.1 Who Is Digital Leisure Shared with?[2]

Sharing digital leisure activities with grandchildren of different genders is very similar in all three time periods studied, although it is true that the percentages are slightly higher in people who share leisure activities with their grandsons, although no significant differences are evident.

In any case, this data confirms that the reduction in the sharing of digital leisure is independent of the gender of the grandchildren of grandparents in Northern Spain, as the percentage has decreased in all three cases (sharing with grandsons, granddaughters, and both) (Fig. 5.5).

5.4.2 Where Is Digital Entertainment Shared?

The sharing of digital leisure between grandparents and grandchildren mostly took place in the homes of grandparents and grandchildren, which greatly limited the comparison between places where this type of leisure activity takes place and those where it does not. This trend remained constant during the three reference periods.

[2] Due to the lack of data on the gender of the respondents' grandchildren, it is not possible to determine whether there are gender-based differences. This is because it is not known whether there are more grandparents with granddaughters in the sample, or whether there is a correlation between the gender of the grandchildren and the practice of shared recreational activities. For this reason, any statistical analysis of the significance of the possible differences would be biased and would not be valid for drawing generalised conclusions.

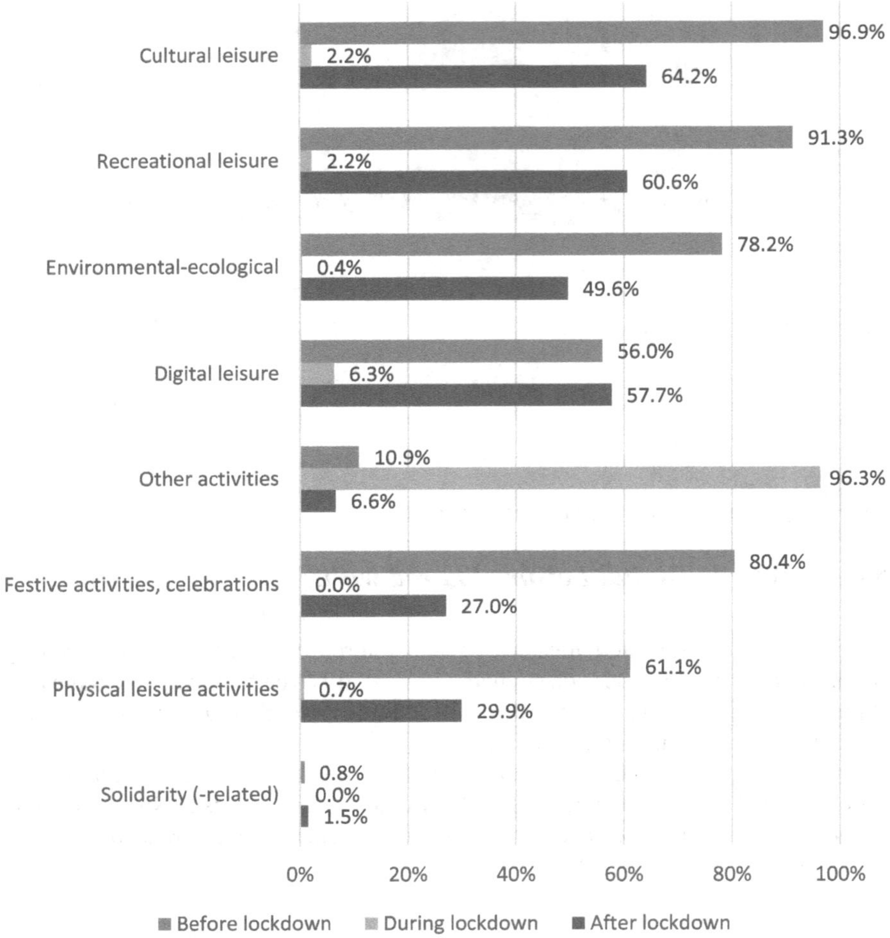

Fig. 5.4 Type of shared leisure, according to time (%)

5.4.3 How Often Is Digital Entertainment Shared?

Distribution over time, as well as the number of people sharing and engaging in such activities, changed significantly during lockdown.

Firstly, due to the disruption of the normal school calendar and the fact that lockdown was imposed during the final months of the school year, there were no cases of digital leisure during the holidays. This hypothesis is corroborated by the usage data and by the fact that no case has gone without sharing this type of leisure time with their grandchildren for a period of less than a week.

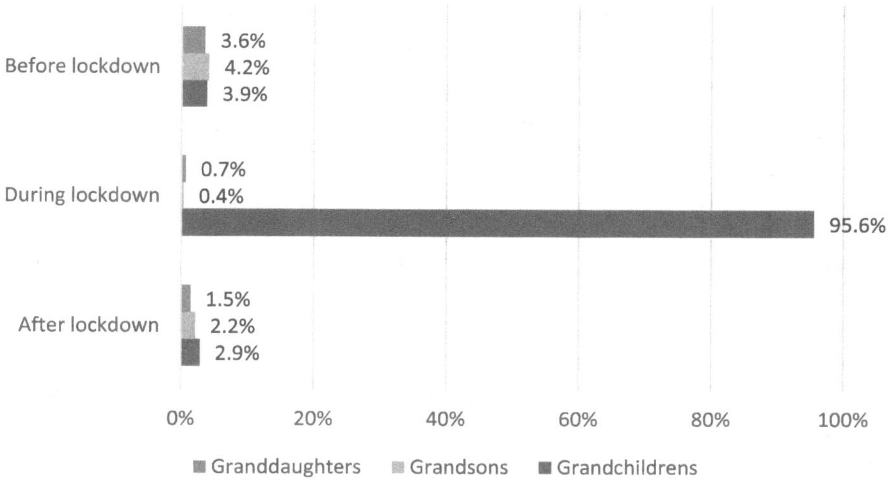

Fig. 5.5 Grandparents sharing digital leisure with their grandsons, granddaughters, or both (%)

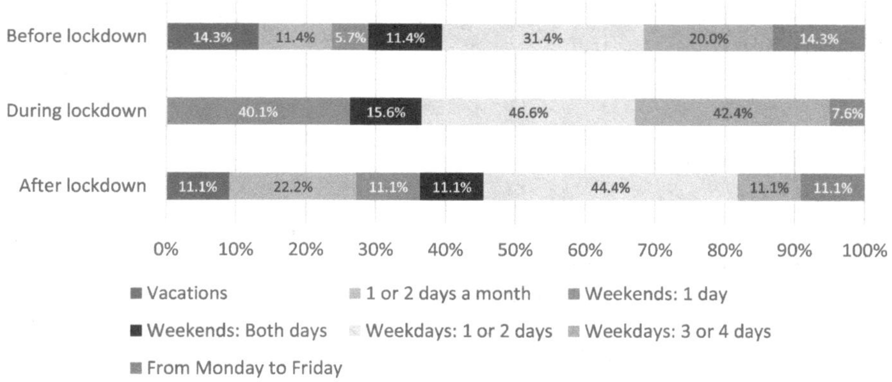

Fig. 5.6 Places where digital leisure is shared, by time (%)

In a similar vein, the decrease that could be perceived in the data on who shares and who does not is also reflected in a slight decrease in the highest frequencies of practice (weekdays 3 or 4 days and 5 days) while, on the other hand, the proportion of grandparents who only share leisure time once or twice a week has doubled (from 11.4% to 22.2%) (Fig. 5.6).

This trend is constant in the two types of digital leisure that make up this category. On the one hand, the proportion of grandparents sharing internet browsing more than twice a week fell from 36.4% before the pandemic to 25.0% after the pandemic, while the use of social networks went from 1 to 2 days a week in 25% of cases to 0% after lockdown (Tables 5.1 and 5.2).

Table 5.1 Places where internet surfing activity is shared, by time (%)

	Before lockdown	During lockdown	After lockdown	Total
Holidays	13.6	0.0	0.0	10.0
Only 1 or 2 days a month	4.5	0.0	25.0	10.0
Weekends, 1 day	9.1	0.0	12.5	10.0
Weekends, 2 days	13.6	0.0	12.5	13.3
Weekdays, 1 or 2 days	31.8	0.0	37.5	33.3
Weekdays, 3 or 4 days	27.3	0.0	12.5	23.3
Weekdays, 5 days	9.1	0.0	12.5	10.0
Total	100.0	100.0	100.0	100.0

Table 5.2 Places where social network use is shared, by time (%)

	Before lockdown	During lockdown	After lockdown	Total
Holidays	10.0	0.0	50.0	1.1
Only 1 or 2 days a month	20.0	0.0	0.0	1.4
Weekends, 1 day	5.0	40.1	0.0	37.3
Weekends, 2 days	5.0	15.6	0.0	14.8
Weekdays, 1 or 2 days	40.0	46.6	100.0	46.5
Weekdays, 3 or 4 days	10.0	42.4	0.0	39.8
Weekdays, 5 days	15.0	7.6	0.0	8.1
Total	100.0	100.0	100.0	100.0

5.5 Discussion

The COVID-19 pandemic demonstrated the resilience of intergenerational relationships, particularly about the use of information and communication technologies (ICTs) as a fundamental tool for maintaining contact between grandparents and grandchildren (Ayuso et al., 2020; Fuchsberger et al., 2021; Lago & Rivoir, 2021).

The results show how digital leisure shared between these two groups increased dramatically during lockdown, highlighting the flexibility and innovation in the way these relationships were kept alive despite the restrictions during this period.

Before the pandemic, only a small percentage of grandparents shared digital leisure activities with their grandchildren. This figure increased considerably during lockdown; a change that underlines how ICTs, and in particular social networks and video calling platforms, became the main means of virtual communication and coexistence (Galiano et al., 2020; Fernández & Sánchez, 2020; Nouwen & Hermine, 2021; Valdemoros et al., 2020).

This phenomenon can be attributed to the lack of alternatives due to the restrictions imposed by the pandemic, which forced families to seek ways to maintain contact and intergenerational relationships through these digital platforms.

Our findings show that the applications most used in times of pandemic were those linked to social networks, seeking a resolution to the need to socialise, in order to avoid negative psychological impacts derived from uncertainty about the unknown, added to a negative impact on mental health, which is a result of absolute loneliness, as stated in previous studies (Piña, 2020; Pineda, 2022).

In contrast, before and after lockdown, internet browsing, and social media use were less prevalent. This change in activity typology may reflect the urgent need for more interactive forms of communication during isolation.

Research such as that of Smith (2021) has pointed out that video calls and online gaming platforms were quickly adopted during lockdown as substitutes for physical interactions. This also aligns with the idea that the type of digital entertainment was adapted to the exceptional circumstances generated by the pandemic.

If we consider the first intergenerational approaches mediated by technology, Barrios and Fajardo (2011) state that current intergenerational relations are based, almost obligatorily, on the use and consumption of ICTs, even dismissing any close relationship with the period of lockdown. This shows that there is no lack of awareness of their being strengthened during the pandemic, but rather a situation of the times, as complemented by the data shown in our results.

Once the restrictions were lifted, participation in shared digital leisure activities dropped again, reaching a level even lower than before the pandemic. This decline suggests that, while digital leisure was an effective solution during lockdown, it has not been sufficiently adopted as part of the usual repertoire of activities shared between grandparents and grandchildren in unrestricted contexts. This trend is consistent with previous studies that have indicated that older adults' ICT use tends to be motivated by need rather than preference, and that once the need is gone, the frequency of use tends to decrease. This pattern is similar to that found by Lee et al. (2023), who observed a decrease in the use of digital platforms for family communication once restrictions were eased.

Our study shows that the frequency of digital interactions varied significantly during the different periods of time studied. Before lockdown, most grandparents shared digital activities 1–2 days per week, while during lockdown this frequency increased to every day. Subsequently, the frequency decreased, with an increase in those who shared activities only once or twice a week.

It is important to note how social networks and video calls became established as the main tools for communication during the pandemic. This changed after the lifting of the restrictions, revealing the low persistence of these digital practices over time. This, together with increased frequency observed during lockdown, suggests that ICT use, while beneficial in times of crisis, has not been sustainably integrated into post-pandemic daily routines (Brooks et al., 2020).

Our data shows that the reduction in digital leisure use was consistent, regardless of the gender of the grandchildren. This suggests that variation in the use of digital leisure was not influenced by gender, but by the general context of lockdown and its subsequent lifting.

It also reveals that digital leisure took place mostly in the homes of both parties, with no significant changes in location during the three time periods, indicating that the mode of sharing was not significantly affected by location during the pandemic.

A limitation of this study is whether social desirability may influence the responses obtained, given that previous studies have verified a tendency for subjects to increase the level of satisfaction in their statements when there are affective and emotional ties (Caputo, 2015).

The prospective provided by this work suggests it may be useful to further explore the importance of the role of technology in intergenerational programmes (Sánchez et al., 2015), given that the experiences provided by technology offer a rare opportunity to strengthen intergenerational relationships, fostering co-learning, autonomy, and a sense of competence, especially in older adults (Nimrod et al., 2019; Tarditi et al., 2022).

All this points to the need to provide training resources for grandparents who lack basic digital skills; their own grandchildren could be the ones to provide technological knowledge as digital natives, thus preventing intergenerational relations from being limited due to the physical separation between the two generations, or to various other situations that may arise.

The web of intergenerational relationships changed during the time of the COVID-19 pandemic. There were significant improvements in the relationships between grandparents and grandchildren, and this has raised awareness of the importance and role of these relationships in the development of both groups (Valiente, 2022).

5.6 Conclusions

People and institutions are starting to have a shared digital identity, which is becoming increasingly integrated due to the ease with which both public and private administrations can develop processes based on the hyper-connectivity, big data and immediacy that characterise the development of processes in the twenty-first century. They also highlight, from the incidence of ICTs themselves, a change today and an adaptation to them that is now synonymous with evolution, making it clear that the virtual situational landscape, which can be synchronous and asynchronous, demands new skills from the traditional education system (Mañas & Roig, 2019).

As a result of the above, digital technology is omnipresent in the everyday life of today's societies, making it evident that digital leisure has changed the way we understand and make use of our free time.

The results of this study highlight several key aspects of the relationship between grandparents and grandchildren in the context of the COVID-19 pandemic.

Firstly, an unprecedented increase in shared digital entertainment took place during lockdown, demonstrating the capacity of ICTs to maintain and strengthen intergenerational ties in situations of physical isolation. However, the significant drop in levels of participation in such activities after lockdown indicates that while ICTs were crucial in an emergency context, they have not been integrated into family dynamics in a lasting way.

This finding suggests a need to promote programmes that continue to support the digital literacy of older adults, encouraging greater continuity in the use of ICTs to maintain intergenerational relationships (Dalton et al., 2020).

Grandchildren, as digital natives, can play a key role in this process, teaching their grandparents how to use digital tools that could enrich their interactions and keep them active even in the absence of a crisis such as the COVID-19 pandemic.

Finally, while the pandemic has been a catalyst for the use of ICTs in the relationship between grandparents and grandchildren, the challenge now is to maintain and foster these digital connections in the future. It is essential to integrate the lessons learned during this period into intergenerational and digital literacy programmes to ensure that these relationships can thrive in all circumstances, contributing to a more connected society.

References

Alonso, R. A., de Jubera, S., de la Jubera, M., Valdemoros, M., & Ponce de León, A. (2022). Digital leisure: An opportunity for intergenerational well-being in times of pandemic? *Journal of New Approaches in Educational Research, 11*(1), 31–48. https://doi.org/10.7821/naer.2022.1.806

Alonso, R. A., Sáenz de Jubera, M., & Sanz, E. (2020). Tiempos compartidos entre abuelos y nietos, tiempos de desarrollo personal. *Revista Española de Pedagogía, 78*(277), 415–433. https://doi.org/10.22550/REP78-3-2020-01

Aveiga, V., Ostaiza, J., Macías, X., & Macías, M. (2018). Uso de la tecnología: entretenimiento o adicción. *Caribeña de Ciencias Sociales, 1*, 1–20.

Ayuso, L., Requena, F., Jiménez-Rodríguez, O., & Khamis, N. (2020). The effects of COVID-19 confinement on the Spanish family: Adaptation or change? *Journal of Comparative Family Studies, 51*(3–4), 274–287. https://doi.org/10.3138/jcfs.51.3-4.004

Barnard, Y., Bradley, M. D., Hodgson, F., & Lloyd, A. D. (2013). Learning to use new technologies by older adults: Perceived difficulties, experimentation behaviour and usability. *Computers in Human Behavior, 29*(4), 1715–1724.

Barrios, A., & Fajardo, C. (2011). Las relaciones intergeneracionales mediadas por el uso y consumos de las nuevas tecnologías de la información y la comunicación (TIC). *ResearchGate*, publication/3056521. https://hdl.handle.net/20.500.12010/10250

Brooks, S. K., Webster, R. K., Smith, L. E., Woodland, L., Wessely, S., Greenberg, N., & Rubin, G. J. (2020). The psychological impact of quarantine and how to reduce it: Rapid review of the evidence. *The Lancet, 395*, 912–920. https://doi.org/10.1016/S0140-6736(20)30460-8

Calzado, M., Cirulli, A., & Lio, V. (2021). La ventana al exterior en la pandemia: tecnologías, hábitos y confianza informativa en Argentina. *Revista CTS, special edition*, 83–100.

Caputo, A. (2015). Sesgo de deseabilidad social en las medidas de bienestar por autoinforme: evidencia de una encuesta en línea. *Universitas Psichologica, 16*(2), 93–102. https://doi.org/10.11144/Javeriana.upsy16-2.sdsw

Chen, C. H., Lyu, K., Li, J., & Shiu, H. (2021). Bridging the digital divide for rural older adults by family intergenerational learning: A classroom case in a rural primary school in China. *International Journal of Environmental Research and Public Health, 19*(1). https://doi.org/10.3390/ijerph19010371

Concepción, A., Corrales, I., Córdoba, M., Acosta, M., Larancuent, O., & De La Cruz, Y. (2020). Sondeo de Casos en Personas Mayores sobre Actividades Cotidianas y Utilización de Tecnologías de la Información y la Comunicación (TIC) en Tiempos de Pandemia. *Revista Tecnológica-Educativa Docentes, 9*(2), 1–19. https://doi.org/10.37843/rted.v9i2.156

Cuenca, J. (2020). El ocio digital: Una perspectiva desde la educación. *Revista de Estudios de Ocio, 10*(2), 123–136.

Dalton, L., Rapa, E., & Stein, A. (2020). Protecting the psychological health of children through effective communication about COVID-19. *The Lancet Child & Adolescent Health, 4*(5), 346–347. https://doi.org/10.1016/S2352-4642(20)30097-3

Esteban-Guitart, M., & Chamarro, A. (2021). La interacción intergeneracional a través de la tecnología digital en el contexto de la pandemia. *Revista de Educación y Cultura, 9*(1), 45–58.

Fernández, R., & Sánchez, M. (2020). Impacto del COVID-19 en personas mayores en España: algunos resultados y reflexiones. *Revista Clínica y Salud, 31*(3), 165–169. https://doi.org/10.5093/clysa2020a25

Fuchsberger, V., Beuthel, J. M., Bentegeac, P., & Tscheligi, M. (2021). Grandparents and grandchildren meeting online: The role of material things in remote settings. *Human Factors in Computing Systems, 478*, 1–14. https://doi.org/10.1145/3411764.3445191

Galiano, M., Prado, R., & Mustelier, R. (2020). Salud mental en la infancia y adolescencia durante la pandemia de COVID-19. *Revista Cubana de Pediatría, 92*(1342), 1–19. https://revpediatria.sld.cu/index.php/ped/article/view/1342/681

García-Peñalvo, F. J., Corell, A., Abella-García, V., & Grande, M. (2021). La covid-19: ≚Un acelerador de la transformación digital en la educación? *Revista Iberoamericana de Educación a Distancia, 24*(1), 7–34.

Gatto, S. L., & Tak, S. H. (2020). Computer, internet, and e-mail use among older adults: Benefits and barriers. *Educational Gerontology, 34*(9), 800–811.

Hess, C., & Schönfeld, F. (2020). Comunicación entre abuelos y nietos en período de aislamiento social obligatorio por COVID-19 en Entre Ríos, Argentina. In *Memorias del XII Congreso Internacional de Investigación y Práctica Profesional en Psicología* (Vol. 3, p. 84).

Hunsaker, A., & Hargittai, E. (2020). A review of internet use among older adults. *New Media & Society, 20*(10), 3937–3954.

Jimena, J. (2020). Programa intergeneracional para combatir la exclusión social adolescente y la brecha digital en personas de la tercera edad. In E. Sánchez, E. Colomo, J. Ruiz, & J. Sánchez (Eds.), *Tecnologías Educativas y Estrategias Didácticas* (pp. 1062–1071). University of Málaga. https://www.researchgate.net/publication/344155062_Programa_intergeneracional_para_combatir_la_exclusion_social_adolescente_y_la_brecha_digital_en_personas_de_la_tercera_edad

Lago, S., & Rivoir, A. (2021). Tecnologías digitales y pandemia: desigualdades, exclusiones y desafíos en América Latina. *América En Alas. Controversias y Concurrencias de Latina, 12*(22), 11–15.

Lee, D., Pollack, S. W., Mroz, T., Frogner, B. K., & Skillman, S. M. (2023). Disability competency training in medical education. *Medical Education Online, 28*(1), 2207773. https://doi.org/10.1080/10872981.2023.2207773

Mañas, A., & Roig, R. (2019). Las Tecnologías de la Información y la Comunicación en el ámbito educativo. Un tándem necesario en el contexto de la sociedad actual. *Revista Internacional d'Humanitats, 45*(1), 75–86. https://core.ac.uk/download/pdf/162130302.pdf

Martín, A. (2020). La brecha digital generacional. *Temas laborales: Revista andaluza de trabajo y bienestar social, 151*(1), 77–93. https://dialnet.unirioja.es/servlet/articulo?codigo=7464144

Nimrod, G., Lemish, D., & Elias, N. (2019). Grandparenting with media: Patterns of mediating grandchildren's media use. *Journal of Family Studies, 28*(1), 70–88. https://www.researchgate.net/publication/336653018_Grandparenting_with_media_patterns_of_mediating_grandchildren's_media_use

Nouwen, M., & Duflos, H. C. M. G. (2021). TikTok as a data gathering space: The case of grandchildren and grandparents during the COVID-19 pandemic. In *Interaction design and children* (pp. 498–502). https://www.researchgate.net/publication/352750545_TikTok_as_a_data_gathering_space_the_case_of_grandchildren_and_grandparents_during_the_COVID-19_pandemic

Pineda, K. (2022). Desarrollo Autónomo de Competencias Comunicativas en el Idioma Inglés. *Revista de lenguas modernas, 35*(1), 211–231. https://doi.org/10.15517/rlm.v0i35.44485

Piña, L. (2020). El COVID-19: Impacto psicológico en los seres humanos. *Revista Arbitrada Interdisciplinaria de Ciencias de la Salud. SALUD Y VIDA, 4*(7), 188–199. https://doi.org/10.35381/s.v.v4i7.670

Sanchez, M., Kaplan, M., & Bradley, L. (2015). Usando la tecnología para conectar las generaciones consideraciones sobre forma y función. *Comunicar, 45*, 95–104.

Seifert, A., Cotten, S. R., & Xie, B. (2021). A double burden of exclusion? Digital and social exclusion of older adults in times of COVID-19. *Journals of Gerontology: Series B, 76*(3), e99–e103.

Smith, M. D. (2021). CALL in a social context: reflecting on digital equity, identity, and interaction in the post-COVID age. *Quality Assurance in Education, 29*(4), 537–549. https://doi.org/10.1108/QAE-10-2020-0122

Tarditi, L., Yuni, J., & Urbano, C. (2022). Comparaciones Intergeneracionales en los Usos y Motivos de Uso de TIC en Personas Adultas Mayores y de Mediana Edad en una Ciudad Argentina. *Anales en Gerontología, 14*(14), 1–26. https://revistas.ucr.ac.cr/index.php/gerontologia/article/view/53226

Valdemoros, M. A., Sáenz de Jubera, M., Alonso, R. A., Santamaría, M., & Medrano, C. (2020). Ocio lúdico y cultural como aportación para la comunicación entre abuelos y nietos. In D. Caldevilla (Ed.), *Unidos por la comunicación: Libro de Actas del Congreso Internacional Latina de Comunicación Social* (p. 318). https://dialnet.unirioja.es/servlet/articulo?codigo=8594917

Valiente, S. (2022). La xarxa intergeneracional i ls influència de la COVID-19. *Anuari de l'envelliment: Illes Balears*, 62–74. https://dialnet.unirioja.es/servlet/articulo?codigo=8781279

Chapter 6
Intergenerational Environmental Leisure Practices in Post-Pandemic Times

José Manuel Martínez-Villar, Rosa Ana Alonso Ruiz, María Ángeles Valdemoros San Emeterio, Cristina Medrano Pascual, and Magdalena Sáenz de Jubera

Abstract Sustainable-ecological leisure activities shared between grandparents and grandchildren contribute to their personal, social, and familial development, promoting cohesion, emotional ties, and well-being. These activities also foster respect for the environment and align with the Sustainable Development Goals outlined in Agenda 2030. This study aims to analyze the practice of sustainable-ecological leisure among grandparents and grandchildren in northern Spain during the post-pandemic era. The research employed a combined methodology: quantitative, using an *ad hoc* questionnaire, and qualitative, through group discussion. The quantitative sample included 350 grandparents with grandchildren aged 6–12, while the qualitative stage involved a discussion group of 9 grandparents with primary school-aged grandchildren. Results revealed that both generations have adopted more pro-environment and prosocial attitudes compared to previous periods. However, grandparents feel the need for more quality time with their grandchildren, as the pandemic has led to a perceived emotional distance. Despite this, grandparents find multiple benefits in these shared leisure practices, primarily enjoying them because they want to spend more time together. The findings highlight the significance of environmental leisure activities, which are seen as satisfying, valuable, and healthy. These activities promote co-learning, intergenerational knowledge, and respect for natural environments.

This paper is connected to the I+D+I Project "Intergenerational leisure in the context of the new normal. Education, opportunities and challenges" (PID2020-119438RB-I00) [2021–2024] funded by the Ministry of Science and Innovation.

J. M. Martínez-Villar · R. A. Alonso Ruiz · M. Á. Valdemoros San Emeterio (✉) ·
C. Medrano Pascual · M. Sáenz de Jubera
University of La Rioja, Logroño, Spain
e-mail: j.mtnez.villar@gmail.com; rosa-ana.alonso@unirioja.es; maria-de-los-angeles.valdemoros@unirioja.es; cristina.medrano@unirioja.es; m-magdalena.saenz-de-jubera@unirioja.es

L. Ronda et al. (eds.), *Leisure and Human Development*, Human Well-Being Research and Policy Making, https://doi.org/10.1007/978-3-031-90778-4_6

6.1 Introduction and Justification

Nowadays, leisure practices are a right of all citizens and integrate different dimensions, among which the recreational, creative, festive, environmental, and solidarity dimensions stand out. These satisfying, free, and valuable experiences enhance the comprehensive development of all human beings (Cuenca, 2016). Additionally, the environmental dimension of leisure is defined as "a specific manifestation of leisure characterized by the experience of satisfying moments motivated by the context, in the sense of being in a place and/or an environment" (Cuenca, 2016, p. 13). Due to its connection with nature and outdoor environments, this dimension of leisure is directly linked to some of the Sustainable Development Goals outlined in the 2030 Agenda, established by the General Assembly of the United Nations (Government of Spain, 2018), which contribute to sustainable development.

Scientific literature has proven that older people show a greater interest in nature than other generations. Thus, we can confirm that getting older is directly linked to natural spaces and outdoor experiences (Kemperman & Timmermans, 2006; Jorgensen & Anthopoulou, 2007; Ding, 2017; Wen et al., 2018). Nevertheless, previous authors have verified that there are different factors affecting these practices, so they must be considered when affirming this (González & de la Fuente, 2007; Attar-Schwartz et al., 2009; Coall & Hertwig, 2010; Kim et al., 2017). In relation to this, when showing a positive and favorable attitude toward natural spaces, older people obtain more satisfaction and well-being (Asah et al., 2012; Taye et al., 2019). Consequently, it is logical to think that this generation might feel uncomfortable when it comes to crowded cities and find themselves more attracted to the countryside or nature (Kim & Byun, 2011; Wen et al., 2018). Some authors manifest that this preference is more closely linked to those leisure activities that are carried out outdoors than to the natural context itself (Brown & Glasgow, 2008; Dzhambov & Dimitrova, 2014).

In recent decades, family structures have experienced significant changes since, due to factors such as the incorporation of women into the workforce (Kanji, 2018), the economic crisis, or the increase in life expectancy, among others, relations among grandparents and grandchildren are closer and more meaningful (Rico et al., 2001). Because of this, several authors have established that grandparents have become important role models for their grandchildren today (González & de la Fuente, 2007; Attar-Schwartz et al., 2009; Sanz et al., 2020).

This generational bond fosters these kinds of relations, and they impact remarkably on the physical, mental, and social development of children (Pinazo, 1999; Rico et al., 2001; Castañeda-García et al., 2017; Noriega & López, 2021; Roa Venegas & Vacas Díaz, 2001). It is necessary to highlight the importance of intergenerational dialogue as an effective tool to strengthen the interactions that occur among different generations, to boost interpersonal communication, and to enable cultural exchange (Carvajal et al., 2020), which benefits both generations (Martínez & Rodríguez, 2018).

Former investigations mention that when shared among grandparents and grandchildren, environmental leisure intensifies and strengthens the intergenerational bond, as it promotes benefits in terms of flexibility in outdoor spaces (Becerril & Bores, 2019; Castell, 2020; Yoo & Russell, 2020), which leads to an improvement in the quality of life and health (Acero et al., 2017).

Among the activities that belong to the environmental dimension of leisure and that have been analyzed in the present study, we can highlight traveling, trips, fishing, hunting, animal and plant care, or gardening, among others. Moreover, González and Temprano (2018) include three environmental leisure activities which play an important part in our society: farm schools, nature classrooms, and interpretation centers.

Recent authors note that those activities that are associated with environmental leisure, such as outdoor walking, interactions with nature, taking care of animals and plants, and gardening, have a significant role in the activities that grandparents and grandchildren practice together (Ponce de León et al., 2022). Also, leisure activities that are carried out in natural contexts on a regular basis are said to provide an increase in emotional, physical, and mental well-being for the participants (Ried, 2015; Rodríguez et al., 2019; Castell, 2020). Thus, rural environments become fabulous locations to practice this kind of activity.

Gardens and farms are considered very relevant when it comes to sharing this environmental leisure since multiple and diverse activities can be carried out: outdoor games, growing fruits and vegetables, farming, digging, taking care of animals, and other practices (Ponce de León et al., 2022). These experiences contribute to values assimilation and exchange, and they involve pro-environmental, social, and civic learning (Wynveen et al., 2011; D'Amore, 2016; Izenstark & Ebata, 2017). Consequently, family or urban gardens play a central role in the environmental dimension of leisure and are considered to be able to transform the environment, having a great impact on the management of spaces, resources, and social relations—individual and group (Esteban & Amador, 2020), thereby promoting intergenerational learning (García et al., 2017; Hake, 2017). These are very promising results, although there are certain authors who believe children are currently distanced from this type of experience (Eduard & Larson, 2020).

From the perspective of grandparents, these interactions allow them to improve their physical and mental development, provide health, comfort, and enjoyment, and support healthy and active aging (Martínez et al., 2017; Rodríguez et al., 2019; Castell, 2020). From the point of view of children, these relationships in nature help them improve their motor and mental skills and the development of habits and routines that will promote a more active adult life (Laaksoharju et al., 2012; Dadvand et al., 2015).

Several investigations confirm that grandparents can transmit their interest in leisure activities in natural environments to their grandchildren (Thompson et al., 2008; Asah et al., 2012; Taye et al., 2019). However, the COVID-19 pandemic hindered contact between grandparents and grandchildren (Valdemoros et al., 2021), as the older generation was particularly affected due to their vulnerability and the fear of contagion (McDarby et al., 2020). Likewise, Vicente Castro (2021) considered this situation a great opportunity to bring both generations together, as technologies helped foster intergenerational learning (Díaz Villalobos, 2021). In this sense, it is important to highlight that during the post-pandemic era, physical activities in natural spaces have decreased, while an increase in exposure to and contact with electronic devices has been noticed (Kotrla et al., 2021), especially among grandchildren (Konok et al., 2020; Yogman et al., 2018). Moreover, this generation has acquired unhealthy eating habits and sedentary lifestyles, although there are differences depending on age, socio-economic level, and other factors (Jenssen et al., 2021).

Nowadays, due to threats such as climate change, a large percentage of people have adopted a more prosocial and pro-environmental attitude compared to previous decades (Wade-Benzoni & Plunkett-Tost, 2009; Clayton, 2018). They have also developed a sense of responsibility toward future generations (Wagner, 2020; Syropoulos & Markowitz, 2021), thereby improving their relationships and fostering intergenerational collaboration (Hurlstone et al., 2020). In this regard, several authors have affirmed that people with an interest in leaving a legacy tend to show more proactive and pro-environmental behavior, as they are aware of the negative consequences of their own actions on the planet (Syropoulos & Markowitz, 2021).

In summary, environmental-ecological leisure experiences developed in family contexts, where both grandparents and grandchildren take an active part, have an attractive and beneficial component for all members. This enables the connection between both generations and creates an interface with natural environments (Becerril & Bores, 2019; Castell, 2020; Ponce de León et al., 2021; Yoo & Russell, 2020). Nature thus becomes an ideal context for family leisure activities, where villages are considered an excellent option for families. Contact with natural locations provides perfect places to practice leisure and obtain learning opportunities, while physical activities are also promoted (Rojek, 2005). This study aims to test how environmental leisure experiences are developed today among grandparents and grandchildren from northern Spain in the aftermath of the COVID-19 pandemic.

6.2 Methodology and Research Design

For the current investigation, both quantitative and qualitative methodologies were employed to conduct an in-depth study with greater scientific rigor. A descriptive cross-sectional design was utilized, and the study was based on a heterogeneous sample to accurately reflect reality and faithfully represent the study population.

6.2.1 Participants

In the quantitative phase, the study population consisted of children aged 6–12 years living in the northern region of Spain, including eight provinces: Cantabria, Vizcaya, Guipúzcoa, Álava, La Rioja, Navarra, Burgos, and Palencia. This selection followed the Nielsen classification, which divides Spain into seven geographical areas with similar characteristics.

Table 6.1 Population and sample of study. Children enrolled in Primary Education (aged 6–12) in the northern regions of Spain. Source: Education Offices and Departments of Cantabria, Basque Country, La Rioja, Navarre, and Castilla León

Provinces	Population	Sample	No. of selected centres
Cantabria	33,608	146	3
Vizcaya	64,813	277	6
Guipúzcoa	44,456	190	4
Álava	20,163	86	2
La Rioja	19,366	83	2
Navarra	40,468	175	4
Burgos	19,774	85	2
Palencia	7709	34	1
Total	250,357	1063	24

The study population was determined based on statistical data published by the Education Offices and Departments from each autonomous community. The data indicated a population size of 250,357 students.

An absolute error of 3% and a confidence level of 95% were set, with the assumption of $p = q = 0.5$. Based on these parameters, the sample size was estimated to be 1075 students. After accounting for an experimental mortality rate of 1.11%, the final sample size was 1063 students. The sampling method used was proportional stratified probabilistic sampling by province. The final sampling units were selected by clusters, with entire educational centers being randomly chosen from each of the eight provinces in the northern region of Spain (see Table 6.1).

14.0% (n=151) of the participants were 6 years old, 15.6% (n=168) were 7 years old, 18.1% (n=195) were 8 years old, 17.7% (n=190) were 9 years old, 17.4% (n=187) were 10 years old, and 17.2% (n=185) were 11 years old (some of whom had just turned 12). Regarding living arrangements, 94.6% of the respondents did not live with their grandparents, 3.7% lived with one grandparent, 1.3% lived with two grandparents, and 0.4% lived with three.

In the qualitative phase, participant selection followed a structural approach, determining group composition based on specific membership criteria. Homogeneity was maintained across the various variables analyzed. Additionally, expert recommendations (González Ríos, 1997; Ibáñez, 2000; Suárez, 2005) were considered to determine the number of participants in the discussion group. This group consisted of nine grandparents (five men and four women) who had grandchildren enrolled in Primary Education, with the grandchildren's ages ranging from 6 to 12 years. All participants resided in the Autonomous Community of La Rioja.

6.3 Research Instrument

In the quantitative stage, an *ad hoc* questionnaire was used to collect relevant information for the study, based on the following six variables:

- *Leisure activities shared with grandparents.* This is a dichotomous variable that records whether participants share leisure activities with their grandparents or not (cultural activities, recreational activities, digital activities, ecological-environmental activities). Categories are yes/no.
- *Ecological-environmental leisure activities shared with grandparents.* This is a dichotomous variable that sets if participants share environmental activities with their grandparents. Categories are yes/no.
- *Locations to share ecological-environmental activities.* This categorical variable was used to record the places where both generations share any type of ecological-environmental activity, giving an answer to the question "Name the place where you practice each of the selected activities" (1=at home—grandparents or grandchildren; 2=associations, clubs, societies, social clubs ("peñas"), understanding that associations are groups of people that practice collective activities on a regular basis with a registered office; 3=municipal areas—sports centers, cultural centers, playrooms, etc.; 4=public open spaces—street, parks in the interior of a municipality, squares, etc.; 5=in nature; 6=in school facilities).
- *Reasons why both generations share ecological-environmental leisure.* This categorical variable gathered the motives and reasons why they practice leisure activities, giving answers to the question "Name the reason(s) why you share leisure activities" (1=simply because I like it; 2=my grandparents take care of me/I take care of my grandchildren while parents are at work; 3=they are the only people with whom I can share these activities; 4=they do not have other people to share these activities with; 5=they know a lot about the activity and they teach me; 6=I know a lot about the activity and I teach them; 7=to entertain them; 8=to spend time together).
- *Physical benefits, emotional well-being; creative benefits, manual benefits, and social benefits.* These variables gathered information on the contributions that ecological-environmental leisure makes to the overall well-being of both generations, through five different questions: (1) "The leisure activities that I share help me to be fitter, to have control over my movements, to keep or improve my physical condition"; (2) "The leisure activities that I share help me to feel happier, to better enjoy the activities and to have more fun"; (3) "The leisure activities that I share help me to be more creative"; (4) "The leisure activities that I share help me to develop new manual skills or to enhance technical skills"; (5) "The leisure activities that I share help me to have a better relationship with them." This information is collected in five categories (1=totally disagree; 5=totally agree).
- *Level of satisfaction with intergenerational ecological-environmental leisure activities.* Five categorical variables gathered information on the satisfaction that ecological-environmental leisure provides to both generations, through five questions: (1) "The leisure activities that I share are as I would like them to be"; (2) "I have achieved important things to me thanks to leisure activities"; (3) "I am satisfied with the leisure activities that I share"; (4) "In the future, I would repeat the leisure activities as they now are"; (5) "The circumstances of my shared leisure activities are positive." This information is recorded through five categories (1=totally disagree; 5=totally agree).

In the qualitative stage, a discussion group was used during the post-pandemic period, as a social-interactive investigation tool, which considers interview elements and participant observation. This technique focused on the dialogue of the participants, which lies in their discourse production, facilitated by a moderator, where they talked and discussed the topic under consideration for the research. Thus, the quantity and variety of dissertations became a reliable source of raw material for the analysis and interpretation of the results (López Francés, 2010).

6.4 Procedure

A questionnaire was developed and administered, specifically designed for children aged 6–12 from different schools in the North of Spain. The study population consists of children from eight provinces: Cantabria, Vizcaya, Guipúzcoa, Álava, La Rioja, Navarra, Burgos, and Palencia. The questionnaire was administered randomly among students from different educational institutions. Prior to its administration, permission was requested from those responsible for ensuring data protection and management.

Five qualified researchers, all holding PhDs in Leisure and Pedagogy, were responsible for contacting the grandparents of the children who provided the required information when completing the questionnaire. Each grandparent was contacted by phone, and their responses were recorded digitally through a structured interview as they were received. The approximate time to record the responses was 30–45 min.

The Ethics Committee of the University of La Rioja approved this procedure. The positive report from the Ethics Committee was registered with the code CE_02_2019.

In the qualitative methodological process, the discussion group technique was used. This dialogic method relies on the production of discourses that emerge from dialogue and debate on the subject of study, which will serve as the raw material for the analysis and interpretation of results (López Francés, 2010).

Based on the objective of this research and the advice of experts to create as many groups as there are segments of the population of interest, it was decided to conduct a discussion group made up of the grandparents.

6.5 Categories of Analysis

Data analysis was conducted in two phases using the statistical program SPSS 23.0. In the first phase, a descriptive study was carried out using frequency statistics. This allowed the researchers to determine which activities were shared among grandparents and grandchildren (aged 6–12), the types of ecological-environmental shared activities, and the perception of well-being improvement in grandparents when practicing ecological-environmental activities with their grandchildren.

In the second phase, an inferential analysis was performed using the Chi-square test (χ^2) to determine the degree of relationship between grandparents' perceived well-being when sharing or not sharing ecological-environmental leisure activities with their grandchildren, in relation to physical condition, movement control, entertainment and fun, creativity, manual skills, and relationships with grandchildren.

The significance level for the entire study was set at $p < 0.05$.

To construct the category system, a theoretical basis on shared environmental leisure practices between grandparents and grandchildren was used, based on a search of articles from prestigious databases such as Dialnet, SciELO, Scopus, and Web of Science, conducted prior to the review of the transcripts (deductive phase). Later, as the testimonies and reflections from participants in the two discussion sessions were analyzed, the categories were expanded and branched into multiple subcategories (inductive phase). This resulted in a system of 8 general categories and 44 subcategories (Table 6.2).

Once the selection was done, the main researcher defined the categories and subcategories of analysis. Specifically, the subcategory of the present investigation was linked to ecological-environmental leisure and garden/farm (places to share leisure).

Finally, the categories and subcategories system of analysis was validated through expert judgment. Six university research professors, all of them holding PhDs in the field of Leisure and Pedagogy, acted as experts.

To measure validity, Cohen's Kappa index (1960, 1968) was used as an indicator of overall agreement among the experts. A nearly perfect level of agreement was obtained with three of the experts (0.862, 0.818, and 0.822), and substantial agreement with the other three (0.742, 0.695, and 0.678). Additionally, Fleiss' (1971) Kappa Coefficient was calculated to examine the degree of agreement between the principal investigator and each of the experts. The scores obtained per category ranged from 0.514 to 0.907, reflecting moderate, good, and very good agreement. The overall score was 0.697, indicating a good level of agreement. Thus, the category validation process was deemed satisfactory.

The qualitative data analysis was also conducted in two phases: In the first, a textual analysis of each category used to analyze the discourses was performed, recording the frequency of occurrences of each category and the percentage of each in relation to the total number of occurrences.

In the second phase, each subcategory of analysis was examined, with the frequency of occurrences and the percentage of each being recorded based on the total number of occurrences within the category. For qualitative data analysis, NVivo Release 1.6 software was used, which allows for data storage and coding, the creation of memos, notes, etc., the importation of files and documents, and their connection to fragments of the discourses (Valdemoros et al., 2011; Dias do Nascimento, 2016; Alonso et al., 2021).

Table 6.2 Categories and subcategories system of analysis

Category 1	**Reasons why they share leisure activities**
Subcategory 1.1	Family feeling
Subcategory 1.2	Time availability
Subcategory 1.3	Entertainment and fun
Subcategory 1.4	Mutual learning
Subcategory 1.5	Mutual help
Subcategory 1.6	Avoid abuse of new technologies
Subcategory 1.7	Caregiver role
Subcategory 1.8	Permissive role
Category 2	**Type of leisure activities**
Subcategory 2.1	Physical-sport leisure activities
Subcategory 2.2	Recreational leisure activities
Subcategory 2.3	Digital leisure activities
Subcategory 2.4	Environmental-ecological leisure
Subcategory 2.5	Cultural leisure activities
Subcategory 2.6	Other
Category 4	**Places to share leisure activities**
Subcategory 4.1	Farm/garden
Subcategory 4.2	Park
Subcategory 4.3	Village
Subcategory 4.4	Home
Subcategory 4.5	Restaurants/cafés
Subcategory 4.6	Lunchroom/Dining area
Subcategory 4.7	Educational center/surroundings of educational center
Category 5	**Time/periods to share leisure activities**
Subcategory 5.1	Summer holidays
Subcategory 5.2	Christmas holidays
Subcategory 5.3	Weekends
Subcategory 5.4	Weekdays
Subcategory 5.5	Bank holidays
Subcategory 5.6	Patron saints' festivities
Category 6	**Shared leisure contribution**
Subcategory 5.1	Positive feelings
Subcategory 5.2	Negative feelings
Subcategory 5.3	Values
Subcategory 5.4	Knowledge and shared experience
Subcategory 5.5	Entertainment and fun
Subcategory 5.6	Intimate communication
Category 7	**People with whom they share leisure activities**
Subcategory 7.1	Maternal grandmother
Subcategory 7.2	Maternal grandfather
Subcategory 7.3	Paternal grandmother
Subcategory 7.4	Paternal grandfather
Subcategory 7.5	Granddaughter on daughter's side
Subcategory 7.6	Grandson on daughter's side
Subcategory 7.7	Granddaughter on son's side
Subcategory 7.8	Grandson on son's side

6.6 Results

Once the methodological procedure has been explained, we can move forward to present the results of both the quantitative and qualitative phases, obtained after the pandemic. Firstly, the results from the quantitative phase are presented, followed by the results from the discussion group, with the objective of determining the current situation of environmental leisure activities shared among grandparents and grandchildren in the North of Spain.

In this way, we can see in Fig. 6.1 that more than 49% of the respondents practice environmental leisure activities, ranking fourth, behind cultural and recreational leisure.

If we observe Table 6.3, we can conclude that almost 40% of the participants practice some kind of environmental leisure activity.

Concretely, after analyzing the activities that belong to the environmental dimension of leisure, trips (38%), plant care or gardening (16.1%), and animal care (14.6%) are the most frequently shared by grandparents and grandchildren (Fig. 6.2).

Likewise, linking the results to the question "Who do you share environmental activities with?" grandparents tend to enjoy these experiences with both grandsons and granddaughters, as seen in Fig. 6.3. However, in cases where the activities are practiced separately, grandsons show a higher percentage (14.6%) of sharing these experiences with their grandparents than granddaughters (8%) (Fig. 6.3).

In relation to the places where these practices are carried out, the results show that nature (80.9%), followed by home (44.1%), are the locations where most environmental leisure activities are shared. The rest of the results show very insignificant percentages (Fig. 6.4).

Regarding the frequency of shared environmental activities, the results are quite revealing, as the highest rates refer to holidays (44.1%) and 1 day on the weekend

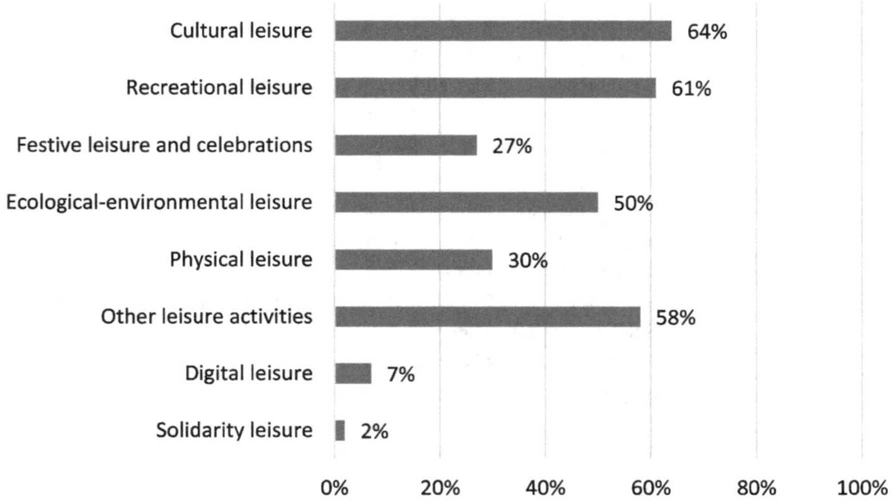

Fig. 6.1 Proportion of the population that shares leisure activities nowadays

Table 6.3 "Do you practice any ecological-environmental leisure activity after the lockdown?" Frequencies and percentages

	Frequency	%
No	54	39.4
Yes	83	60.6

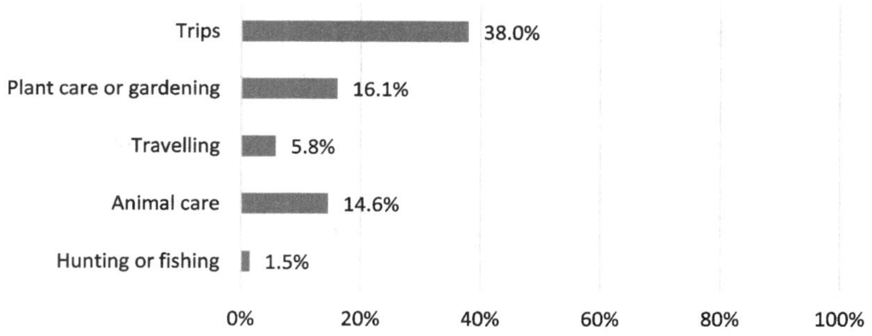

Fig. 6.2 Proportion of the population that shares environmental activities nowadays

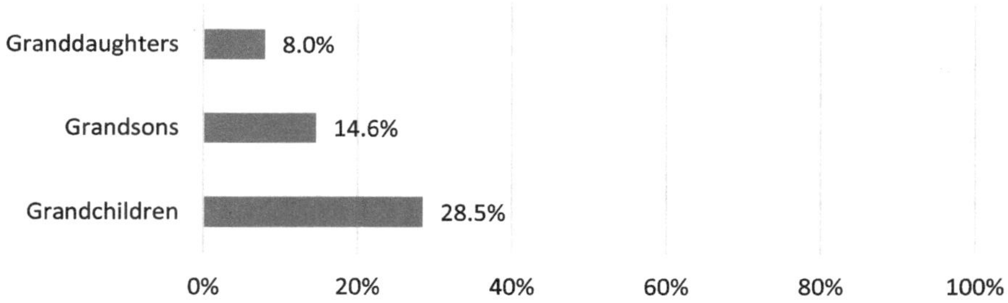

Fig. 6.3 Proportion of grandparents who share environmental leisure with their grandson(s), granddaughter(s), or both

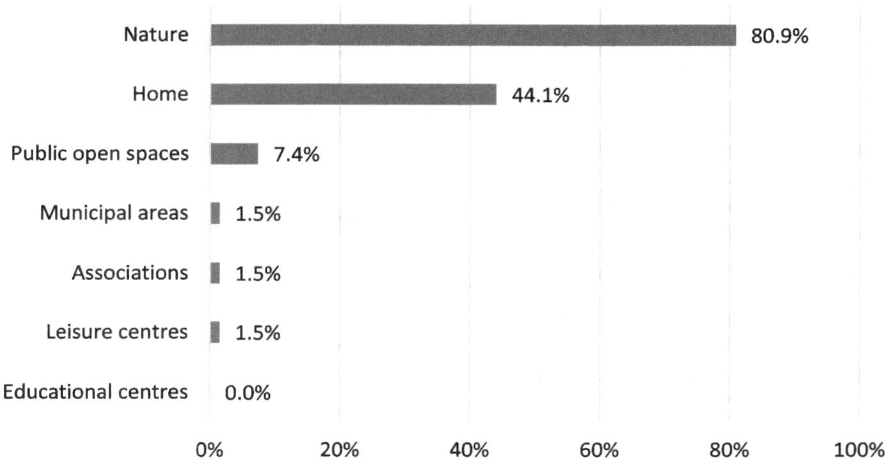

Fig. 6.4 Places where environmental leisure activities are carried out (%)

(36.8%). The other options have much lower incidence, showing equal values, as can be seen in Fig. 6.5.

Moreover, the most relevant reasons for grandparents to share leisure experiences with their grandchildren are, first, to spend more time together (68.7%), and second, because they enjoy it (64.2%). The other reasons have much lower percentages (Fig. 6.6).

From the grandparents' perspective, in relation to the benefits provided by environmental leisure shared experiences, and as shown in Table 6.4, these activities help them feel happier when shared with their grandchildren (92.2%) and help them build better relationships (87.6%). Other options did not show significant results.

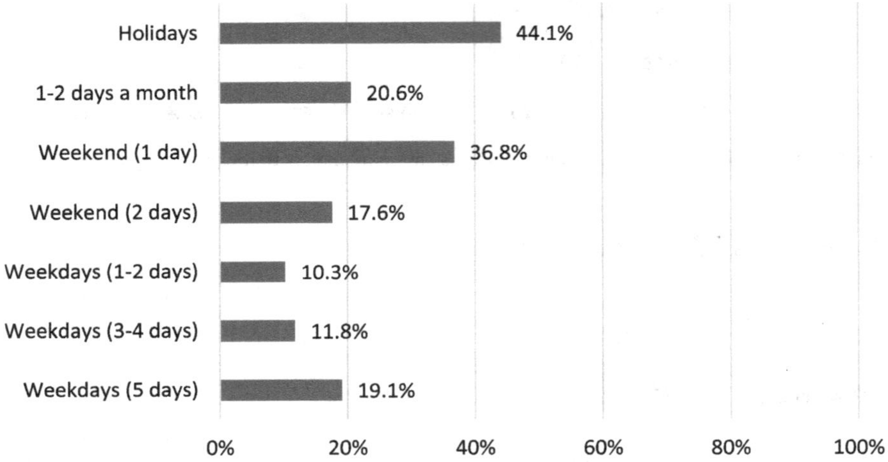

Fig. 6.5 Frequency of shared environmental leisure (%)

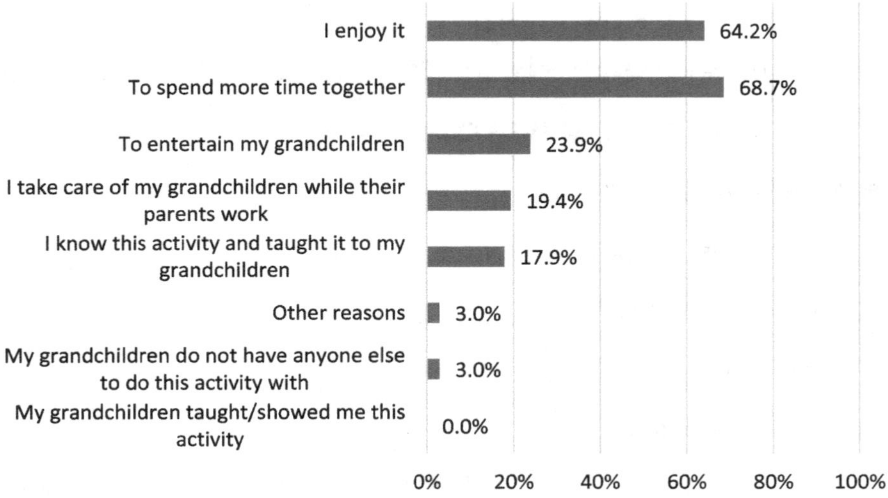

Fig. 6.6 Reasons why environmental leisure is shared (%)

During the post-pandemic era, results confirm that, in relation to participants' perception of the level of satisfaction when sharing leisure activities, grandparents are generally satisfied with the type of leisure they share with their grandchildren. Additionally, they would repeat the activities as they are now (Table 6.5).

Alternatively, once the results from the quantitative phase are presented, the analysis of the textual units derived from the discussion group is conducted, highlighting the following results. The general feeling that grandparents have regarding outdoor activities shared with their grandchildren is positive, although they would like to have more contact with them. Such statements are confirmed by utterances like these:

"Yes, now more than ever." (Ni)

"Doing more activities, definitely." (F)

"…social relations are lost. People have less enthusiasm. They don't feel like going out, to the bars, or socializing with friends or with people they used to have contact with before the pandemic." (F)

"In my case, I get to see them more often. But activities, no. Their parents don't let me practice any activities with them. And if we are together, we have to be apart." (Te)

"Well, we go to see them many days, and we see them in the countryside. They go skating, and we just watch them. I enjoy my grandchildren a lot." (Ti)

Table 6.4 Level of agreement (1 = totally disagree, 5 = totally agree) with statements related to grandparents' well-being after the lockdown

Statement	Totally disagree	2	3	4	Totally agree
It helps me stay fit	10.2%	7.8%	14.8%	14.1%	53.1%
It helps me feel happier	0.8%	0.0%	1.6%	5.4%	92.2%
It helps me become more creative	6.3%	9.4%	18.8%	15.6%	50.0%
It helps me develop new manual or technical skills	6.3%	10.2%	18.0%	17.2%	48.4%
It helps me have a better relationship with my grandson/granddaughter/grandchildren	0.8%	0.0%	3.1%	8.5%	87.6%

Table 6.5 Level of agreement (1 = totally disagree, 5 = totally agree) with statements related to satisfaction levels after the lockdown

Statement	Totally disagree	2	3	4	Totally agree
In general, the leisure activities that I share with my grandchild/grandchildren are the way I want them to be	5.3%	2.3%	11.3%	17.3%	63.9%
I have so far achieved things that are important to me through the leisure I share with my grandchild/grandchildren	0.0%	0.0%	8.4%	13.7%	77.9%
I am satisfied with the leisure I share with them	3.0%	4.5%	10.5%	12.0%	69.9%
In the future, I would repeat the leisure activities shared with my grandchild/grandchildren as they are now	0.8%	2.3%	11.5%	11.5%	74.0%
The circumstances of my shared leisure activities are positive	9.8%	3.0%	7.6%	13.6%	65.9%

"Yes, in the garden." (Ni)

"Nobody had ever seen what a potato was like, how to plant and grow it." (Jo)

Regarding the places where these activities are shared, as well as the frequency with which they are shared among grandchildren and grandparents, weekends and weekdays stand out, along with the farm and the garden as preferred locations. These testimonies support this:

"At the weekend, at least mine, my children, I might go to my village. Because we do have grandmothers too, of course. And they stay here and go to Mount Corvo." (E)

"Well, I normally, every Saturday…" (Mar)

"Because in summer, for example, we spend time with our grandchildren in the patio, at our village house, the house of everyone. We even set up a pool; if there's no swimming pool anywhere, then you can put one in your patio, and we spend the summer there." (F)

"And in August, I am every day with my grandchildren in my village." (V)

Moreover, regarding the feelings these activities evoke in grandparents and the reasons why they engage in them, the results are clear. Currently, they are preoccupied with the loss of contact due to the pandemic, especially because of the alarm system that was in place for more than a year. Nevertheless, grandchildren feel anguish when they cannot help with daily tasks, such as picking up or taking children to school. They feel the social distance both within their family environment and in their circle of friends.

In conclusion, they long for the times before the pandemic, as they feel anxious when they reflect on the fact that they have lost part of their lives—a part that will never come back. For this reason, grandparents need to regain physical and emotional contact, because it was they who cultivated these bonds with great effort and dedication over the year.

"And in August, I am every day with my grandchildren in my village." (V)

"Hugging your children and grandchildren is the best thing we have in life. Because you need more affection, you feel all alone." (V)

"Due to this, social relationships have been lost." (Ni)

"In my case, I want to be with them." (Te)

"You feel like going to the village more often. Walking, because you can go to the mountain, where you don't need your facemask… It's something different." (V)

"What I miss the most is hugging people." (Jo)

"And it's true, I like playing with them. And I like them to learn things they do not have, because they only play computer games." (Vi)

"It'll never be the same. Nothing can be the same. Everything is different." (Te)

"They go to the mountain and take some sandwiches with them, and they try, not with us, maybe with their parents, to be outdoors at the weekend, when it's possible, when it doesn't rain…"

6.7 Discussion and Conclusions

Our results reveal that grandparents consider rural places the ideal location to share and develop leisure activities, as previously evidenced by other authors (Ponce de León et al., 2022). Although the COVID-19 pandemic has soured relations between grandparents and grandchildren, it has also provided an opportunity to explore new ways of leisure, largely due to new technologies, which can be seen as an excellent tool for learning and bringing different generations together, as confirmed in previous investigations (Díaz Villalobos, 2021; Valdemoros et al., 2021; Vicente Castro, 2021). However, it is necessary to note the importance of intergenerational dialogue, as it strengthens relations between both generations and facilitates communication and cultural exchange, providing multiple benefits to the quality of their relationships, which are fully aligned with Martínez and Rodríguez (2018) and Carvajal et al. (2020).

The findings affirm that walking outdoors, having experiences in natural environments, taking care of animals and plants, or gardening are activities closely related to environmental leisure. These activities play an important role in practices shared between grandparents and grandchildren, positively impacting their lives, as stated in previous studies (Barnett, 2013; Becerril & Bores, 2019; Castell, 2020; Yoo & Russell, 2020; Ponce de León et al., 2021, 2022). These studies also emphasize that shared experiences are crucial to building stronger relationships, creating quality intergenerational moments, and connecting their relationships with natural environments, thus preventing grandparents from being limited to household tasks and caregiving.

Additionally, the present investigation proves that a high percentage of grandparents and grandchildren enjoy spending time together, recognizing the mutual benefits of shared leisure practices. This contrasts with Eduard and Larson (2020), who assert that such shared activities lead to intergenerational alienation.

Finally, results derived from the discussion group highlight that shared environmental leisure activities generate various learnings related to the environment and its conservation, as asserted by D'amore (2016), Izenstark and Ebata (2017), and Wynveen et al. (2011). This investigation provides diverse benefits to grandparents and grandchildren alike, a statement echoed by numerous studies (Dadvand et al., 2015; Castell, 2020; Laaksoharju et al., 2012; Martínez et al., 2017; Rodríguez et al., 2019).

Shared experiences, such as animal and plant care or trips, result in significant gains in strengthening affective bonds. This has been confirmed by much of the scientific literature (Becerril & Bores, 2019; Castell, 2020; D'amore, 2016; Izenstark & Ebata, 2017; Wynveen et al., 2011; Yoo & Russell, 2020).

We are pleased to note that grandparents perceive these shared activities as bringing various benefits, such as the improvement of physical, mental, and social development, which also contribute to active aging (Castell, 2020; Martínez et al., 2017; Rodríguez et al., 2019). Moreover, findings reveal that leisure experiences shared among grandparents and grandchildren in natural contexts provide a source of relaxation and joy for the participants (Castell, 2020; Rodríguez et al., 2019; Ried, 2015).

Furthermore, grandparents involved in this study feel that activities shared in natural spaces promote social relations and foster pro-environmental learning, as stated in previous investigations (D'amore, 2016; Izenstark & Ebata, 2017; Wynveen et al., 2011).

It has also been proven that the older generation exhibits a more pro-environmental attitude, which provides high levels of personal satisfaction, as established by other authors (Asah et al., 2012; Taye et al., 2019). This investigation presents a significant result: Gardens have the potential to connect grandparents and grandchildren, enabling knowledge and values transmission, enhancing co-learning, and promoting environmental sensitivity, as reflected in previous studies (Esteban & Amador, 2020; García et al., 2017; Hake, 2017; Jamieson, 2016; Kala & Galcanová, 2016; Ried, 2015; Rivera et al., 2014).

Moreover, results show that environmental issues, such as climate change, are making grandparents more prosocial and pro-environment, as mentioned in previous papers (Clayton, 2018; Wade-Benzoni & Plunkett-Tost, 2009). Additionally, it has been verified that grandparents love leisure activities in nature, where a favorable climate is created for them to transmit their love for natural environments to their grandchildren, as supported by earlier studies (Asah et al., 2012; Taye et al., 2019).

Nevertheless, this study confirms that after the pandemic, grandparents and grandchildren have distanced themselves due to the situation caused by COVID-19, as noted by Valdemoros et al. (2021). Findings from this research affirm that villages and rural areas, far from the noise and hectic pace of cities, are ideal contexts for practicing these types of leisure activities, in agreement with Ponce de León et al. (2022).

Once the results have been compared with the previous scientific literature, the main conclusions of this study are outlined below. The objective is to clarify, specify, and highlight the fundamental aspects of the research conducted.

- The ecological-environmental leisure activities hold an intermediate position among the leisure practices that grandparents and grandchildren share during post-pandemic periods, ranking fourth, behind those related to cultural and recreational leisure. The least frequent practices are those related to festivities, digital leisure, and solidarity leisure.
- Trips, animal and plant care, and gardening stand out as preferred environmental activities.
- Most of the environmental leisure activities shared among grandparents and grandchildren take place during holidays, as traveling or going on trips require more free time.
- "Short" or "instant" activities, such as trips, are carried out more frequently, since they do not require many prerequisites for their practice, compared to other activities like traveling, which requires more time and planning, or those related to animal care or gardening, conditioned by the prior availability of schedules and materials, which are enjoyed less frequently.
- Places where these experiences are usually shared are nature and home.
- In relation to frequency, results show that it mainly occurs during holiday periods.
- The lockdown drastically halted the leisure practice shared among grandparents and grandchildren, and it created distance between them.

- Technologies played a fundamental role in keeping and fostering intergenerational relationships interactively, improving the living conditions of the elderly and supporting both generations.
- Nowadays, environmental activities have been resumed, and in some cases, with greater intensity than before, as outdoor spaces are safer than indoor spaces, which makes it possible to have safe, satisfying, and enriching experiences.
- Older people who share environmental activities with their grandchildren perceive the benefits for their physical fitness and their level of satisfaction.
- Environmental practices shared among grandparents and grandchildren help them feel better and build better relationships.
- Sharing ecological-environmental leisure activities contributes to the improvement of physical, mental, and emotional development for both generations, since it boosts the assimilation of healthy habits, the pro-environmental awareness and commitment to environmental care, intergenerational bonds, and the co-learning process.

References

Acero, A. R., Cano-Prous, A., Castellanos, G., Martín-Lanas, R., & Canga-Armayor, A. (2017). Identidad familiar & enfermedad mental grave: una síntesis temática de estudios cualitativos. *Revista Europea de Psicología Social, 47*(5), 11–627. https://doi.org/10.1002/ejsp.2240

Alonso, R. A., Sáenz de Jubera, M., Sanz, E., Valdemoros, M. A., & Ponce de León, A. (2021). Selección de participantes en la investigación: ejemplificación para un contexto intergeneracional. In M. C. Ortega, F. J. García, & A. de Juanas (Eds.), *Guía para la elaboración de trabajos fin de máster de investigación educativa* (pp. 85–95). Octaedro.

Asah, S. T., Bengston, D. N., & Westphal, L. M. (2012). The influence of childhood: Operational pathways to adulthood participation in nature-based activities. *Environment and Behavior, 44*(4), 545–569.

Attar-Schwartz, S., Tan, J. P., & Buchanan, A. (2009). Adolescents' perspectives on relationships with grandparents: The contribution of adolescent, grandparents, and parent-grandparent relationship variables. *Children and Youth Services Review, 31*, 1057–1066.

Barnett, L. A. (2013). What people want from their leisure. *Journal of Leisure Research, 45*(2), 150–191.

Becerril, R., & Bores, N. (2019). Claves para el diseño de propuestas educativas intergeneracionales a partir de una experiencia de actividad física. *Ágora para la Educación Física & el Deporte, 21*, 111–124. https://doi.org/10.24197/aefd.0.2019.111-124

Brown, D. L., & Glasgow, N. (2008). *Rural retirement migration, 21*. Springer Science & Business Media.

Carvajal, G., Ojeda, D., Díaz, E., & Tabares, Y. (2020). Convivencia escolar & procesos intergeneracionales: Encuentros & tensiones. *Cult Educ Soc, 11*(1), 101–116. https://doi.org/10.17981/cul-tedusoc.10.2.2020.7

Castañeda-García, P. J., Valle-Sanz, C., & Gutiérrez-Barroso, J. (2017). From grandparenthood to great-grandparenthood. Exploring a family role. *Journal of Psychology, 47*(3), 115–122. https://doi.org/10.1016/j.anpsic.2018.01.003

Castell, C. (2020). Naturaleza and salud: una alianza necesaria. *Gaceta Sanitaria, 34*(2), 194–196.

Clayton, S. (2018). The role of perceived justice, political ideology, and individual or collective framing in support for environmental policies. *Social Justice Research, 31*, 219–237. https://doi.org/10.1007/s11211-018-0303-z

Coall, D. A., & Hertwig, R. (2010). Grandparental investment: Past, present, and future. *Behavioral and Brain Sciences, 33*(1), 1–19. https://doi.org/10.1017/S0140525X09991105
Cohen, J. (1960). A coefficient of agreement for nominal scales. *Educational and Psychological Measurement, 20*, 37–46.
Cohen, J. (1968). Multiple regression as a general data-analytic system. *Psychological Bulletin, 70*(6), 426–443.
Cuenca, M. (2016). *Las culturas del ocio*. Universidad de Deusto.
Dadvand, P., Nieuwenhuijsen, M. J., & Esnaola, M. (2015). Green spaces and cognitive development in primary schoolchildren. *Proceedings National Academy of Sciences of USA, 112*(26), 7937–7942. https://doi.org/10.1073/pnas.1503402112
D'amore, C. (2016). Family nature clubs: An intergenerational opportunity to foster love of the natural world. *Families, Relationships and Societies, 5*(3), 431–446. https://doi.org/10.1332/204674316X14758471234542
Dias do Nascimento, J., Meireles, I., Ribeiro, M., Braga de Camargo, T., Catafesta, F., & Bernardino, E. (2016). Uso del software NVivo® en una investigación con Teoría Fundamentada. *Index de Enfermería, 25*(4), 263–267.
Díaz Villalobos, R. (2021). "El otro" al teléfono. Relatos desde la pandemia causada por el COVID 2019. *Revista INFAD de Psicología. International Journal of Developmental and Educational Psychology, 2*(2), 379–386. https://doi.org/10.17060/ijodaep.2021.n2.v2.2245
Ding, Y. (2017). Personal life satisfaction of China's rural elderly: Effect of the new rural pension programme. *Journal of International Development, 29*(1), 52–66.
Dzhambov, A. M., & Dimitrova, D. D. (2014). Elderly visitors of an urban park, health anxiety and individual awareness of nature experiences. *Urban Forestry and Urban Greening, 13*(4), 806–813.
Edwards, R. C., & Larson, B. M. H. (2020). When screens replace backyards: Strategies to connect digital-media-oriented young people to nature. *Environmental Education Research, 26*(7), 950–968. https://doi.org/10.1080/13504622.2020.1776844
Esteban, M., & Amador, L. (2020). El huerto social como estrategia para la educación ambiental. *Agricultura Sociedad & Desarrollo, 17*(2), 321–347. https://doi.org/10.22231/asyd.v17i2.1348
Fleiss, J. (1971). Measuring nominal scale agreement among many raters. *Psychological Bulletin, 76*(5), 378–382.
García, J. C., Gutiérrez, J. G., Balderas, M. A., & Araújo, M. R. (2017). Beneficios socioculturales & ambientales de los huertos familiares en el altiplano mexicano. *Bois et Forêts des Tropiques, 329*, 10.19182/bft2016.329.a31310.
Gobierno de España. (2018). Plan de acción para la implementación de la Agenda 2030. Hacia una Estrategia Española de Desarrollo Sostenible.
González Ríos, M. J. (1997). *Metodología de la investigación social. Técnicas de recolección de datos*. Aguaclara.
González, F., & Temprano, R. (2018). Actividades de ocio & tiempo libre. *Paraninfo*, 101–109.
González, J., & de la Fuente, R. (2007). Intergenerational grandparent/grandchild relations. The socioeducational role of grandparents. *Educational Gerontology, 34*(1), 67–88. https://doi.org/10.1080/03601270701763993
Hake, B. J. (2017). Gardens as learning spaces: Intergenerational learning in urban food gardens. *Journal of Intergenerational Relationships, 15*(1), 26–38. https://doi.org/10.1080/15350770.2017.1260369
Hurlstone, M. J., Price, A., Wang, S., Leviston, Z., & Walker, I. (2020). Activating the legacy motive mitigates intergenerational discounting in the climate game. *Global Environmental Change-Human and Policy Dimensions, 60*, 102008. https://doi.org/10.1016/j.gloenvcha.2019.102008
Ibáñez, J. (2000). *Más allá de la sociología. El grupo de discusión: Técnica & crítica*. Siglo XXI.
Izenstark, D., & Ebata, A. T. (2017). The effects of the natural environment on attention and family cohesion: An experimental study. *Children, Youth and Environments, 27*(2), 93–109. https://doi.org/10.7721/chilyoutenvi.27.2.0093

Jamieson, L. (2016). Families, relationships and 'environment': (Un)sustainability, climate change and biodiversity loss. *Families, Relationships and Societies, 5*(3), 335–355. https://doi.org/10.1332/204674316X14758387773007
Jenssen, B. P., Kelly, M. K., Powell, M., Bouchelle, Z., Mayne, S. L., & Fiks, A. G. (2021). COVID-19 and changes in child obesity. *Pediatrics, 147*(5). https://doi.org/10.1542/peds.2021-050123
Jorgensen, A., & Anthopoulou, A. (2007). Enjoyment and fear in urban woodlands – does age make a difference? *Urban Forestry and Urban Greening, 6*(4), 267–278.
Kala, L., & Galčanová, L. (2016). *Intergenerational Transmission of Pro-Environmental Values and Lifestyles: How Is the Ecological Habitus Reproduced?* Third ISA Forum - The Futures We Want: Global Sociology and the Struggles for a Better World.
Kanji, S. (2018). Grandparent care: A key factor in mothers' labour force participation in the UK. *Journal of Social Policy, 47*(3), 523–542. https://doi.org/10.1017/S004727941700071X
Kemperman, A. D., & Timmermans, H. J. (2006). Heterogeneity in urban park use of aging visitors: A latent class analysis. *Leisure Sciences, 28*(1), 57–71.
Kim, C. H., & Byun, P. S. (2011). *Retirement of baby boom generation and the strategy for revitalization of rural areas in Korea*. Research Institute for Human Settlements.
Kim, H.-J., Kang, H., & Johnson-Motoyama, M. (2017). The psychological well-being of grandparents who provide supplementary grandchild care: A systematic review. *Journal of Family Studies, 23*, 118–141. https://doi.org/10.1080/13229400.2016.1194306
Konok, V., Bunford, N., & Milós, Á. (2020). Associations between child mobile use and digital parenting style in Hungarian families. *Journal of Children and Media, 14*(1), 91–109. https://doi.org/10.1080/17482798.2019.1684332
Kotrla, M., Varga, V., & Jelovčić, S. (2021). Digital technology use during the COVID-19 pandemic and its relations to sleep quality and life satisfaction in children and parents. *Društvena istraživanja: časopis za opća društvena pitanja, 30*(2), 249–269. https://doi.org/10.5559/di.30.2.04
Laaksoharju, T., Rappe, E., & Kaivola, T. (2012). Garden affordances for social learning, play, and for building nature-child relationship. *Urban Forestry & Urban Greening, 11*, 195–203. https://doi.org/10.1016/j.ufug.2012.01.003
López Francés, I. (2010). El grupo de discusión como estrategia metodológica de investigación: aplicación a un caso. *Edetania, 38*, 147–156.
Martínez, S., Moreno, P., Escarbajal, A. (Eds.) (2017). *Envejecimiento activo, programas intergeneracionales y educación social*. Dykinson.
Martínez, N., & Rodríguez, A. M. (2018). Educación intergeneracional: un nuevo reto para la formación del profesorado. *Revista Estud & Exp Educ., 17*(33), 113–124. https://doi.org/10.21703/rexe.20181733nmartinez7
McDarby, M., Ju, C. H., & Carpenter, B. D. (2020). Frequency of contact and explanations for increased contact between grandchildren and their grandparents during the COVID-19 pandemic. *Journal of Intergenerational Relationships, 19*(2), 163–178. https://doi.org/10.1080/15350770.2020.1852995
Noriega, C., & López, J. (2021). Fortalezas & estilos educativos en abuelos con nietos de 6 a 12 años. *Revista INFAD de Psicología. International Journal of Developmental and Educational Psychology, 2*(2), 121–134. https://doi.org/10.17060/ijodaep.2021.n2.v2.2217
Pinazo, S. (1999). Significado social del rol de abuelo [Social meaning of the grandparent role]. *Revista Multidisciplinar de Gerontología, 9*, 169–176. https://www.academia.edu/3223898/
Ponce de León, A., Valdemoros, M. A., Sanz. E., Sáenz de Jubera, M., & Alonso, R. A. (2021). Ocio ambientalecológico compartido entre abuelos/as y nietos/as. In J. Escribano Pizarro & A. Ferrandis Martínez (Eds.), *TERRA, Desarrollo local y dinámicas territoriales: Homenaje a Joan Noguera (pp. 145–161). Universitat de València.*
Ponce de León, A., Valdemoros, M. A., Sanz, E., Sáenz de Jubera, M., & Alonso, R. A. (2022). *Ocio compartido entre nietos & abuelos ≚libertad o imposición?* In A. Madariaga & M. P. Rodrigo (Eds.), *Ocio saludable & construcción de ciudadanía* (pp. 163–180). Thomson Reuters Aranzadi.

Rico, C., Serra, E., & Viguer, P. (2001). *Abuelos & nietos: abuelo favorito, abuelo útil*. Pirámide.

Ried, A. (2015). La experiencia de ocio al aire libre en contacto con la naturaleza, como vivencia restauradora de la relación ser humano-naturaleza. *Polis, Revista Latinoamericana, 14*(41), 499–516. https://doi.org/10.4067/S0718-65682015000200029

Rivera, A. L., Magaña, D., Gómez, M., Fernández, F., & Loske, A. M. (2014). Physical methods for genetic transformation of fungi and yeast. *Physics of Life Reviews, 11*(2), 184–203. https://doi.org/10.1016/j.plrev.2014.01.007

Roa Venegas, J. M., & Vacas Díaz, C. (2001). Perfiles de abuelidad [Grandparenthood profiles]. *Pedagogía Social: Revista Interuniversitaria, 6–7*, 205–219. https://dialnet.unirioja.es/servlet/articulo?codigo=2658836

Rodríguez, V., Ramírez, Y., & Alarcón, Y. (2019). La dimensión ambiental en las actividades físico-recreativas con el adulto mayor de la comunidad Nuevo Veguitas. *Revista Caribeña de Ciencias Sociales*. https://www.eumed.net/rev/caribe/2019/07/dimension-ambiental-actividades.html

Rojek, C. (2005). *Teoría del ocio: Principios & prácticas*. Palgrave Macmillan.

Sanz, E., Valdemoros, M. A., Ponce de León, A., Alonso, R. A., & Sáenz de Jubera, M. (2020). Ocio & bienestar en clave intergeneracional. In J. A. Caride, M. B. Caballo, & R. Gradaílle (Eds.), *Tiempos, educación & ocio en una sociedad de redes* (pp. 139–152). Octaedro.

Suárez, F. A. (2005). *El grupo de discusión. Una herramienta para la investigación cualitativa*. Alertes.

Syropoulos, S., & Markowitz, E. M. (2021). Prosocial responses to COVID-19: Examining the role of gratitude, fairness, and legacy motives. *Personality and Individual Differences, 171*, 110–488. https://doi.org/10.1016/j.paid.2020.110488

Taye, F. A., Abildtrup, J., Mayer, M., Ščasný, M., Strange, N., & Lundhede, T. (2019). Childhood experience in forest recreation practices: Evidence from nine European countries. *Urban Forestry and Urban Greening, 46*, Article 126471.

Thompson, C. W., Aspinall, P., & Montarzino, A. (2008). The childhood factor: Adult visits to green places and the significance of childhood experience. *Environment and Behavior, 40*(1), 111–143.

Valdemoros, M. A., Alonso, R. A., Sáenz de Jubera, M., Ponce de León, A., & Sanz, E. (2021). Intergenerational leisure and family reconciliation. *Psychology, Society, & Education, 13*(3), 1–13. https://doi.org/10.25115/psye.v13i3.4809

Valdemoros, M. A., Ponce de León, A., & Sanz, E. (2011). Fundamentos en el manejo del NVIVO 9 como herramienta al servicio de estudios cualitativos. *Contextos educativos: Revista de educación, 14*, 11–30. https://doi.org/10.18172/con.637

Vicente Castro, F. (2021). Introducción de "Aprendiendo en positivo: la respuesta al COVID-19". *Revista INFAD de Psicología. International Journal of Developmental and Educational Psychology, 2*(2), 1–16. https://revista.infad.eu/index.php/IJODAEP/article/view/2257

Wade-Benzoni, K., & Tost, P. (2009). The egoism and altruism of intergenerational behavior. *Personality and Social Psychology Review, 13*(3). https://doi.org/10.1177/1088868309339317

Wagner, A. F. (2020). What the stock market tells us about the post-COVID-19 world. *Nature Human Behaviour, 4*(440). https://doi.org/10.1038/s41562-020-0869-y

Wen, C., Albert, C., & Von Haaren, C. (2018). The elderly in green spaces: Exploring requirements and preferences concerning nature-based recreation. *Sustainable Cities and Society, 38*, 582–593.

Wynveen, C., Kyle, G., Absher, J., & Theodori, G. (2011). The meanings associated with varying degrees of attachment to a natural landscape. *Journal of Leisure Research, 43*, 290–311.

Yogman, M., Garner, A., Hutchinson, J., Hirsh-Pasek, K., Golinkoff, R. M., & Committee on Psychosocial Aspects of Child and Family Health. (2018). The power of play: A pediatric role in enhancing development in young children. *Pediatrics, 142*(3), e20182058. https://doi.org/10.1542/peds.2018-2058

Yoo, J., & Russell, D. W. (2020). Caring for grandchildren and grandparents' physical and mental health changes. *Journal of Child and Family Studies, 29*(3), 845–854. https://doi.org/10.1007/s10826-019-0

Chapter 7
The Role and Future of Art Fair Audiences: Visitors' Perspectives on the Hybrid Art Fair in Madrid

Alexandra Zagrebelnaia

Abstract The social role of art fairs has often been overlooked in academic discussions, which have primarily emphasized their commercial aspects. However, as these events are open to the public, it is important to consider audience perceptions and examine how art fairs can contribute socially as well as economically. This study, based on a post-visit survey of 71 visitors to the Hybrid art fair in Madrid (March–April 2022), found that despite their commercial nature, the public perceives art fairs as spaces for education and cultural engagement. Audience expectations for social commitment remain consistent regardless of prior experience with art fairs. These findings indicate that art fair organizers should prioritize audience development and social impact, paving the way for future research and potential evolution of the art fair model.

7.1 Introduction

The art market has undergone significant transformation in recent years, with art fairs playing a diminished role in sales. This shift has sparked debates among art dealers about potential reforms to the fair format. The UBS Art Market Reports of 2022 and 2023 underscore the need for innovation and collaborative strategies to ensure the sustainability of art fairs. Given their dual commercial and cultural nature, and their appeal to both industry professionals and the general public, understanding the diverse perspectives of these audiences is essential for informed planning and decision-making.

Additionally, reports such as those by Artsy (2022) and McAndrew (2023) highlight gradual but stable changes in the socio-demographic profiles of art buyers. Notably, some prominent art collectors are reducing their attendance at fairs due to age, while younger generations increasingly favour purchasing art online. To regain

A. Zagrebelnaia (✉)
University of Deusto, Bilbao, Spain
e-mail: zagrebelnaia@gmail.com

L. Ronda et al. (eds.), *Leisure and Human Development*, Human Well-Being Research and Policy Making, https://doi.org/10.1007/978-3-031-90778-4_7

their former significance and navigate this evolving landscape, art fair managers must explore innovative ways to attract both audiences and galleries, grounded in a comprehensive understanding of these trends.

Scholars like Falk (1998) have long championed systematic visitor studies, urging arts organizations to gather and apply data about their audiences. While some countries have issued national-level audience research guidelines (Close, 1998; Tomlinson & Roberts, 2006), such practices are rarely applied to art fairs despite their unique blend of commercial and cultural elements. For uninformed visitors, these events may be perceived through a limited lens, shaped by varying levels of familiarity and experience.

This chapter presents an exploratory analysis of visitor perceptions regarding the mission of art fairs and their expectations for the future, based on a post-visit online survey of 71 attendees of the emerging art fair Hybrid in Madrid. The analysis segments responses according to independent variables such as *familiarity with art fairs* and *connection to the art world* to determine whether these factors significantly influence visitor perceptions. Although conducted on a small scale, this research provides a foundation for identifying key priorities for art fair organizers and serves as a starting point for further investigation in this field.

7.2 Socially Oriented Audience Development for the Art Fairs

With a general decrease in attendance of cultural institutions (Institutul Național pentru Cercetare și Formare Culturală, 2022; Rosenberg, 2023), an audience-centred approach seems even more relevant for their future development (Ayala et al., 2019). It is imperative not to overlook the fact that, apart from being a marketing strategy (Diggle, 1994; Hill et al., 2000; Kolb, 2005; Colbert & Cuadrado, 2012), audience development strategies also encompass a significant social component (European Commission, 2012). Recent trends in audience development indicate that the audience now actively participates in what Lusch and Vargo (cited in Etgar, 2008) refer to as the "co-creation of value".

Since the 1990s, cultural institutions have been adapting to new social missions by offering innovative forms of internal organization, reimagining more accessible exhibition designs, and introducing inclusive programming. There is still, however, a large space for improvement in 2024. Lindelof (2014) asserts that the discourse on audience development explores the influence of arts marketing and the social and historical contingencies of artistic value. Cuenca-Amigo and Makua (2019) identify the social approach to audience development as one of the most significant, while Hadley (2021) proposed the tradition of *social justice*, which prioritizes the participants' belief systems and values the outcomes of engagement over the specific forms and expressions of art.

Numerous studies (Daykin & Byrne, 2006; Arts Council England, 2007; KEA, 2009) have demonstrated that artistic encounters can enrich people's lives, foster personal growth, contribute to overall well-being, and positively impact the public sphere. However, it is crucial to acknowledge that these benefits are contingent upon a specific type of aesthetic experience that actively engages the audience's senses, emotions, and intellect.

For instance, Ayala et al. (2021) propose that museums should not only provide leisure experiences but also fulfil a social mission. Nevertheless, given the subjective nature of visitors' experiences, which depend on multiple factors, it may be challenging for art institutions to ensure the achievement of these social goals (Monteagudo & San Salvador del Valle, 2017), particularly in the context of art fairs, where this challenge becomes even more critical. Referring to the principles of new institutionalism (Bryan-Wilson, 2003), Barragán (2008) suggests introducing the term "New *Fairism*" into the discourse surrounding art fairs as a new way of understanding and redefining the function of the fair as an institution and artistic structure. This concept can be associated with the more traditional notion of New Museology (Vergo, 1989), which emphasizes the importance of cultural diversity and social inclusion of different groups (Cho & Jolley, 2016; Ayala et al., 2021). Additionally, concepts such as cultural democratization and cultural democracy can be incorporated, advocating for the transformation of cultural institutions into accessible organizations that foster societal participation (Hadley & Belfiore, 2018).

Although virtual exhibitions in museums or OVRs of the art fairs can be conditionally considered as "museums without walls", following the utopian idea of absolute inclusion (Malraux, 1965), and can be seen as tools for socially oriented audience development, this experience does not necessarily foster diversification of the socio-demographic profile of the visitors of these exhibitions (Zagrebelnaia, 2021), which questions the practical implications of this tool.

In general, the clear commercial nature of art fairs calls into question the possibility of their social compromise. At first glance, sponsored mainly by private entities, art fairs seem to enjoy relative freedom in their programming, accessibility, and orientation. However, a closer examination reveals that most of them, in fact, have public connections at the state or local level, which underscores the importance of their social commitment. Although some galleries and art fairs acknowledge their social responsibility and commitment (Zagrebelnaia & Bayón, 2022), it is necessary to study the perceived mission of art fairs more deeply, including the perceptions of different stakeholders.

Since the seminal work of Baumol and Bowen in 1966, it has been widely acknowledged that individuals with higher levels of education, income, and social status are more inclined to attend art-related events. On the one hand, the existence of such social gradients is unsurprising, given that individuals with higher incomes tend to have greater access to material, financial, and experiential resources. However, these pronounced social differentials remain consistent regardless of pricing considerations and are evident even in arts events that do not require an admission fee (Throsby, 1994). Additionally, educational attainment and social class often serve as more reliable indicators of attendance compared to income levels. In general, studying the demand for art events encompasses various approaches, with this strand of cultural economics heavily relying on orthodox consumer theory. Considering the difficulty of attracting diverse groups of people to even less elitist art events than art fairs, it is naive to assume that audience development strategies will open these events to the full variety of socio-demographic groups. However, understanding the perception and vision of art fairs within the already existing social groups can foster their loyalty (Falk & Dierking, 1992) and may even help convert them into potential art collectors by engaging them, building relationships, and demonstrating the value of art.

7.3 Mission of the Art Fairs

Many authors (Mehring, 2008; Thompson, 2011; Vermeylen, 2015) focus on the business-related side of the fairs, seeing them primarily as commercial events. Following this approach, Haisch and Menzel (2022) suggested evaluating the fairs as temporary markets, akin to trade fairs. There is no doubt that there is a resemblance to classical trade fairs, starting with the design of the exhibition space and a special focus on art professionals. However, Bathelt et al. (2014) deliberately exclude art fairs from the framework of trade shows, arguing that, unlike the latter, art fairs target consumers rather than professional.

Besides that, an important mission of art fairs, supported by many authors (Barragán, 2008, 2020; Ricci, 2020; Ruiz, 2021), is clearly the cultural one. Baia Curioni (2012) summarizes that culture and economics are interconnected. Poli (2011) emphasizes the importance of the artistic components of the fairs, whereas Sigle (2020) highlights their significant contribution to the popularization of contemporary art. Gerlis (2021) went further, claiming that art fairs make the "rarefied art world seem more accessible" (p. 13). Additionally, art fairs have been studied from different perspectives: as field-configuring events, in connection with other creative industries, as gatekeepers to the art world, as a map of the art world, as a site for re-enactment of the art world, and as a place for selected encounters.

According to Barragán (2008), from trade shows with cultural impact, art fairs have transformed into real experiences. The entire concept of consuming contemporary art is represented as a social and cultural experience (Velthuis, 2012), where the quality of art on display sometimes seems less important than the quality of the "experience" that the art fair offers (Barragán, 2008). This can be clearly seen in the fact that most fairs are supplemented by "experimental" and non-commercial events (Ricci, 2020), including artist talks, lectures, workshops, edited publications, bookshops, and additional curated exhibitions (Smith, 2006; Altshuler, 2020; Haisch & Menzel, 2022).

Art fairs continue to hold significant value for individuals new to collecting, serving as a valuable platform for engaging with art dealers and gaining first-hand exposure to a diverse range of artistic creations. An art advisor highlighted the importance of bringing new collectors to art fairs, as it allows them to see a multitude of artworks in one place and provides the opportunity to observe their tastes and guide them towards the best examples of the art they are most attracted to (Bryce, in an interview with Halperin & Schneider, March 11, 2019).

Additionally, art fairs are important meeting points for various actors in the art world (Yogev & Grund, 2012). They provide significant networking opportunities (Poli, 2011; Yogev, 2010; Yogev & Grund, 2012; Morgner, 2014; Ruiz, 2021), serving as unmissable society events (Vermeylen, 2015). Morgner (2014) even suggested applying network theory to art fairs, seeing them as suitable venues for exploring the relationships between producers and consumers of cultural artefacts. In fact, despite their short duration, art fairs provide opportunities to meet more people than during a regular month at a gallery (Poli, 2011).

Some authors consider art fairs as important manifestations and driving forces of integration into the international art world (Velthuis & Baia Curioni, 2015) and tools for the globalization of art (Baia Curioni, 2012; Velthuis, 2012; Quemin, 2013; Vermeylen, 2015). Sigle (2020) suggests that by participating in fairs, galleries can extend their geographical range beyond their regional and national dimensions and gain access to transnational art markets.

In fact, representatives of the Hybrid art fair distinguished "important cultural and educational experiences" and "visibility" among the crucial missions of contemporary art fairs, reflecting on the responsibility of all participating galleries to educate their audience. Interestingly, a similar discussion emerged during the panel talk "Art Fairs in the Times of Change", held at ARCO Madrid 2021, when the director of Galerie Krinzinger, Thomas Krinzinger, also mentioned the social responsibility of art galleries (Zagrebelnaia & Bayón, 2022).

7.4 The Case of the Hybrid Art Fair: Brief Description and Justification

In recent years, there has been increasing research attention on art fairs, with a focus on renowned events such as ARCO, Bologna Artefiera, and MiArt. However, smaller art fairs have received less scrutiny, leading to a gap in the general understanding of the art fair landscape. This study aims to address this gap by offering a more comprehensive examination of art fairs in Spain. To ensure a diverse representation of art fairs, a set of predetermined criteria based on the theoretical framework was used for the selection of the case study. These criteria included factors such as sustainability, innovation, consolidation, visibility, connection to public institutions, utilization of urban settings, and relevance to various artistic sectors. By applying these criteria, the study seeks to achieve a more varied and comprehensive understanding of the art fair landscape.

The selection of the Hybrid Art Fair as a case study was based on several factors. Firstly, the fair's association with public institutions and grants, as well as its commitment to openness and a diverse public programme, made it an intriguing subject for investigation. Additionally, the fair's unique location within the Petit Palace Santa Bárbara hotel in central Madrid, providing a less formal and unconventional setting, was deemed noteworthy. This approach aims to attract a broader range of audiences beyond those typically interested in art fairs. In contrast, larger art fairs like ARCO Madrid, held in an exhibition centre outside the city, may have a more specific target audience. Thus, the choice of Hybrid Art Fair as a case study offers an opportunity to examine an emerging art fair situated conveniently in Madrid.

Initially, in the pursuit of studying an emerging art fair in Madrid, several art fairs occurring during the city's art week were approached with offers to collaborate. However, many of these fairs exhibited a lack of responsiveness or were unwilling to participate in research. While initially perceived as obstacles, these circumstances raised important questions about the openness and willingness of art fairs to engage in academic research projects and assessments. This also highlighted the potential influence of public grants and proximity to public institutions in fostering cooperation and collaboration.

It has been suggested that art fairs benefiting from public grants are potentially more open to collaboration with researchers, primarily because such funding typically comes with stipulations that encourage or even mandate scholarly engagement. Often, these grants are designed not just to support the arts economically but also to ensure that the funded activities contribute to broader cultural and academic discourse. Consequently, art fairs with significant public funding, such as Hybrid Art Fair, seem more responsive to academic collaborations as they strive to fulfil these requirements, using insights gained from researchers to justify public investment in their activities. On the other hand, art fairs without this type of funding might not feel the same impetus to engage with the academic world. Without the external push from funding bodies, immediate commercial pressures and market-driven priorities often take precedence.

The Hybrid Art Fair, established in 2017, is a small-scale, emerging contemporary art fair. The management team, currently led by Ana Sanfrutos and Aida Chaves, oversees art fair-related activities throughout the year, while hiring external agencies and specialists (e.g. press, PR, visitors' department, graphic design) for short-term collaborations before and during the fair. Each edition typically features 31 to 35 galleries and takes place once a year during Madrid art week. Drawing an average of over 5000 visitors per edition, the fair has garnered attention for its affordability. With a single-entrance ticket priced at nine euros and a *multipass* option priced at fifteen euros, the fair provides a more accessible and democratic environment compared to larger, higher-priced art fairs. This emphasis on affordability highlights the fair's relevance to this research, which seeks to explore the dynamics of emerging art fairs in Madrid.

As a young art fair focused on emerging art practices, Hybrid unites commercial art galleries with independent artist spaces, special projects, and even selected individual artists as part of a curated section called Displaced. According to its official description, this section represents "a program of ephemeral interventions by independent artists in the fair's transit places", such as halls, lounge areas, or staircases. The organizers emphasize the fair's experimental nature, stating: "Hybrid Art Fair is much more than an art fair with exhibitions. The fair is committed to a dynamic program of activities, creating a unique experience for each visitor" (Hybrid Art Fair, n.d.).

7.5 Methodology

Following the foundation of visitor studies, a quantitative analysis was chosen, conducted through a visitor survey. This section outlines the design of the questionnaire used for data collection, the sample selection and description, and the various data evaluation methods.

7.5.1 Questionnaire Design

The questionnaire was specifically tailored to the theoretical framework surrounding the perceived mission of art fairs and other cultural organizations, the significance of social implications for cultural institutions, and insights from the PUBLICUM project, which focused on museum audiences and was supported by prior scientific publications (Ayala et al., 2019). The survey incorporated previously validated scales and variables, tested in the context of museum audiences, and complemented by ad-hoc variables reflecting the specific context of art fairs. The questionnaire was pre-tested and slightly reformulated before distribution. It included 17 mandatory questions and one open-ended, non-compulsory question, divided into standard statistical questions and those directly related to the art fair visit.

However, due to the focus of this study, not all questions were included in the analysis. The focus was placed on questions 9 (Fig. 7.1) and 11 (Fig. 7.2) of the survey, which evaluated public perceptions of the mission of art fairs and potential avenues for their development. These questions were chosen under the belief that understanding diverse audience perspectives on art fairs could influence their future growth and adaptations.

In line with the social orientation of cultural institutions and its implications for visitor perceptions, it is worth noting the role of art fairs as leisure spaces (Amigo, 2014; Frost & Laing, 2017). Additionally, aligned with theories of cultural democracy (Hadley & Belfiore, 2018; Pinochet & Güell, 2018) and new *fairism* (Barragán, 2008), the importance of embracing cultural diversity and inclusion (Cho & Jolley, 2016) as well as a gender perspective (Hein, 2007; Bergsdóttir 2016) is highlighted.

Following the idea of strategic areas of audience development (Bollo et al., 2017) as well as the results of interviews with key figures of art fairs (organizers and participating galleries), it was important to evaluate visitors' willingness to participate in the co-creation of artistic programmes (Simon, 2010); their opinion on the pedagogical role of cultural institutions (Hanquinet & Savage, 2012); the importance of the introduction of digital tools; and the importance of increasing the number of visitors.

9) Art Fairs are developing new ways of interaction with their audience. To what extent do you think they should carry out these actions? *

Please indicate your level of agreement with the following statements from the lowest "Strongly Disagree" to the highest "Strongly Agree", in case you are not sure about the answer or it doesn't apply to your case you can indicate N/A (No Answer)

	strongly disagree	disagree	neither agree nor disagree	agree	strongly agree	N/A
Become places of leisure and enjoyment	○	○	○	○	○	○
Offer a vision that respects cultural diversity	○	○	○	○	○	○
Involve audience in co-creation of Artistic and/or Educational program	○	○	○	○	○	○
Include the gender perspective in their activities	○	○	○	○	○	○
Increase the number of visitors to reach more people	○	○	○	○	○	○
Become spaces for social inclusion of people with any kind of disability	○	○	○	○	○	○
Compensate for education and knowledge that audiences may not possess	○	○	○	○	○	○
Provide more transparent pricing of the exhibited artworks	○	○	○	○	○	○
Provide special programs for families with kids	○	○	○	○	○	○
Use more digital tools and/or organize more online activities	○	○	○	○	○	○
Provide more information about other Art Events happening in the city during the Art Fair	○	○	○	○	○	○
Involve local communities and local artists in their programming	○	○	○	○	○	○
Introduce Membership plans for the visitors	○	○	○	○	○	○

Fig. 7.1 Presentation of question 9 from the visitors' survey

11) Due to a commercial and cultural nature, Art Fairs can have a different meaning for different types of visitors. *

Please indicate to which extent do you agree with the following statements about the Art Fairs from the lowest "Strongly Disagree" to the highest "Strongly Agree", in case you are not sure about the answer or it doesn't apply to your case you can indicate N/A (No Answer)

	Strongly Disagree	Disagree	Neither Agree Nor Disagree	Agree	Strongly Agree	N/A
Art Fair is a commercial event aimed mainly on selling art objects	○	○	○	○	○	○
Art Fair creates great environment for meeting people from art industry and making professional connections	○	○	○	○	○	○
Art Fair is an entertaining activity to attend during your free time	○	○	○	○	○	○
Art Fair provides aesthetic and cultural experience	○	○	○	○	○	○
Art Fair can help me to learn more about Contemporary Art	○	○	○	○	○	○
Art Fair is a place to meet new people and socialize	○	○	○	○	○	○
Art Fair can attract tourists and new people to the city	○	○	○	○	○	○
Art Fair is a good place to go with family and children	○	○	○	○	○	○

Fig. 7.2 Presentation of question 11 from the visitors' survey

Additionally, other more generic variables were introduced to test their applicability to the context of art fairs. According to Mikulic et al. (2015), implementing membership programmes with exclusive benefits, such as early access, discounts, or invitations to special events, can incentivize repeat attendance and create a sense of belonging. Furthermore, some items addressed specific issues noted as problematic areas for art fairs, such as the lack of sufficient knowledge among the general audience (Gerlis, 2020a, 2020b) and lack of transparency (Scorcu et al., 2021; Prieto-Rodriguez & Vecco, 2021).

In the context of the heterogeneous nature of art fairs, it is worth evaluating what meaning they may hold for the audience, based on the characteristics indicated in the theoretical framework. Researchers see art fairs as commercial events (Thompson, 2011; Baia Curioni 2020), networking tools (Morgner, 2014; Yogev & Grund, 2012), cultural activities (Mehring, 2008; Ricci, 2020; Ruiz, 2021), and experiences (Barragán, 2008), or as tools for disseminating persuasive social messages and promoting tourism (Frost & Laing, 2017). Additionally, following the idea of their resemblance to other cultural events, it is important to evaluate if art fairs can be considered leisure activities (Monteagudo, 2020) and suitable venues for families with children.

The response choices for all items were designed in the form of five-point ordinal-type Likert scales. In this scale, each subject has five different response choices for each item, and a sixth option for "Not applicable". The choice of this type of scale was based on its proven efficiency and suitability for visitor surveys (Elejabarrieta & Iñiguez, 2008; Joshi et al., 2015).

7.5.2 Sample Selection and Data Collection

Prior to conducting the fieldwork, the adapted questionnaire was verified and approved by an external researcher with expertise in audience development for cultural organizations. The distribution of the survey was carried out through an email campaign initiated by the art fair organizers, utilizing their existing mailing list. Additionally, advertisements were placed on the art fair's social media channels, specifically Instagram. The survey distribution took place between March eighth and April eighth, 2022, after the conclusion of the Hybrid Art Fair 2022 edition. The survey was conducted online using the Survey Hero platform.

On average, participants spent 7.03 minutes completing the questionnaire. The survey was available in both Spanish and English to accommodate a wider range of respondents. The decision to administer the survey online was influenced by the prevailing post-pandemic circumstances under which the research was conducted. While the art fairs in Madrid were held in person in 2022, certain COVID-related precautions were still necessary. This decision subsequently influenced the final sample size, as it was not possible to directly affect the number of respondents.

A total of 73 valid questionnaires were obtained from participants of various age groups and genders, resulting in a participation rate of 54.9% among individuals who opened the survey, meaning that only 133 individuals opened the survey in total. Although the sample size was smaller than initially planned, it was decided to proceed with analysing and including it in the final research as a basis for further considerations.

During the data analysis stage, 2.74% of the questionnaires (completed by 2 individuals) were excluded due to their response to the opening question of the survey regarding their attendance at the art fair in 2022. Consequently, only the answers from respondents who had physically attended the fair ($n = 71$) were considered for further analysis. According to the Hybrid Art Fair internal report, the total number of visitors in 2022 was 4600 (N). Considering this as the size of the population, the present research may be considered statistically representative (Krejcie & Morgan, 1970) with a confidence level of 95% and a margin of error of 11.54%, which was considered when analysing the survey results.

7.5.3 Description of the Sample

The sample consists of 71 individuals who completed the questionnaire. Table 7.1 shows the socio-demographic classification of the respondents.

The survey was held online, and anyone could participate, so it was impossible to maintain gender balance. As a result, the significant majority of the respondents are female (69.86%). Since the fair did not provide any socio-demographic data on the attendees, it is impossible to determine whether this reflects a general socio-demographic trend for attendance or whether women are simply more responsive to surveys (Smith, 2006). However, it may also reflect a broader trend of higher attendance at museums and cultural institutions among the female population (Ayala et al., 2019).

Analysis of the age groups revealed a stable balance between the Young and Adult groups, each comprising 27.40% of the overall attendance rate. This confirms that the event is aimed at diverse age groups. However, due to the focus of this research, these socio-demographic variables were not further considered for evaluation or cross-referencing.

Nevertheless, following Peterson's (1992) idea that audience segmentation helps in understanding the diverse needs, preferences, and behaviours of different audience segments, additional variables were introduced, segmenting respondents according to the frequency of attendance at art fairs and their connection to art, as illustrated in Table 7.2.

Analysis of the results showed that most respondents have some connection to the art world, whether through their job, education, or specific hobby. Those who selected "other" clarified that they were art professors (2), partners of artists (2), painters (1), or art collectors (1). These individuals can also be included in the group "connected to the art world". This question was introduced to assess the participants' involvement in related activities without categorizing specific profiles. Therefore, multiple choices were allowed. The result illustrates the general trend of visitors' connection to art rather than segmenting them based on the specific nature of that connection.

Table 7.1 Socio-demographic characteristics of the sample

Independent variable	Group	Absolute frequencies	Relative frequencies
Gender	Female	51	69.86%
	Male	19	26.03%
	Non-binary	0	0%
	Prefer not to say	3	4.11%
Age	>18	0	0%
	18–24	4	5.48%
	25–34	20	27.40%
	35–44	24	32.88%
	45–64	20	27.40%
	65<	5	6.85%

Table 7.2 Classification of the respondents

Independent variable	Group	Sub-group	Absolute frequency	Relative frequencies
Relation to art	Art-related	I am a professional artist, designer, architect, active in the creative industry	22	30.99%
		I have an art-related hobby	21	29.58%
		I have an art or culture-related education/training	21	29.58%
		I am an art/creative industry professional (producer, curator, manager, gallerist, publisher etc.)	9	12.68%
	Not related to art	No relation	12	16.09%
		Other	6	8.45%
Experience in visiting art fairs	Newcomer	This is the first time I have visited an art fair	8	11.27%
	Some experience	Between 1 and 2 times	16	22.54%
	Medium experience	Between 3 and 5 times	22	30.99%
	Experienced visitor	More than 5 times	25	35.21%

At the same time, Question 2 focused on familiarity with art fairs. It revealed that most respondents had attended an art fair at least three times, which suggests a certain degree of knowledge of the event's structure. This also indicates their interest in the art world and/or the art market, as well as loyalty to this type of event.

Although this segmentation was initially introduced to provide more specific information about the visitors' profiles, it ultimately led to a deeper understanding of the art fairs' audiences and the need to study this phenomenon in more detail to create audience spectrum personas.

7.6 Results Analysis and Discussion

This section presents an overview of the scores obtained for each individual item in questions nine and eleven. Tables 7.3 and 7.4 display the items in ascending order according to the mean of the responses for each of them.

The analysis of the responses to question nine shows that 10 out of 15 items received a score higher than 4, which was considered statistically significant. The results illustrate how visitors believe that art fairs should become more involved in society (Ayala et al., 2019), suggesting the importance of the social orientation of the event. This implies that, despite the obvious organizational and functional differences between art fairs and other cultural events, general visitors do not perceive

Table 7.3 Results of the measures of each item of question 9 analysed

Variables	Strongly disagree (1)	Disagree (2)	Neither agree nor disagree (3)	Agree (4)	Strongly agree (5)	Ø
Offer a vision that respects cultural diversity	0.00%	1.41%	4.23%	23.94%	70.42%	4.63
Organize cultural activities in the city throughout the year	0.00%	0.00%	4.23%	39.44%	56.34%	4.52
Become spaces for social inclusion of people with any kind of disability	0.00%	0.00%	4.23%	42.25%	53.52%	4.49
Involve local communities and local artists in their programming	0.00%	0.00%	9.86%	43.66%	46.48%	4.37
Include the gender perspective in their activities	2.82%	4.23%	11.27%	22.54%	59.15%	4.31
Provide more transparent pricing of the exhibited artworks	0.00%	0.00%	15.49%	46.48%	38.03%	4.23
Provide information about other events happening in the city during the fair	0.00%	4.23%	7.04%	53.52%	35.21%	4.2
Introduce free consultancy services for people interested in collecting art	0.00%	1.49%	16.42%	43.28%	38.81%	4.19
Involve audience in co-creation of artistic and/or educational programme	0.00%	5.63%	16.9%	36.62%	40.85%	4.13
Compensate for education and knowledge that audiences may not possess	2.86%	8.57%	7.14%	37.14%	44.49%	4.11
Introduce membership plans for the visitors	1.54$	3.08%	29.23%	38.46%	27.69%	3.88
Increase the number of visitors to reach more people	1.45%	5.0.8%	28.99%	36.23%	27.54%	3.83
Become places of leisure and enjoyment	2.86%	15.71%	10%	41.43%	30%	3.8
Provide special programmes for families with kids	1.49%	10.45%	20.9%	49.25%	17.91%	3.72
Use more digital tools and/or organize more online activities	0.00%	14.71%	26.47%	35.29%	23.53%	3.68

a significant difference between them. However, as in previous examples, this could also indicate a social desirability bias (Krumpal, 2013) frequently encountered in surveys.

Table 7.4 Results of the measures of each item of question 11 analysed

Variables	Strongly disagree (1)	Disagree (2)	Neither agree nor disagree (3)	Agree (4)	Strongly agree (5)	Ø
Art fair can help me to learn more about contemporary art	0%	0%	1.43%	40%	58.57%	4.57
Art fair provides aesthetic and cultural experience	0%	0%	2.86%	41.43%	55.71%	4.53
Art fair creates great environment for meeting people from art industry and making professional connections	0%	0%	4.41%	52.94%	49.65%	4.38
Art fair can attract tourists and new people to the city	0%	1.47%	11.76%	44.12%	42.45%	4.28
Art fair is an entertaining activity to attend during your free time	0%	4.29%	14.29%	54.29%	27.14%	4.04
Art fair is a place to meet new people and socialize	1.43%	2.86%	25.71%	31.14%	32.86%	3.97
Art fair is a good place to go with family and children	4.41%	16.18%	20.59%	35.29%	23.53%	3.57
Art fair is a commercial event aimed mainly on selling art objects	1.43%	25.71%	21.43%	40%	11.43%	3.34

This can also be seen in the third most demanded action perceived by visitors, with a mean score of 4.49, where art fairs should "Become spaces for social inclusion of people with any kind of disability", and the fifth most demanded action with a mean score of 4.31, "Include the gender perspective in their activities". These results, however, should not be overlooked and require further managerial consideration, as they may have important implications for the art fairs' organizers to reconsider the social orientation and impact (Murray, 2012) of their events.

Additionally, among the most demanded actions, those related to community engagement (Borwick, 2012) can be identified, such as the demand for constant engagement and continuity of relations with the audience throughout the year. Interestingly, in the case of the Hybrid Art Fair, they organize several activities throughout the year, including an art festival, introducing artists' studios in different districts of Madrid (Zagrebelnaia & Bayón, 2022), and encouraging local participation.

At the same time, the idea of art fairs "Using more digital tools and/or organizing more online activities", based on the importance of digital transformation (Bollo et al., 2017), seems to be the least appealing to visitors. This can be partially explained by "digital fatigue" (Gerlis, 2020a, 2020b, June 15), caused by oversaturation with online activities during the pandemic not long before. Although representatives of the art world acknowledge the importance of rapid digital transformation

(Zagrebelnaia, 2021), the implementation and distribution of digital tools should be approached with care.

The analysis of the responses to question eleven (Table 7.4) shows that visitors tend to generally agree with all the listed statements and assumptions regarding the art mission of art fairs, suggesting some confusion or lack of clarity about the nature of the event. Nevertheless, the least popular response was about the primarily commercial nature of the event. Although some art specialists and collectors highlight the importance of sales and the trade fair nature of the event, the survey shows that the general audience does not perceive art fairs as such or does so to a lesser extent.

The analysis shows that five out of eight items received a score higher than 4, which was considered statistically significant. It illustrates that visitors believe in the educational role of art fairs (Zagrebelnaia & Bayón, 2022), with a score of 4.57, followed by cultural experience (Barragán & Helguera, 2020) with a score of 4.53, and as a networking tool (Morgner, 2014) with a score of 4.38. These results highlight the importance of these elements for the success of art fairs and should not be overlooked by the organizers. For example, the assumption that "Art fairs can help me learn more about contemporary art". Additionally, after analysing the general opinions on which changes were demanded to a greater or lesser extent, it is worth considering the data, keeping in mind the independent variables of familiarity with art fairs.

Following the discoveries based on the analysis of questions eight and ten, it became important to examine the potential relationship between the respondents' familiarity with art fairs and their connection to the art world, in relation to their perceptions of the art fair's mission and the actions they believe art fair organizers should undertake. However, upon a thorough review and cross-referencing of the data, no connection was found. This suggests that neither familiarity with the art fair nor involvement in the art world influences visitors' perceptions of the fair. It also highlights that certain facets of the art fair experience are considered significantly more important across all target groups, and thus should be carefully considered by the organizers of art fairs.

7.7 Conclusions

To conclude, one of the major implications of this research is to explore the social role of art fairs and their potential impact on the dynamics of the art system, based on the vision perceived by the art fair visitors. Additionally, the survey examined the social role of art fairs and their potential impact on the art system dynamics. By addressing the issue from an audience development perspective, this chapter has highlighted the perception and expectations of the general audience, emphasizing the need for social commitment and orientation from art fair organizers.

The visitors' perspectives analysed in this chapter reveal their aspirations for enhanced social engagement, inclusivity, and sustained community involvement. They emphasize the alignment between the educational and cultural dimensions of art fairs with their personal beliefs. Visitors expect art fairs to provide opportunities for artistic discovery, social interaction, and cultural enrichment. They also expect art fairs to be inclusive, diverse, and accessible to all. However, achieving this is unrealistic due to the commercial focus of the events, making it unsuitable for some visitor groups.

Additionally, the analysis revealed that these assumptions, despite seeming discriminatory, biased, or exclusive, actually point to the complexity and intricacies of such events. For those unfamiliar with the format of art fairs and the art market, the experience can be difficult to grasp and navigate, potentially resulting in an unbeneficial experience for unprepared visitors, as well as additional discomfort for galleries. Expanding on insights from prior PhD research (unpublished), there is a clear need to "prepare" or "equip" the public to unlock and appreciate the multifaceted dimensions of events like art fairs. This foundational idea carries profound implications. By integrating knowledge of the art ecosystem into educational programmes, it can contribute to both interest and understanding of the art world. This foundational exposure can serve multiple purposes. It can act as a catalyst, inspiring individuals to pursue careers in the arts, whether as artists, discerning critics, visionary curators, or even educators. With a comprehensive understanding of the art world, some may also lean towards the business side of the spectrum, as collectors or art dealers, bridging creators with connoisseurs. Furthermore, a solid grounding in art can help cultivate a new generation of enthusiasts who not only appreciate art but actively participate in its economy.

The findings have shown that the general audience perceives art fairs as places for education and cultural experience and expects them to be socially committed and oriented. This contrasts sharply with the perceptions of the participating galleries, as evidenced in the previous chapter, and may present a significant challenge for art fair organizers, who must satisfy both groups.

In essence, this chapter has established the focus areas for art fairs that organizers need to consider and laid the groundwork for further research in this field. The combination of commercial and cultural aspects in art fairs contributes to their social role by fostering a dynamic and inclusive art ecosystem. However, it is important to note that the practical implications and social compromise of art fairs are subjects of ongoing debate. Though this study is based solely on a Spanish context and limited in scope, the insights may be applicable to other smaller art fair scenarios. A broader survey across diverse fairs could offer more comprehensive insights.

References

Amigo, M. L. (2014). *Ocio estético valioso*. Universidad de Deusto.

Arts Council England. (2007). *A prospectus for arts and health*. Arts Council. Retrieved from www.artscouncil.org.uk/publication_archive/a-prospectus-for-arts-and-health

Artsy. (2022). *Art market recap: An Artsy report 2022*. Artsy. Retrieved from https://partners.artsy.net/resource/2022-art-market-recap/

Ayala, I., Cuenca-Amigo, M., & Cuenca, J. (2019). Examining the state of the art of audience development in museums and heritage organisations: A systematic literature review. *Museum Management and Curatorship*. https://doi.org/10.1080/09647775.2019.1698312

Ayala, I., Cuenca-Amigo, M., & Cuenca, J. (2021). The future of museums: An analysis from the visitors' perspective in the Spanish context. *Journal of Arts Management, Law, and Society, 51*(3), 171–187.

Baia Curioni, S. (2012). A fairy tale: Art system, globalization, and the fair movement. In M. Lind & O. Velthuis (Eds.), *Contemporary art and its commercial markets: A report on current conditions and future scenarios* (pp. 115–151). Sternberg Press.

Baia Curioni, S., Equi Pierazzini, M., Forti, L. (2020). Philosophic money. *The contemporary art system as a market and cultural agent. Arts, 9(4):110.* https://doi.org/10.3390/arts9040110

Barragán, P. (2008). *The art fair age: On art fairs as urban entertainment centers, art fair curators, expanded painting, collecting, and new fairism*. Charta.

Barragán, P., & Helguera, P. (2020). *From Roman feria to global art fair, from Olympia festival to neo-liberal biennial: On the 'biennialization' of art fairs and the 'fairization' of biennials*. Artium Media.

Bathelt, H., Golfetto, F., & Rinallo, D. (2014). *Trade shows in the globalizing knowledge economy*. Oxford University Press. https://doi.org/10.1093/acprof:oso/9780199643080.001.0001

Bergsdóttir, A. (2016). Museums and feminist matters: Considerations of a feminist museology. *NORA – Nordic Journal of Feminist and Gender Research, 24*(2), 126–139. https://doi.org/10.1080/08038740.2016.1182945

Bollo, A., DaMilano, C., Gariboldi, A., & Torch, C. (2017). *Study on audience development: How to place audiences at the center of cultural organizations (Final Report)*. Engage Audiences. Retrieved from http://engageaudiences.eu/files/2017/04/NC0116644ENN_002.pdf

Borwick, D. (2012). *Building communities, not audiences*. Arts Engaged.

Bryan-Wilson, J. (2003). A curriculum for institutional critique, or the professionalization of conceptual art. In *New Institutionalism*. Office for Contemporary Art (OCA).

Cho, H., & Jolley, A. (2016). Museum education for children with disabilities: Development of the nature senses traveling trunk. *Journal of Museum Education, 41*(3), 220–229. https://doi.org/10.1080/10598650.2016.1193313

Close, H. R. (1998). *Who's my market? Guide to researching audiences and visitors in the arts*. Australia Council.

Colbert, F., & Cuadrado, M. (2012). *Marketing de las artes y la cultura*. Ariel Patrimonio.

Cuenca-Amigo, M., & Makua, A. (2019). El desarrollo de audiencias: Una aproximación comparada en el contexto europeo. In N. Cuenca-Amigo & J. Cuenca (Eds.), *El desarrollo de audiencias en España: Reflexiones desde la teoría y la práctica* (pp. 55–74). Universidad de Deusto.

Daykin, N., & Byrne, E. (2006). The impact of visual arts and design on the health and wellbeing of patients and staff in mental health care: A systematic review of the literature. *Centre for Public Health Research, University of the West of England, UK*. Retrieved from http://eprints.uwe.ac.uk/4829

Diggle, K. (1994). *Arts marketing*. Rhinegold.

Elejabarrieta, F., & Iniguez, L. (2008). Construcción de escalas de actitud tipo Thurstone y Likert. *Revista Electrónica: La Sociología en sus Escenarios, 17*. Retrieved from https://revistas.udea.edu.co/index.php/ceo/article/view/6820

Etgar, M. (2008). A descriptive model of the consumer co-production process. *Journal of the Academy of Marketing Science, 36*(1), 97–108.

European Commission. (2012). *European audiences: 2020 and beyond*. Publications Office of the European Union.

Falk, J. H. (1998). A framework for diversifying museum audiences: Putting heart and head in the right place. *Museum News, 77*(5), 35–43.

Falk, J. H., & Dierking, L. D. (1992). *The museum experience*. Whaleback Books.

Frost, W., & Laing, J. (2017). *Exhibitions, trade fairs, and industrial events*. Routledge.
Gerlis, M. (2020a, May 5). How Covid-19 has forced the art market's speedy digital conversion. *The Art Newspaper*. Retrieved from https://www.theartnewspaper.com/analysis/how-covid-19-fored-the-art-market-s-speedy-digital-conversion
Gerlis, M. (2020b, June 15). Who are the art market's virtual winners? *The Art Newspaper*. Retrieved from https://www.theartnewspaper.com/comment/who-are-the-virtual-winners
Gerlis, M. (2021). The art fair story: A rollercoaster ride. Lund Humphries Publishers, Limited.
Hadley, S. (2021). *Audience development and cultural policy*. Springer.
Hadley, S., & Belfiore, E. (2018). Cultural democracy and cultural policy. *Cultural Trends, 27*(3), 218–223. https://doi.org/10.1080/09548963.2018.1474009
Haisch, T., & Menzel, M. P. (2022). Temporary markets: Market devices and processes of valuation at three Basel art fairs. *Environment and Planning A: Economy and Space, 55*(2). https://doi.org/10.1177/0308518X221128309
Hanquinet, L., & Savage, M. (2012). Educative leisure and the art museum. *Museum and Society, 10*(1), 42–59.
Hein, H. (2007). Redressing the museum in feminist theory. *Museum Management and Curatorship, 22*, 29–42.
Hill, E., O'Sullivan, C., & O'Sullivan, T. (2000). *Creative arts marketing*. Butterworth-Heinemann.
Hybrid Art Fair. (n.d.). *Google Arts & Culture*. Retrieved from https://artsandculture.google.com/story/hybrid-art-fair-boreal-project/MAXhvLdG1PyAIA?hl=en
Institutul Național pentru Cercetare și Formare Culturală. (2022). *Barometrul de consum cultural 2022: Participare culturală și perspective democratice*. Culturadata. Retrieved from https://www.culturadata.ro/barometrul-de-consum-cultural-2022-participare-culturala-si-perspective--democratice/.
Joshi, A., Kale, S., Chandel, S., & Pal, D. (2015). Likert scale: Explored and explained. *British Journal of Applied Science and Technology, 7*, 396–403.
KEA. (2009). *The impact of culture on creativity*. European Commission.
Kolb, B. M. (2005). *Marketing for cultural organizations: New strategies for attracting audiences to classical music, dance, museums, theater, and opera* (2nd ed.). Thomson Learning.
Krejcie, R.V., & Morgan, D.W. (1970). Determining sample size for research activities. Educational and psychological measurement, 30 (3).
Krumpal, I. (2013). Determinants of social desirability bias in sensitive surveys: A literature review. Quality & quantity, 47(4): 2025–2047. https://doi.org/10.1007/s11135-011-9640-9 S2CID 143045969.
Lindelof, A. M. (2014). Audience development and its blind spot: A quest for pleasure and play in the discussion of performing arts institutions. *International Journal of Cultural Policy, 3*. https://doi.org/10.1080/10286632.2014.891585
Malraux, A. (1965). *Le musée imaginaire: Voix du silence*. Gallimard.
McAndrew, C. (2023). *The art market 2023: An art basel and UBS report*. Art Basel and UBS.
Mehring, C. (2008). Emerging market: The birth of the contemporary art fair. *Artforum, 46*(8), 322–334.
Mikulic, J., Krešić, D., Prebezac, D., Milicevic, K., & Seric, M. (2015). Identifying drivers of destination attractiveness in a competitive environment: A comparison of approaches. *Journal of Destination Marketing and Management, 5*. https://doi.org/10.1016/j.jdmm.2015.12.003
Monteagudo, M. J. (2020). Las experiencias museísticas y sus beneficios: Una reflexión desde los estudios de ocio. In F. Bayón & J. Cuenca (Eds.), *Públicos en transformación: Una visión interdisciplinar de las funciones, experiencias y espacios del público actual de los museos* (pp. 63–72). Dykinson.
Monteagudo, M. J., & San Salvador del Valle, R. (2017). Leisure experience in consumer society: Characteristics, possibility conditions, and threats. In M. J. Monteagudo (Ed.), *Leisure experience in consumer and contributions to human development* (pp. 37–61). Universidad de Deusto.

Morgner, C. (2014). The art fair as network. *The Journal of Arts Management, Law, and Society, 44*(1), 33–46.
Murray, M. (2012). Art, social action and social change. In C. Walker, K. Johnson, & L. Cunningham (Eds.), *Community psychology and the economics of mental health: Global perspectives* (pp. 253–265). https://doi.org/10.13140/2.1.1291.1049
Peterson, R. A. (1992). Understanding audience segmentation: From elite and mass to omnivore and univore. *Poetics, 21*(4), 243–258. https://doi.org/10.1016/0304-422X(92)90008-Q
Pinochet, C., & Güell, P. (2018). Visitantes, audiencias, públicos: Apuntes para un estudio desde las prácticas culturales. *Revista Atenea, 518*, 151–166. https://doi.org/10.4067/S0718-04622018000200151
Poli, F. (2011). *Il sistema dell'arte contemporanea: Produzione artistica, mercato, musei*. Universale Laterza.
Prieto-Rodriguez, J., & Vecco, M. (2021). Reading between the lines in the art market: Lack of transparency and price heterogeneity as an indicator of multiple equilibria. *Economic Modelling, 102*. https://doi.org/10.1016/j.econmod.2021.102205
Quemin, A. (2013). International contemporary art fairs in a globalized art market. *European Societies, 15*(2), 162–177.
Ricci, C. (2020). Between a fair and a biennial. In C. Baldacci, C. Ricci, & A. Vettese (Eds.), *Double trouble in exhibiting the contemporary: Art fairs and shows* (pp. 63–72). Scalpendi.
Rosenberg, E. (2023, October 18). *NEA study finds sharp decline in arts audiences since the pandemic*. The Washington Post. Retrieved from https://www.washingtonpost.com/entertainment/2023/10/18/nea-study-arts-audience-decline/
Ruiz, N. (2021). *ARCO: Una historia de arte y mercado* (1st ed.). Contextos.
Scorcu, A. E., Vici, L., & Zanola, R. (2021). To fake or not to fake: An empirical investigation on the fine art market. *Journal of Cultural Economy, 45*, 143–152. https://doi.org/10.1007/s10824-020-09394-0
Sigle, E. (2020). The art fair boom and its contradictions. In A. Glauser, P. Holder, T. Mazzurana, O. Moeschler, V. Rolle, & F. Schultheis (Eds.), *The sociology of arts and markets: New developments and persistent patterns* (pp. 365–385). Palgrave Macmillan.
Simon, N. (2010). *The participatory museum*. Museum 2.0, USA.
Smith, M. K. (2006). *Tourism, culture, and regeneration*. CAB International.
Thompson, D. (2011). Art fair: The market as medium. In B. Moeran & J. Strandgaard Pedersen (Eds.), *The creative industries: Fairs, festivals and competitive events* (pp. 59–72). Cambridge University Press.
Throsby, D. (1994). The production and consumption of the arts: A view of cultural economics. *Journal of Economic Literature, 32*, 1–29. Retrieved from www.jstor.org/stable/2728421
Tomlinson, R., & Roberts, T. (2006). *Full house: Turning data into audiences*. Creative New Zealand.
Velthuis, O. (2012). The contemporary art market between stasis and flux. In M. Lind & O. Velthuis (Eds.), *Contemporary art and its commercial markets: A report on current conditions and future scenarios* (pp. 17–50). Sternberg Press.
Velthuis, O., & Baia Curioni, S. (2015). *Cosmopolitan canvases: The globalization of markets for contemporary art*. Oxford University Press.
Vermeylen, F. (2015). The India art fair and the market for visual arts in the Global South. In O. Velthuis & S. Baia Curioni (Eds.), *Canvases and careers in a cosmopolitan culture: On the globalization of contemporary art markets* (pp. 125–140). Oxford University Press.
Yogev, T. (2010). The social construction of quality: Status dynamics in the market for contemporary art. *Socio-Economic Review, 8*(3), 511–536.
Yogev, T., & Grund, T. (2012). Network dynamics and market structure: The case of art fairs. *Sociological Focus, 45*(1), 23–40.
Zagrebelnaia, A. (2021). State of the art fair post-COVID: Audience development strategies in post-digital context. *European Journal of Cultural Management and Policy, 11*(2), 34–51.

Zagrebelnaia, A., & Bayón, F. (2022). Hacia un modelo social para las ferias de arte: El caso de Hybrid Art Fair. In A. Madariaga & P. Rodrigo-Moriche (Eds.), *Ocio saludable y construcción de ciudadanía* (pp. 130–138). Aranzadi.

Chapter 8
The Significance of Ethnographic Museums in the BizkaiKOA Network

Sofía Moreno-Domínguez

Abstract This chapter explores the impact of cultural participation in the neo-rural ecosystem of Bizkaia, Spain, with a focus on digitalisation as a new space for audience communities. The study examines two ethnographic museums in the BizkaiKOA network near Bilbao and their connection to local audiences, using a matrix specifically designed to evaluate their rootedness. By measuring the identity variable, this research provides an in-depth understanding of each museum. The results compare two museums that provided informed consent: the Txakolin Museoa, or Txakolingunea, in Bakio, and the Euskal Herria Museoa in Gernika-Lumo. The chapter analyses the differing realities and public perceptions of the museums, considering factors such as the naming of the cultural space and its impact, the location and accessibility of the museum, collaboration with local associations, involvement in local festivals, and the commitment of the local community. The analysis also highlights the importance of the museum director's background in fostering local connections, as well as the effective presentation of museum content, including the role of technology and its potential challenges. The chapter concludes that, despite the potential of digitisation, the museums studied still prioritise face-to-face visits, emphasising that maintaining a physical presence remains a preferred mode of engagement.

8.1 Introduction

This research project focuses on the impact of cultural participation and highlights the need to rethink alternative ways of fostering human development, linking these actions to their relationship with contemporary territories.

Current human development strategies must include, or at least consider, cultural participation, as outlined in the Universal Declaration of Human Rights (UDHR).

S. Moreno-Domínguez (✉)
Mondragon Unibertsitatea/University of Deusto, Bilbao, Spain
e-mail: smoreno@mondragon.edu; sofiamoreno@opendeusto.es

L. Ronda et al. (eds.), *Leisure and Human Development*, Human Well-Being Research and Policy Making, https://doi.org/10.1007/978-3-031-90778-4_8

This 1948 declaration includes an article, number 27, which states in its first paragraph: "Everyone has the right to take part freely in the cultural life of the community (…)" (United Nations, 2024), as will be discussed in greater detail in the conclusions of this paper.

In recent discourse, there has been increasing emphasis on audience development and social inclusion, focusing on the recognition of minorities within broader communities. This perspective has been developed in this study, building on prior research conducted by Bayón and Cuenca (2020), Cuenca-Amigo et al. (2019), and Walker-Kunhe (2005). In terms of territories, another significant consideration in this new dimension of cultural management is the expansion beyond the urban domain to include alternative ways of living, such as the neo-rural, suburban, and metropolitan spheres. Some examples of prior studies relevant to this area, included in this bibliography, are those of Camarero (1993), Chamboredon (1980), Chevalier (1981), Ferrara and Pisano (2019), Izquierdo Vallina (2019), and Roseman (2013), among many other authors.

The neo-rural ecosystem, in particular, is emerging as a habitat increasingly shaped by demographic policies linked to sustainable development in relation to culture. This topic is growing exponentially as a research focus, as evidenced by papers and documents authored by Dessein (2015), Duxbury et al. (2017), Kagan (2021), and Soini and Dessein (2016), among others. These trends are now entering the socio-political arena and, apart from underscoring the importance of the issues addressed in this chapter, provide the backdrop for further scientific exploration of related aspects that fall beyond the scope of this research.

It is important to clarify that this study focuses primarily on the loss of culture and tradition in inhabited or potentially inhabited rural or neo-rural areas, particularly in light of new urban residents relocating to these regions. The aim is to transform these spaces into platforms for cultural expression, encompassing its many facets and complexities. Indeed, to construct such platforms, it is common to draw upon the contemporary trend of hybridisation, both in terms of actions and spatial configurations.

8.1.1 Research Objectives

The main aim of this research is to understand the drivers of change in cultural management introduced by specific neo-rural projects. This will be demonstrated by assessing the innovations generated through audience development. To achieve this, we will explore how the new forms of cultural participation emerging from the neo-rural ecosystem of Bizkaia integrate local actors within their communities.

A secondary objective is to adapt the definition of neo-ruralism to the current phenomenon of delocalisation that characterises our fast-moving society in the early decades of the twenty-first century. This focus involves particular attention to the attributes that make this movement a key element in developing strategies for building audiences and maintaining their loyalty as part of a circular process.

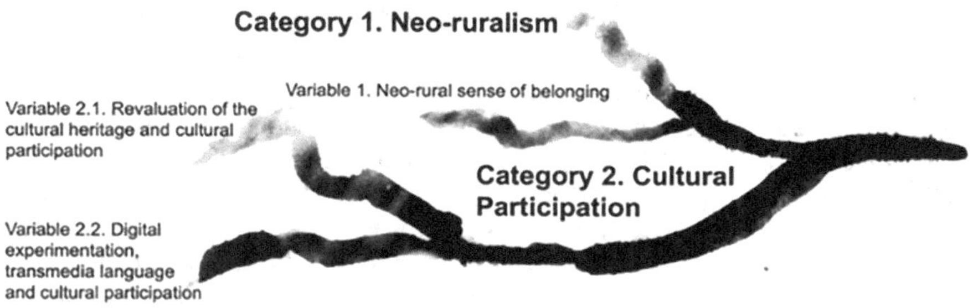

Fig. 8.1 Categories and variables

To guide the reader and provide context for this study, we have developed a figure representing our research framework and situating it within the larger thesis from which this contrasting information originally derives (Fig. 8.1).

8.1.2 *Hypotheses*

The initial hypotheses are divided into two parts. The first part focuses on neo-ruralism, or urban migration, as a movement whose characteristics are fundamental to generating new strategies for developing audience communities and fostering their engagement.

The second part examines how cultural participation is essential for integrating minority groups within less densely populated communities. This is analysed using a self-designed methodology, the matrix of rootedness, to measure the participation variable in relation to the identity of each museum.

8.1.3 *Research Questions*

The following research questions guide this study, focusing on the intersection of neo-ruralism, cultural participation, and community integration:

1. What new forms of cultural participation are emerging in the context of neo-ruralism/urban migration?
2. Do sparsely populated areas hold an advantage over densely populated areas in terms of integration and social dissemination of the cultural content that organisations are working with?

8.2 Case Study: Description of the BizkaiKOA Network

The BizkaiKOA network of museums and cultural sites was established by the Council of Bizkaia. Based on a semi-structured interview conducted via Zoom with the manager of the BizkaiKOA network, identified by the initials A.M., on 30 June 2022, we can gain a broader understanding of the functioning of the two ethnographic museums selected as case studies.

This public network was created rapidly in 2011. However, as noted by A.M. (2022), this rapid development underestimated the importance of some processes, such as the intention of openness that the network was meant to embody.

The origin of the BizkaiKOA project lies in the Council of Bizkaia's recognition of the large number of museums, most of them small, which require support in areas such as management, storage, economic resources, and human resources. Excluding the most renowned museums in Bizkaia, such as the Guggenheim and the Bilbao Fine Arts Museum, the remaining museums are smaller and fall into two categories of ownership: (1) fully owned by the Council of Bizkaia and (2) partially (50%) owned by the Council or reliant on it through annual subsidies. Although there are sporadic collaborations, including some exhibition exchanges, these connections are primarily personal. The aim is to develop a more structured and coherent management approach for the network in the future.

The head of the BizkaiKOA network (A.M.) operates with a dual focus on two missions: (1) ensuring comprehensive care for the museums owned by the regional government and (2) assisting in the management of other museums in Bizkaia through specific services designed to achieve transversality.

Reflecting on Biscayan identity is also key to understanding this network. This identity is deeply connected to local trades, customs, and traditions. For this reason, the two selected museums partially incorporate the memory of local inhabitants, as these individuals provide the most authentic insight into the quality of life in the villages where the museums are located, drawing from their own experiences.

One of the most significant events, according to A.M. (2022), is the European Heritage Days, which have been held in Bizkaia for more than 20 years. These events, celebrated under a different theme each year chosen by European organisations, are brought to Bizkaia by the Council. Bizkaia stands out in European forums for its success with this initiative.

Bizkaia's best practice involves collaboration with dynamic actors such as associations, centres, and other entities. This is particularly evident in the European Heritage Days, which represent the most transversal action coordinated by BizkaiKOA. The network seeks to extend the transversal dynamics of this initiative to other actions within its coordination.

8.2.1 *Euskal Herria Museoa (Gernika-Lumo)*

The current Euskal Herria Museum was originally built as a private summer house in 1733. The building was constructed on the remains of a medieval tower that was almost destroyed during the "Matxinada de Aduanas"—a social uprising that took place in the Basque Country in the eighteenth century.

Its restoration was undertaken by Don Juan de Mezeta, who adhered to the urban and domestic trends of the Basque Baroque style. This style divided spaces into areas for people and those for carriages and included open spaces such as the gardens of the Europe Park (Fig. 8.2), which recreate the different ecosystems of the continent. The garden is also one of the few elements that survived the bombing of Gernika in 1937.

In 1982, the Council of Bizkaia acquired the building, preserving its symbolic essence. The museum was officially opened to the public in 1991, following a complete restoration of the building's interior (Fig. 8.3). Little evidence remains of the original interior apart from a few photographs and oral testimonies. In this way, the summer residence of the Allende-Salazar family was transformed into a monumental legacy for the people of Gernika.

The Euskal Herria Museoa is dedicated to explaining who the Basque people are. It seeks to answer questions such as where their territories have been defined over the years through territorial management strategies centred on the "anteiglesias" or "elizateak" (the oldest form of social organisation in which resources like forests and water were communally shared), how they sound, how they dance, how they prepare food, and how they present themselves. These elements, which form the

Fig. 8.2 The Gernika Tree (left) and the gardens of Europe Park (right). Photographs taken during the technical visit to the museum in January 2022

Fig. 8.3 Interior of the Euskal Herria Museum (left) and an exhibition on women racket players (right). Photographs taken during the technical visit to the museum in January 2022

soul of Basque culture, are displayed in a physical and tangible way through the museum's permanent exhibition.

On 21 January 2022, a technical visit to the museum's facilities was conducted, along with an in-depth interview with the museum's director at the time, L.I., an employee with 22 years of experience in the organisation.

The interview flowed naturally, allowing both parties to discuss internal challenges and the museum's aspirations for the future. The conversation touched on all the key points to be measured within the arithmetic matrix of rootedness, as will be elaborated upon later.

8.2.2 Txakolin Museoa (Bakio)

In 2014, the Txakolingunea was opened to the public as a centre dedicated to the interpretation of "chacolí" (in Spanish) or "txakoli" (in Basque), its culture, production, and consumption.

Although the launch of this space was positively assessed by the Council of Bizkaia a year after its inauguration, with the optimistic headline "More than 4000 people visited the Txakolingunea in Bakio (Fig. 8.4) in its first year of activity" (Council of Bizkaia, 2015), it also faced criticism. A news item published by the digital newspaper Gara in 2014 highlighted neighbourhood protests demanding, "Kiroldegia publikoa Txakolingunearen truke" (a public gym instead of Txakolingunea) (Goikoetxea, 2014).

Fig. 8.4 Three images showing the exterior and the interior of the Txakolin Museoa, as well as its museography. Source: BizkaiKOA website, 2023

Focusing on the positive aspects of the centre's first year of activity, the majority of visitors were initially residents from the region of Uribe and the rest of Bizkaia. Originally named Txakolingunea, the centre was recently renamed Txakolin Museoa to better reflect its content.

The mission of the Txakolin Museoa is to promote and disseminate knowledge about txakoli, a wine with roots dating back to the fourteenth century, highlighting its connection to the municipality of Bakio and its surrounding areas. However, local perceptions of the centre remain sharply divided, with little middle ground.

The centre has gained visibility through the initiative and openness of its team, who have worked with an attitude of active listening to adapt the space to local initiatives. Their approach has avoided imposing decisions, instead favouring collaboration with those who contribute to the centre's activities within the community.

On 2 February 2022, a semi-structured interview was conducted with the director of the Txakolin Museoa, A.G., and the visitor guide, S.S. After explaining the interview protocol, its stages, and the procedure for measuring responses using the matrix of rootedness, the conversation centred on identity. According to A.G., the old name (Txakolingunea) was deemed too long and difficult for visitors to understand. Moreover, the initial interactions with the rebranded name appear to be an effective way of generating interest in the "txakoli" ecosystem—encompassing its production, tradition, consumption, marketing, and significance in Basque culture.

8.3 Methodology: What Is the Matrix of Rootedness?

Before examining the results of the arithmetic matrix of rootedness in territorial dynamisation, as provided by two ethnographic museums in the BizkaiKOA network, we will take a moment to explore the concept of the arithmetic or matrix of rootedness in order to fully understand it.

The goal of adapting the Likert scale into a more human-centred version is to gain an overview of the attachment to the territories where these two museums were situated at the time of the interviews (2022). These reports result from an analysis of the total number of responses obtained in the interviews, along with the perceptions gathered from the technical visits to the sites.

This tool introduces a variable that changes according to interpretation. The necessary reformulation to adapt it to a new object of study involves considering the variable of identity, and examining what defines a cultural action as belonging to the location where it occurs.

The adapted table, shown in Table 8.1, is based on identity and represents the version that was applied to the semi-structured in-depth interview protocols. This was applied both in the interview script and in the analysis of the two case studies, which incorporate ethnography into the BizkaiKOA network.

Table 8.1 Arithmetic of rootedness adapted to dynamisation tools

Matrix of rootedness adapted to territorial dynamisation			
Measurement	Low degree of rootedness (0–1)	Medium degree of rootedness (2, 3)	High degree of rootedness (4, 5)
The answers to the questions shall be graded from 0 to 5 (where 0< and 5>)			
Identity	Imported and disconnected	Partially hybridised	Hybridised and linked to local memory

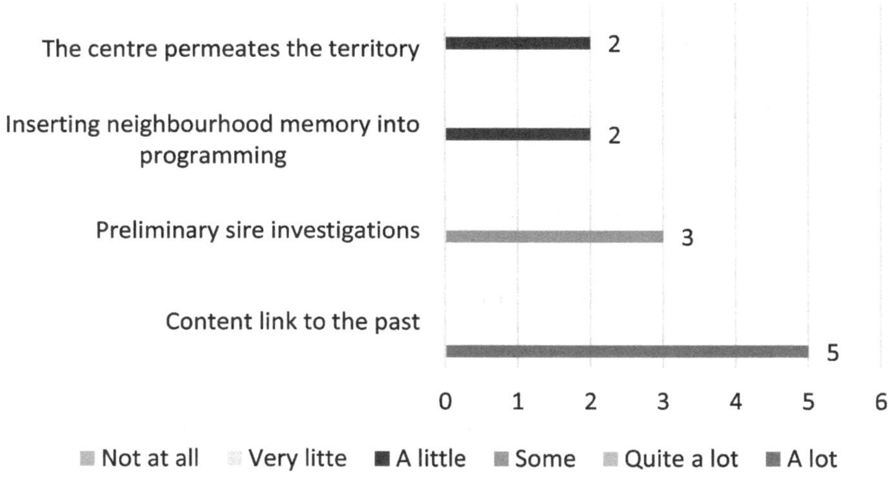

Fig. 8.5 Identity variable responses (Euskal Herria Museoa, Gernika-Lumo)

8.3.1 The Matrix of Rootedness in the Euskal Herria Museoa

The specificity of the Euskal Herria Museoa, whose subject matter is based on Basque culture and traditions, makes it essential to disseminate, maintain and revise Basque identity as a whole, as well as to have a certain spontaneity outside the network of the Council, according to A.M. (2022).

The structure of the semi-structured in-depth interview conducted with the director of the museum in 2022, L.I., yielded the following results, subjectively classified by measuring the answers to the following questions and subsequently validated with the interviewee in 2023 as feedback (Fig. 8.5).

The Euskal Herria Museoa has obtained a medium degree of rootedness (3/5), as its programme is partially linked to the local memory of the area through the use of an emblematic historical building, but it does not manage to be fully understood as a project intended for the immediate public.

8.3.2 The Matrix of Rootedness in the Txakolin Museoa

The biggest challenge of the Txakolin Museoa is overcoming the initial problem that the people of Bakio had in understanding its importance and use as a centre. The people's desire to use the facilities for sports and other purposes has meant that this centre is the most challenging and complex of those found in the network.

Another recent challenge has been the change from being known as Txakolingunea (the place of the txakoli) to a nomenclature more in line with the rest of the centres of BizkaiKOA: Txakolin Museoa. The museum team insists on being understood by

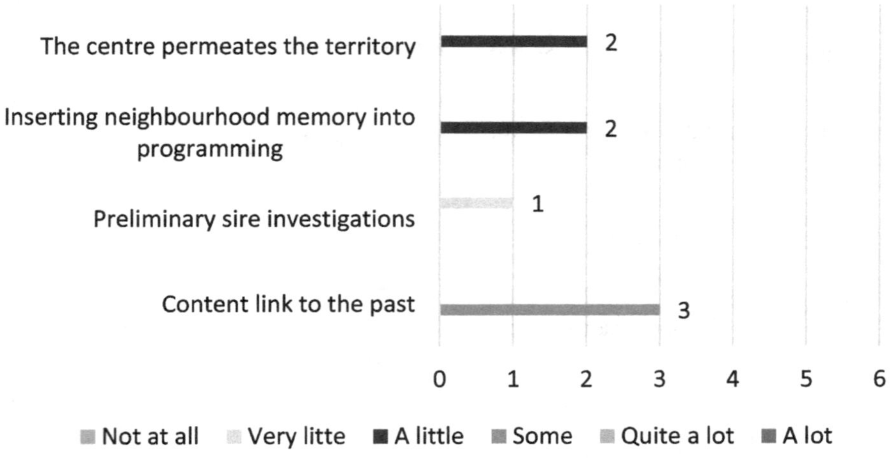

Fig. 8.6 Identity variable responses (Txakolin Museoa, Bakio)

visitors, and they are aware that they have neither an archive nor a collection, so it is more appropriate to refer to themselves as a centre for the interpretation of txakoli.

The answers obtained in the interview with the director, A.G., and her colleague and museum guide, S.S., in 2022 highlight these subjectively extracted values, which were further contrasted in 2023 (Fig. 8.6).

The sum of all these measures results in a medium score (2/5) for the identity variable, due to the fact that the Txakolin Museoa, although close to the "txakoli" wineries of Bakio, is not a centre whose mission is fully understood by part of the local population.

This is due to the neighbourhood conflict that led to its construction under political pretensions, which still needs to be addressed today, with innovative interventions to bring the public, and especially the locals, closer to the facilities.

8.3.3 Crossed Data Between the Two Case Studies

The identity variable has referential elements for institutions that represent what brings us together, especially when they are public and their mission is to have an impact on society.

In general, there was a clear separation between the local population and tourists, who are more focused on creating memorable images and mental frames when travelling.

This difference in the way museums are visited is quite important to understand both case studies in order to develop strategies for current and future audiences that make sense in terms of bringing essence to the institutions and creating different kinds of expectations when visiting them.

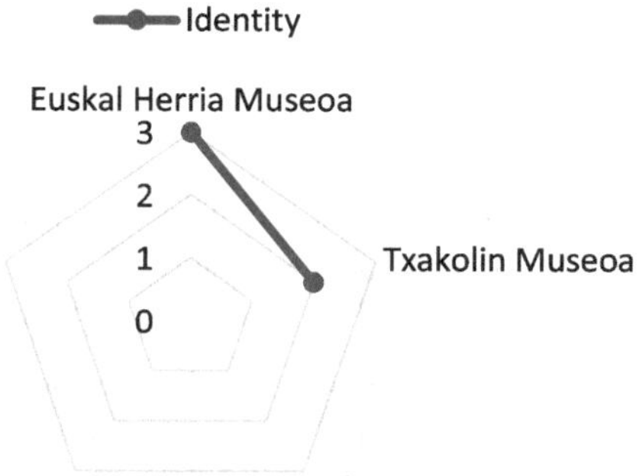

Fig. 8.7 The identity variable in the two ethnographic museums of BizkaiKOA

In addition to all this, the fact that identities are fickle and change regularly is present throughout this research process. It is therefore necessary to address current issues that will help develop each museum in line with the advances taking place in the field.

Although culture alone will not prevent diasporas or forced migrations, as these depend more on access to quality employment, housing, or other essential services such as shops, schools, or medical centres, culture can help make problems visible in the contemporary world.

In the two ethnographic museums of the BizkaiKOA network, the identity variable has obtained the following common data, based on the interviews conducted in these institutions in 2022 and revised in 2023 (Fig. 8.7).

Without wishing to make any comparisons, the graph shows that the Txakolin Museoa has achieved a medium degree of rootedness (2/5), as it started its journey with some complications, and at the time of the interview (in 2022), was still working hand in hand with the local community to become a centre highly valued by its surroundings.

The Euskal Herria Museoa, on the other hand, also has a medium degree of rootedness (3/5), slightly higher in this case, due to its proximity to the very famous Gernika Tree and the General Courts of Bizkaia, also known as the Palacio Alegría, but with the obstacle of limited opening hours. Despite this negative aspect, all these factors make this museum a symbol of the Gernika-Lumo region.

8.4 Analysis: Opening the Floor to the International Dimension

Having researched the topic of this chapter: *"The Significance of Ethnographic Museums in the BizkaiKOA Network"*, we will briefly summarise some specific key points before addressing the results and lines for future research.

The categories and variables introduced here reflect the same theme: how living in a specific habitat affects cultural participation and how, on the other hand, cultural participation is essential for developing the sense of belonging of local inhabitants, without forgetting contemporary constraints, such as the intangible dimension of the digital world, and considering the importance of rootedness, particularly in rural areas.

These issues are complex in themselves, but we also need to add a new layer of complexity to the way cultural management operates sustainably by including it in the framework of the Sustainable Development Goals (SDGs) of the Global 2030 Agenda, to which this study specifically refers as follows:

- SDG 4 (Quality Education), as we consider the value of cultural heritage transmission for the development of neo-rural societies.
- SDG 11 (Sustainable Cities and Communities), which understands sustainability as something broader that also affects culture and cultural participation.
- SDG 17 (Partnerships for the Goals), which refers to the cultural work developed in networks and its further steps.

We can also imagine other SDGs being discussed as possibilities across Europe, such as the #Culture2030Goal campaign promoted by Arterial Network, Culture Action Europe, ICOMOS (International Council on Monuments and Sites), IFCCD (International Federation of Coalitions for Cultural Diversity), IFLA (The International Federation of Library Associations and Institutions), International Music Council and the Culture 21 UCLG Committee (Culture2030Goal, 2022).

Returning to the time dimension and regarding less densely populated areas, in Spain there is a path that the inhabitants could follow to understand their relationship with these types of territories, and we must highlight here: the Rural Development Plans (from 1980 to the present).

These changes are very much influenced by socio-cultural and political factors, such as glocalisation (the integration of global and local strategies) and an increased number of migrations and population movements, such as commuting.

All these movements have a great impact on the way we interact with our habitats and also create new stratifications that deal with the subjective perspective of territories. This becomes highly visible when we also focus on feelings such as the sense of belonging, which is why this theme naturally becomes the backbone of this project.

Generally speaking, museums see themselves as custodians of the heritage of the past, but not as owners of the goods and treasures that represent our collective memory as a society. And this is problematic because they don't see themselves as having enough agency to act and promote the change needed to transform culture in a sustainable way.

To return to the consideration of spontaneity and cultural sustainability as essential tools for registering and preserving the collective memory of our territories, we have referred to some new behavioural theories such as nudge theory (the idea of self-control by society for the common good of the social group) (Thaler & Sunstein, 2009).

In order to understand culture as sustainability, we have used Dessein's (2015) perception, which is not to understand culture for sustainability or the culture of sustainability, but to include all social or political progress in the cultural sector to make it sustainable in itself with its own agency and power.

To address the issue of cultural participation in the context of contemporary institutions, we can take a look at some new theories and policies that seek to transform museums into more participatory organisations.

Following this idea, and in an English-speaking context, we have the well-known research on the participatory museum by Simon (2010). This book, published and conceived in the United States of America, gives us a perspective in which cultural institutions must change their way of interacting due to the new sources of entertainment, learning and communication that are entirely linked to the digital environment.

The main question addressed in Simon's (2010) book is: How can cultural institutions reconnect with the public and reposition themselves in contemporary life? And the answer the author proposes is: by inviting people to actively engage as cultural participants and not simply as consumers (Simon, 2010).

We can clearly see that the role of museums is changing. It is inevitable that the network effect that reproduces today's digital communication will influence the perception of today's audiences. Every choice made by an audience is conditioned by its preferences, as a group and as an individual, and knowing these preferences plays an important role as data in the mission to find a suitable model for each cultural institution.

Without wishing to add new themes and levels of research to this chapter, it is important to highlight some specific examples that my stay abroad in the ECC (Economics, Comparisons, Connections) research group at the Department of Public History of the University of Ghent (Belgium) has given me. Specifically, I found one interesting case: Jessy Koeiman's curatorial experience of collective learning at Kunstinstituut Melly, Rotterdam, as an example of how to work with audiences, not passively involving them, but allowing young audiences to be important actors in the future of the museum or cultural centre.

Since 2018, Koeiman (2024) has been focused on bringing innovative methods of education and visualisation of art and culture. She has created various programmes to connect with people on different levels, always sticking to the principle of solidarity whenever possible.

With the main goal of meeting and sharing around "art as a bridge to overcome differences" (Koeiman, 2024) and also allowing the cultural institution to learn from its audience, she created three different programmes:

1. SESSIONS is a series of multidisciplinary events in which different disciplines combine to entertain the audience, who can also be the main actors by sharing their art forms (such as spoken word, dance or music).
2. CLIP (Collective Learning In Practice) is a programme in which a group of young people from different backgrounds, based in Rotterdam and aged between 17 and 24 years, work on a 6-month project at Kunstinstituut Melly to get involved in some decision-making processes within the cultural institution in order to increase the bottom-up mentality of the cultural centre.

3. Neighbours, to mention activities that involve collaborations with people from the surrounding area, such as Barber Bob, a nearby business on the corner of Boomgrardstraat (the street where Kunstinstituut Melly is located), or a memorandum entitled "The Cool Project" to revisit a social project carried out by artists John Ahearn and Rigoberto Torres in 1991, involving their old local participants from that time.

These examples not only have inspiring points of contact and connection with each other, but also use contemporary artivist codes to engage with communities.

This fact leads us to think that, in terms of increasingly successful participatory techniques, the museums that seem to be more advanced in this matter, at least between the years of this study (2020 and 2024), are the artistic ones, so that all the others can follow and hopefully learn from them.

The way people interact with and experience culture today is changing dramatically. As a result, cultural, artistic and ethnographic institutions must also change in order to respond to this new scenario, not only in the way they operate (as we have seen in the two examples described above), but also in the way they organise themselves, whether within or outside a network.

8.5 Conclusions: A Broader Perspective on Ethnographic Museums and Network

After weaving in some other European and global cultural initiatives of interest as a contrasting round, with the commitment to renewing the perspective of this chapter in order to create a proper diagnosis in a broader context, it is now time to present the conclusions of our case studies in detail.

If we start from a global perspective and then return to a local one, rural Spain is a vast and extensive territory. So, with this as a starting point, let's look closer at the locations of the two ethnographic museums: Are they neo-rural, rural, suburban, rurban, or metropolitan? Addressing the issue of definition in these two territories means, above all, confronting an unusual understanding of each habitat for each inhabitant.

These territorial constraints are also evident in the research of the selected case studies. Both of them felt that they were something more than a village: a suburb of Bilbao, or small places with a great history behind them that couldn't be described by the traditional definition of rural.

As the two museums compared, received, and reviewed their data after each individual analysis, some new questions emerged, such as: Is it more useful for each selected museum to work independently or as a network?

These museums have a very strong identity that allows them to function well without highlighting too many common activities or dates. There are also some strategies that would need to be explored further, such as museum passes or a card that allows visitors to access multiple museums with the same ticket (by paying a fixed amount of money in advance each year). This could motivate people to visit more museums than the typical or more famous ones. However, in other circumstances, it is important to reflect on whether this idea is beneficial or not for going beyond the most popular museums.

Moreover, being part of a larger network does not negate the fact that logistical and administrative tasks are easier when working as part of an institution, rather than independently. This raises a debate on whether it is better to work individually or as a network that is not well understood. In Spain, we have another example of this kind, similar to the BizkaiKOA network, but on a national scale and based in Madrid.

This other example is the National Museums Network, which links some museums in Madrid, such as the Museo del Traje (Fashion Museum), the Museo del Romanticismo (Romanticism Museum), or the Casa Sorolla (the former house of the painter Joaquín Sorolla), with many other institutions that share a brand name, a bonus (similar to the museum pass described above), or some promotional material, such as catalogues, flyers, or merchandise to distribute to tourists, in order to increase the number of visitors each year (Ministry of Culture, s.f.).

Since this is a larger network and it operates in Madrid, the capital of Spain, the resources used are greater, but the management and coordination problems are similar or almost the same.

After cross-referencing all the data relating to these two museums, it was possible to extract some information that could give an idea of how difficult it might be to develop a common brand identity for them. One of these challenges is the fact that these museums do not currently feel very comfortable using digital tools in their daily lives. This issue is especially relevant when it comes to actively participating in some of the network's online marketing strategies. The reason for this is that most of them do not feel able to work with these new media, as they only have a small number of multi-tasking staff officially involved in each project.

With all this in mind, the aim of this paper is to interpret the sense of belonging of two subjects of study: two ethnographic museums of a wider network called BizkaiKOA, where we can also find (in a broader sense) other types of museums and archaeological and historical sites.

It is also important to note that we chose ethnographic museums over other types of institutions and sites in the BizkaiKOA network because ethnography is a qualitative social science whose research method systematically describes and interprets the culture of different human groups or communities. This definition of ethnography has recently been updated by the digital humanities and the proliferation of practices such as audience development in cultural management to re-humanise social media, and the use of new technologies today has translated into new methodologies, such as the matrix of rootedness developed in this study as a feedback loop.

After extracting all the data related to these two museums and using a critical approach as an analytical position, we have one main question in mind: Is working in a network an effective strategy for cultural work in Spain today?

The sample institutions moved between two clear positions. Firstly, we realised that internally these two museums are aware that they have areas for improvement. Secondly, we also noticed that externally, when we focus on how other organisations and institutions see these museums, there are some blind spots to be benchmarked. This lack of freedom could happen because we can't forget that one of the main expectations of culture today is to be self-sufficient and sustainable.

We are still aware of the need to contrast this matrix of rootedness as a methodology for measurement with other case studies and cultural projects in order to validate its use and perfect it through these repetitions.

However, being connected in a network is the main essence of some actions that we also perceived during the semi-in-depth interviews, and it is increasingly a core part of the dynamics of change, where mutual help and collective care become two parts of today's scenario (at least in the healthy self-managed initiatives we observed in rural areas). As an organisation, embracing change means understanding and being prepared for the constraints that you will have to face in order to change for good.

References

Bayón, F., & Cuenca, J. (2020). *Públicos en transformación: Una visión interdisciplinar y de las funciones, experiencias y espacios del público actual de los museos*. Editorial Dykinson, S.L.

Camarero, L. A. (1993). *Del éxodo rural y del éxodo urbano: Ocaso y renacimiento de los asentamientos rurales en España*. Ministerio de Agricultura, Pesca y Alimentación.

Chamboredon, J. C. (1980). Les usages urbains de l'espace rural: Du moyen de production au lieu de récréation. *Revue Française de Sociologie, 21*(11), 97–119.

Chevalier, M. (1981). Les phénomènes néo-ruraux. *L'Espace Géographique, 1*, 33–47.

Cuenca-Amigo, M., Macaracena, J., & Cuenca, J. (2019). *El desarrollo de audiencias en España: Reflexiones desde la teoría y la práctica* (Documentos de Estudios de Ocio 64). Universidad de Deusto.

Culture2030Goal. (2022). *Culture 2030 Goal*. https://culture2030goal.net/our-culture-goal-proposal. Accessed February 21, 2024.

Dessein, J., et al. (2015). Conclusions from the Cost Action IS1007 investing cultural sustainability. *Culture in, for and as Sustainable Development*. https://doi.org/10.13140/RG.2.1.3380.7844

Diputación Foral de Bizkaia. (2015). Más de 4.000 personas visitan el Txakolingune de Bakio en su primer año de actividad. *BizkaiKOA*. https://www.bizkaikoa.bizkaia.eus/detalleContenido.asp?id=583&t=3. Accessed February 20, 2024.

Duxbury, N., et al. (2017). Cultural policies for sustainable development: Four strategic paths. *International Journal of Cultural Policy, 23*, 214–230. https://doi.org/10.1080/10286632.2017.1280789

Ferrara, B., & Pisano, L. (2019). Manifesto of Rural Futurism. *Rethinking a New Rurality*. Rural Futurism. https://www.ruralfuturism.com/. Accessed February 18, 2024.

Goikoetxea, A. (2014, March 20). Las protestas vecinales marcan la inauguración de Txakolingunea. *Gara*.

Izquierdo Vallina, J. (2019). *La ciudad agropolitana: La aldea cosmopolita*. Krk Ediciones.

Kagan, S. J. (2021). Creativity in spaces of possibilities for sustainable urban development: An empirical study of four cultural initiatives in Hannover, Germany. *World Futures: The Journal of General Evolution, 77*(1), 1–27. https://doi.org/10.1080/02604027.2021.1984157

Koeiman, J. (2024). Curating/Melly. *Jessy Koeiman*. The Netherlands. https://www.jessykoeiman.com/?p=14926. Accessed February 19, 2024.

Roseman, S. R., et al. (2013). Antropología y nuevas ruralidades. *Gazeta de Antropología, 29*(2). https://doi.org/10.30827/Digibug.28509

Simon, N. (2010). *The participatory museum*. MUSEUM 2.0. https://participatorymuseum.org. Accessed February 18, 2024.

Soini, K., & Dessein, J. (2016). Culture-sustainability relation: Towards a conceptual framework. *Sustainability, 8*(2), 167. https://doi.org/10.3390/su8020167

Thaler, R. H., & Sunstein, C. R. (2009). *Nudge: Improving decisions about health, wealth, and happiness*. Penguin Books.

United Nations. (2024). *Universal Declaration of Human Rights*. https://www.un.org/en/about-us/universal-declaration-of-human-rights. Accessed February 19, 2024.

Walker-Kunhe, D. (2005). *Invitation to the party: Building bridges to the arts, culture, and communities*. Theatre Communication Group, Inc.

Chapter 9
The Impact of Platform Economy on Spanish Sun and Beach Destinations: A Case Study of Free Tours

Asunción Fernández-Villarán, Jorge Rivera-García, and Ricardo Pastor-Ruiz

Abstract This chapter examines the impact of the platform economy on Spanish sun and beach destinations, focusing on free tours. As the collaborative economy reshapes tourism, platform-mediated free tours have gained attention but raised concerns about overcrowding and mass tourism in city centres. While much research on the platform economy centres on accommodation, studies on free tours remain scarce. This research addresses this gap by analysing the spatial impacts of free tours in mature sun and beach destinations and comparing the findings with previous studies. The analysis examines GuruWalk, Spain's largest free tour platform, investigating tour concentration in space and time and the regulatory frameworks in the selected destinations. The findings highlight how platform-mediated free tours contribute to overcrowding in already saturated areas. Additionally, the chapter underscores the importance of local governance in regulating free tours, though few national examples are noted. This chapter offers insights for destination management organisations and policymakers to address the challenges of the platform economy and promote sustainable tourism in sun and beach destinations.

A. Fernández-Villarán
University of Deusto, Bilbao, Spain
e-mail: asun.fvillaran@deusto.es

J. Rivera-García (✉)
Faculty of Economics and Business Studies, Universitat Oberta de Catalunya (UOC), Barcelona, Spain
e-mail: jriveraga@uoc.edu

R. Pastor-Ruiz
Universidad Internacional de La Rioja, Logroño, Spain
e-mail: ricardo.pastor@unir.net

L. Ronda et al. (eds.), *Leisure and Human Development*, Human Well-Being Research and Policy Making, https://doi.org/10.1007/978-3-031-90778-4_9

9.1 Introduction

The rapid growth and high valuations of companies like Airbnb and Uber have drawn significant attention to the impact of the sharing economy on tourism (Dredge & Gyimóthy, 2015). Similarly, the activity of platform-mediated free tours in the tourism sector, although more fragmented and lacking a central platform, is as notable as Airbnb within its domain and mirrors the model of the short-term accommodation platform. Koerts (2017) explains that the relationship between free tours and paid guided tours is comparable to that between Airbnb and the hotel industry.

Platform-mediated free city tours, also known as free tours or free walking tours, have become an increasingly popular trend in tourism, sparking a burgeoning debate about their potential effects on the sustainability of tourist destinations. These tours are guided experiences distinguished by two main features: (1) They do not have a set price, instead, participants are encouraged to give a tip at the end of the tour; and (2) the guide often lacks official certification as a local tourist guide (García & Ruiz, 2022). Free walking tours are a prevalent phenomenon, especially in cities with a high volume of tourists. The distribution of free guided tours through digital platforms, within the framework of the collaborative economy, has generated increasing interest in the field of tourism (see de Waal & Arets, 2022). Among other reasons, it contributes to the marketing, image, and visibility of destinations, especially in cities with the highest volume of cultural tourism.

A review of the literature shows that free tours have been studied from different perspectives. Some authors analyse the relationship between the organisers of free guided tours and tourists (Rátz, 2016), highlighting the research line that emphasises the role of new technologies, especially social media, in such interactions (Widtfeldt Meged & Zillinger, 2018). These studies are conducted either within the framework of the concepts and principles proposed by evolutionary economic geography, such as knowledge and innovation (Leal Londoño & Font Medina, 2018), or on concepts of geolocation, place, and narrative (Nilsson & Zillinger, 2020) and, especially, on the controversy that its current model is generated about the initial collaborative economy (Leal Londoño & Font Medina, 2018).

One consequence of the surge in free guided tours is their contribution to the overcrowding and substantial tourist influx in city centres. The concept of overtourism is linked to the discomfort felt by residents and the social opposition to tourism (Smith et al., 2019). This social issue, rooted in the expansion of global mobility (Cheer et al., 2019; UNWTO, 2019a), is exacerbated by the growing ease of access to new destinations, the proliferation of short-term rental services like Airbnb, and tourists' desire to experience authentic local life (Smith et al., 2019). Nevertheless, free tours have not been thoroughly examined. Morales-Pérez et al. (2020) explore the socio-spatial negative effects on tourist destinations, such as rising rental prices, population displacement, and the occupation of public and private spaces, while de Waal and Arets (2022) emphasise social impacts. Most research on the tourism platform economy focuses on the accommodation sector, analysing the social, economic, and environmental impacts of different types of accommodation in large cities (Richards et al., 2020). To date, no studies have addressed the contribution of free tours to spatial impacts like crowding or overcrowding at tourist destinations.

Academic interest in free guided tours has primarily focused on large cities known for their cultural tourism where the impact has been most significant, such as Berlin, Amsterdam, and Barcelona. Moreover, the phenomenon of free tours can influence the image of a destination, which is evident in the way this activity is marketed online (Leal Londoño & Font Medina, 2018). Similar to the major cities where short-term holiday rentals have surged uncontrollably, cultural destinations are experiencing a notable increase in the prevalence of free tours.

There are few studies on the impact of the platform economy, with most of them focusing on the case of accommodation platforms, such as Airbnb, and concentrating their research on urban destinations. In these studies, it is observed that the impact varies significantly depending on the type of destination analysed. In line with this, a previous study conducted by the authors of this chapter (Rivera-García et al., 2023), which focused on cultural destinations, concluded that the impact of free tours depended on the destination's life cycle phase. However, there is a gap in the literature regarding the collaborative economy in more traditional and medium-sized tourist destinations. Therefore, this chapter focuses on sun and beach destinations to better understand how the shared economy affects different types of tourist destinations.

As a result, the main objective of this research is to expand knowledge in an area that has not been studied adequately to date, analysing how this activity affects sun and beach environments. The specific objectives are to identify the socio-spatial impacts produced by this activity in sun and beach destinations. This includes verifying the hypothesis that platform-mediated free tours contribute to increased tourist agglomerations and the overcrowding of sun and beach destinations. Additionally, the research aims to examine the importance of local governance in the regulation of free tours according to each phase of the destination's life cycle.

Empirically, 22 mature sun and beach destinations in Spain have been selected to analyse the socio-spatial impact of free tours. The results help to understand the differences that this activity generates in each destination.

9.2 Conceptual Framework

9.2.1 The Platform Economy in Tourism: From Airbnb to Free Tours

As the sharing economy evolved, it transitioned into the platform economy, dominated by large digital platforms that control market access (Pastor & Rivera-García, 2020). Platforms can be described as marketplaces accessible via computers and mobile devices, where users can directly book services from providers, theoretically bypassing traditional tourism intermediaries. Thus, platforms function as digital infrastructures that enable interaction between two or more groups (García & Ruiz, 2022). These platforms use network effects to expand rapidly across sectors like accommodation, transport, and freelance work (Kenney & Zysman, 2016). Unlike the sharing economy, the platform economy relies on data analytics, algorithms, and substantial capital, increasing consumer efficiency and convenience but also raising market concentration issues and regulatory challenges (Srnicek, 2017). Online short-term holiday rental platforms are among the best-known in the tourism industry, having transformed not only the accommodation sector but also global travel. The impact of the platform economy on tourism has attracted attention primarily because of the speed at which it is growing and the valuations of companies, such as Airbnb and Uber (Dredge & Gyimóthy, 2015).

As the discussion surrounding the collaborative economy model progressed and short-term holiday rentals dominated the scene, experts began to focus on the economic and social implications of platforms in other tourism sectors, such as free tours. The tourism activity of platform-mediated free tours, while much more atomised and without any platform as prominent as Airbnb in its sector, replicates the accommodation platform model. The concept of free guided walking tours was first established in Berlin in 2003 and has, since, spread internationally (Widtfeldt Meged & Zillinger, 2018). Academic interest in free guided tours has focused on large cities where cultural tourism is predominant and where the tourism impact has been greatest, such as Berlin, Amsterdam, and Barcelona, where the volume of tourism is particularly significant (García & Ruiz, 2022). Free guided tours can be defined as very similar to paid tours (Koerts, 2017; Leal Londoño & Font Medina, 2018; Widtfeldt Meged & Zillinger, 2018), except for two main factors. First, there is no pre-established price. However, tipping is always recommended if one enjoys a tour (García & Ruiz, 2022). Second, guides are mostly young, with less than 10 years of experience in the profession, with many of them without any official accreditation (Navalón-García & Mínguez, 2021). Koerts (2017) summarises that the free tour is perhaps to the guided tour what Airbnb is to the hotel industry.

9.2.2 *Impact of Free Tours on Destinations*

Scholars have initiated analyses on how this emerging phenomenon in tourism might impact local economies and conventional tour operators. Some researchers, such as Oskam and Boswijk (2016), contended that free tours have the potential to generate positive economic impacts in cities by attracting more visitors and boosting spending in local businesses. However, others have highlighted that these benefits may not be evenly distributed and that free tours may exacerbate existing inequalities within the tourism industry, leading to a concentration of power among a few large platforms, to the detriment of small and medium-sized enterprises (Koerts, 2017).

In addition, the phenomenon of free tours could impact the image of the destination, which is reflected in the way this activity is marketed online (Leal Londoño & Font Medina, 2018). Similar to the situation in several major cities where short-term holiday rentals have proliferated uncontrollably, cultural destinations are experiencing an increased prevalence of free tours.

In recent years, terms such as *tourismphobia*, *overexploitation*, and *overtourism* have gained a presence in the academic glossary and public discourse. Overtourism is considered a turning point for tourist destinations, marking a new stage in the understanding of the impacts of tourism (Namberger et al., 2019). This concept describes the problems that arise in destinations due to the high and growing influx of visitors (Blázquez-Salom et al., 2021). However, there is some confusion among researchers regarding terms related to over-tourism. It is essential to distinguish between density, overcrowding, saturation, and overtourism. Density is an indicator that measures tourist activity, while overcrowding is a psychological response to this density, reflecting the overload of people in an area that can affect both resources and economic or social objectives, impacting both mature and emerging destinations. Saturation refers to a negative impact perceived as undesirable by tourists and residents (Peeters et al., 2021). Overtourism, in turn, describes a situation where the impact of tourism exceeds the physical, ecological, social, economic, psychological, and/or political capacity of a place (Peeters et al., 2021).

The literature review reveals that research on the impact of the platform economy has focused on two aspects of over-tourism. Firstly, it is associated with the number of visitors, which is related to tourist density, identified as the main cause of overtourism and the most relevant indicator for its evaluation (Peeters et al., 2021). In our context, the number of guided tours available is the basic reference to measure the density of this activity. Secondly, although density is often a necessary precursor to saturation, according to Stokols (1972), it is not sufficient on its own. In addition to the number of visitors and tourist congestion, the relevance of factors such as seasonality, spatio-temporal concentration, type of use, and tourist behaviour is considered (Koerts, 2017; UNWTO, 2019b). That is, the impacts of tourism activities depend not only on the number of tourists but also, and possibly more significantly, on their behaviour and the characteristics of the local offer. The concentration of tourists in the main points of interest (Koerts, 2017; Nilsson, 2020) emerges as a key indicator for measuring spatiotemporal concentration.

9.2.3 The Role of Tourism Governance

Some of the quantitative effects of the increase in tourists in urban centres and central areas include congestion, noise and waste generation, exploitation of environmental resources, and the consumption of potentially scarce resources such as water, electricity, and gas. Additionally, there is real estate speculation and a rise in the cost of living (Martín et al., 2018). The impacts of overtourism on urban areas are multifaceted and go beyond mere physical congestion. Noise pollution, often intensified by increased tourist activity, disrupts the daily lives of residents and can lead to long-term health issues such as stress and sleep disturbances. The accumulation of waste presents significant challenges for local sanitation services, which may struggle to keep up with the influx of tourists. This can lead to unsanitary and unattractive conditions, deteriorating the quality of life for residents and the overall appeal of the destination.

The exploitation of environmental resources is another critical issue. The high demand for water, electricity, and gas by tourists can strain local supplies, especially in areas already facing scarcity. This excessive consumption can lead to resource depletion, higher costs for residents, and increased pressure on infrastructure. Moreover, the speculative real estate market driven by tourism can inflate property prices, making it difficult for locals to afford housing and contributing to the displacement of long-term residents (Cohen & Hopkins, 2019). According to Pasquinelli and Trunfio (2020) and Morales-Pérez et al. (2020), there are three governance approaches to mitigate the negative impacts of excessive tourism in cities. Firstly, the normative approach involves public administration actions that can include taxation, activity control, licensing, or restricting access to certain areas. For example, cities like Venice and Amsterdam have implemented tourist taxes and entry fees to manage the flow of visitors and generate revenue for local maintenance and infrastructure improvements (Pasquinelli & Trunfio, 2020). Secondly, the management approach includes non-coercive actions aimed at developing destinations in ways that limit pressure on the most affected areas. This involves engaging all stakeholders in the co-creation of a destination, developing alternative itineraries or experiences, and encouraging a more even distribution of tourists across different areas. By promoting lesser-known attractions and off-peak travel times, cities can alleviate congestion in hotspots and distribute the economic benefits of tourism more widely (Morales-Pérez et al., 2020). Finally, the marketing approach includes communication strategies aimed at promoting responsible attitudes and reducing pressure on the city. Effective marketing campaigns can raise awareness about the impacts of over-tourism and encourage behaviours that minimise these effects. For instance, the “Be a Local” campaign in Barcelona encourages tourists to respect local customs and environments, aiming to foster a more harmonious relationship between visitors and residents (Morales-Pérez et al., 2020).

9.2.4 Sun and Beach Tourism

Sun and beach tourism represents one of the most popular segments of tourism markets (Femeniás Rosselló, 2019). This form of tourism, also known as coastal tourism, encompasses a wide array of tourism, leisure, and recreational activities that occur in coastal regions. As defined by Bigné et al. (2007), citing Hall (2001), it includes sectors such as accommodation, catering, food, and second homes; infrastructure like shops; and providers of leisure and water-based activities such as sailing, marine ecotourism, cruises, swimming, fishing, diving, and more. Sun and beach tourists primarily seek relaxation and recreation, falling under the category of leisure tourism (Bigné et al., 2007).

Sun and beach destinations, which have traditionally been linked to a Fordist production model and mass tourism, are not immune to shifts in tourism demand.

These destinations also grapple with the challenges of seasonality and modernisation, particularly in the case of mature destinations. Furthermore, they must navigate the repercussions of crises and alterations in their surrounding environment.

The appeal of the Sea, Sun, and Sand ("3S"), along with scenic beauty and recreational activities, is driving the steady global growth of coastal tourism (Lithgow et al., 2019). In locations where cultural attractions and activities are in close geographical proximity to the coast, 3S tourism and cultural tourism—initially separate segments of the tourism market—can be developed in a complementary manner (Khakzad, 2018).

The substantial annual influx of tourists raises concerns about both the sustainability and the carrying capacity of these destinations. Economically, these areas are heavily reliant on tourism and have now reached their social and environmental limits. This situation exemplifies the phenomenon of overtourism, which is marked by issues such as overcrowding (Insch, 2020; Peeters et al., 2021).

Nonetheless, traditional sun and beach tourism has seen a general downturn (Aguiló et al., 2005). As a countermeasure, some destinations have revamped their tourism strategies to incorporate principles of sustainable development. This form of tourism should be viewed as a multidimensional phenomenon. As per Prebensen et al. (2010), its "body" dimension is defined by the sun and warmth, while the "mind" dimension consists of two primary elements: escapism and culture/nature. The satisfaction of tourists largely hinges on effectively addressing this complexity, that is, the motivations tied to both the body and mind.

While this variety of tourism brings a multitude of advantages to host destinations, it also presents a series of challenges. These include environmental degradation or loss of competitiveness, among others. Given this backdrop, it becomes compelling to explore the influence exerted by free guided tours. These tours, often seen as a cost-effective way for tourists to explore a destination, could have a significant impact on the local economy, environment, and social fabric. Understanding this impact could provide valuable insights for stakeholders, helping them balance the benefits of tourism with sustainable practices and responsible growth.

9.3 Methodology

This study employs a mixed-methods approach, incorporating both quantitative and qualitative analyses. The methodology involves internet data analysis and participant observation. Data were sourced from the Guruwalk platform, selected for being the leading provider of free tours and the only platform offering all tours for free (Gutiérrez-Duarte & Roldán-Martínez, 2020). Guruwalk provided information on tour routes, tour frequency, and user feedback. Secondary data were also utilised, offering insights into tourist infrastructure and spatial usage in selected destinations.

The study focuses on sun and beach destinations, selecting the top 22 beach destinations in Spain based on their popularity and the number of visitors they receive annually, according to official figures from the Annual Review of the Municipal Register (INE, 2024). The destinations analysed were: Benidorm, Palma, Calviá, Torremolinos, Lloret de Mar, Málaga, Alicante, Donostia/San Sebastián, Roquetas de Mar, Peñíscola, Cartagena, A Coruña, Gijón, Almería, Sitges, Cádiz, El Puerto de Santa María, Castellón de la Plana, Elche, Llanes, Ribadeo, and Viveiro, and are shown in Fig. 9.1.

As observed in Table 9.1, the destinations are located on various coasts, including Costa Blanca, Mallorca, Costa del Sol, Costa Brava, Basque Coast, Costa de Almería, Costa del Azahar, Costa Cálida, Costa da Morte, Green Coast, Costa del Garraf, Costa de la Luz, and Costa de Lugo. Many of these destinations are famous for their beaches, promenades, and unique natural landscapes such as cliffs, natural parks, and estuaries. The destinations offer a variety of cultural attractions, including castles, museums, historical sites, cathedrals, and old towns. Some destinations are also known for their nightlife, water sports, and local cuisine, such as tapas and seafood.

The next step is to identify the variables and indicators to analyse each of the previously identified variables and indicators:

- Tourist density is measured by the number of tours offered.
- Temporal concentration is measured by the frequency, day of the week, and schedule.
- Tourism policy is measured by the existence of guided tours regulation.

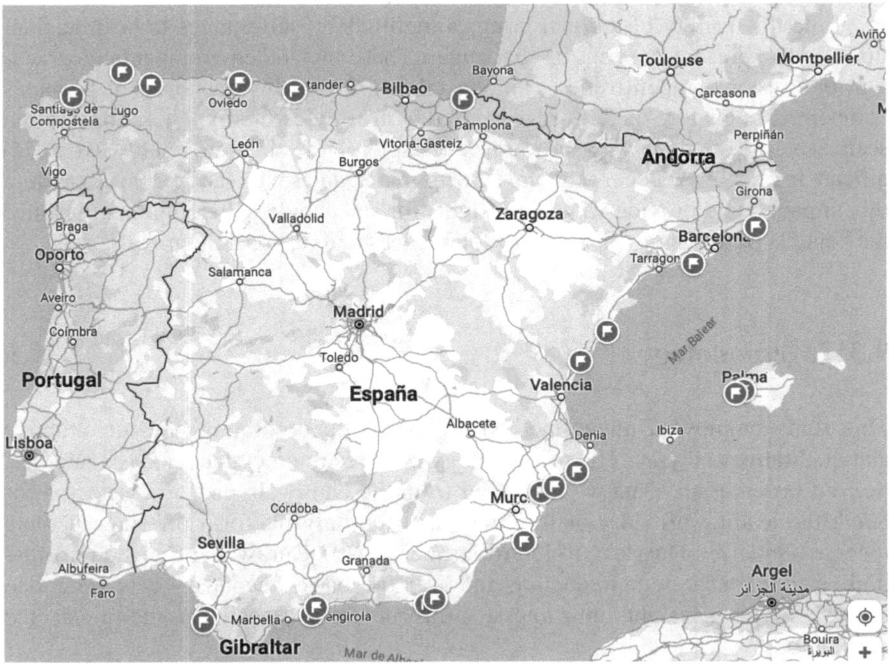

Fig. 9.1 Destinations analysed

Table 9.1 Tourist attractions in selected destinations

Destination	Coast	Natural resources	Cultural resources
Benidorm	White coast	Beaches	Nightlife and skyline, historic Old Town, Balcón del Mediterráneo
Palma	Mallorca	Waterfront promenade	Palma Cathedral (La Seu), Bellver Castle, and old city
Calviá	Mallorca	Beaches	Historic village of Calviá and water sports
Torremolinos	Costa del sol	Beaches	Lively bars and La Carihuela fishing district. Crocodile Park and old town
Lloret de Mar	Costa Brava	Cliffs	Historic Santa Clotilde Gardens. Castle of Sant Joan
Málaga	Costa del Sol	Beach promenade	Alcazaba Fortress, Picasso Museum, and Atarazanas Market and tapas in the city centre
Alicante	Costa Blanca	Postiguet Beach	Santa Bárbara Castle, Explanada de España promenade, Barrio de la Santa Cruz (colourful houses and narrow streets)
Donostia/San Sebastián	Costa Vasca (Basque Coast)	La Concha Beach, Ondarreta Beach	Old Town (Parte Vieja), and Kursaal Congress Centre. Pintxos (Basque tapas) in local bars
Roquetas de Mar	Costa de Almería	Playa Serena and Punta Entinas-Sabinar Natural Park	Castillo de Santa Ana, Water activities and historic sites
Peñíscola	Costa del Azahar	Beaches	Peñíscola Castle (used in the film "El Cid"), and old town
Cartagena	Costa Cálida		Roman ruins, including Roman Theatre and Punic Wall. Naval Museum and harbour
A Coruña	Costa da Morte	Riazor Beach. Panoramic views from Monte de San Pedro	Tower of Hercules (a Roman lighthouse), historic Old Town
Gijón	Costa Verde (Green Coast)	San Lorenzo Beach, Waterfront promenade	Elogio del Horizonte sculpture, Laboral Ciudad de la Cultura, and botanical garden
Almería	Costa de Almería	Cabo de Gata-Níjar Natural Park. Desert-like landscapes and beaches	Alcazaba fortress, Cathedral of Almería,
Sitges	Costa del Garraf	Beaches	Nightlife. Church of Sant Bartomeu i Santa Tecla
Cádiz	Costa de la Luz	La Caleta Beach	Historic Old Town, Cathedral of Cádiz, and Lively atmosphere, seafood, and flamenco music

(continued)

Table 9.1 (continued)

Destination	Coast	Natural resources	Cultural resources
El Puerto de Santa María	Costa de la Luz	Beaches along the Bay of Cádiz	Sherry bodegas, Castle of San Marcos
Castellón de la Plana	Costa del Azahar	Grao de Castellón beach area	Fadrí bell tower, Llotja del Cànem
Elche	Costa Blanca	Palm groves (El Palmeral)	Basilica of Santa María and Mystery Play of Elche (Misteri d'Elx)
Llanes	Costa Verde (Green Coast)	Cliffs	Cubes of Memory (Cubos de la Memoria) and historic old town
Ribadeo	Costa de Lugo	Playa de las Catedrales (Cathedrals Beach), and estuary landscape	Historic Ponte dos Santos
Viveiro	Costa de Lugo	Viveiro estuary	Castle of San Felipe

For each destination, the context indicators, defined in the previous section, help interpret the data obtained. For each city, a data file has been created that collects the spatio-temporal variables of each route: (1) Frequency/day; (2) Operating days; (3) Departure times; (4) Visited points (POI). Microsoft Excel is used to filter the data, so we can know, for spatial concentration, the frequencies of the different meeting points and visited points in each population, and for temporal concentration, the number of visits offered each day and hour of the week.

Table 9.2 presents information about the destinations analysed. Firstly, the most visited destinations are Benidorm, Palma, and Calvià, with visitor counts of 2,232,959, 2,488,914, and 1,693,096 respectively. These locations attract a significant number of tourists each year, making them popular choices for travellers. In terms of the ratio of visitors to inhabitants, Peníscola/Peñíscola, Calvià, and Benidorm stand out. Peníscola/Peñíscola has an impressive 45.46 visitors for each inhabitant, followed by Calvià with 31.85, and Benidorm with 30.87. On the other hand, Alacant/Alicante, Elx/Elche, and Castelló de la Plana have the lowest ratios, with 0.43, 0.90, and 1.35 visitors per inhabitant respectively. When we look at seasonality, which is the percentage of visitors in July and August, Llanes, Roquetas de Mar, and Ribadeo have the highest figures at 38.53%, 37.25%, and 36.91% respectively. This suggests that these destinations are particularly popular during the summer months. Conversely, Málaga, Alacant/Alicante, and Elx/Elche have the lowest seasonality figures, indicating a more even distribution of visitors throughout the year. Lastly, it's worth noting that most of the destinations are considered "Smart Destinations". However, Alacant/Alicante, Roquetas de Mar, Cartagena, Coruña, A, Cádiz, Puerto de Santa María, El, Castelló de la Plana, Elx/Elche, and Ribadeo do not fall into this category.

The data sample includes an analysis of tour routes, points of interest, and the temporal and spatial distribution of tourists across various destinations. Data collection instruments included the Guruwalk website for obtaining data on tours. Additionally, direct observation was conducted to assess the influence of free tours on the use of public spaces in some of these locations. Descriptive statistics were

Table 9.2 Contextual indicators

Destination	Number of visitors	Inhabitants	Visitors/ inhabitants	Smart destination	Seasonality = % (Visitors in July and august)/total
Benidorm	2,232,959	72,342	30.87	Yes	23.41
Palma	2,488,914	423,350	5.88	Yes	27.17
Calvià	1,693,096	53,162	31.85	Yes	33.92
Torremolinos	1,199,912	70,434	17.04	Yes	25.20
Lloret de Mar	1,131,785	41,559	27.23	Yes	30.72
Málaga	1,517,239	586,384	2.59	Yes	18.05
Alacant/ Alicante	830,046	1,950,357	0.43	No	19.94
Donostia/San Sebastián	916,649	188,743	4.86	Yes	20.26
Roquetas de Mar	507,291	106,510	4.76	No	37.25
Peníscola/ Peñíscola	384,123	8449	45.46	Yes	29.01
Cartagena	332,192	218,050	1.52	No	28.84
Coruña, A	466,221	247,376	1.88	No	20.55
Gijón	394,966	268,313	1.47	Yes	24.16
Almería	348,073	200,578	1.74	Yes	23.89
Sitges	267,949	31,954	8.39	Yes	23.28
Cádiz	287,411	111,811	2.57	No	21.52
Puerto de Santa María, El	213,847	89,813	2.38	No	23.16
Castelló de la Plana	238,690	176,238	1.35	No	21.70
Elx/Elche	214,380	238,293	0.90	No	20.40
Llanes	121,638	13,524	8.99	Yes	38.53
Ribadeo	61,623	9828	6.27	No	36.91
Viveiro	40,280	15,221	2.65	No	27.63

employed to examine the frequency of tours, the number of participants, and areas with high and low activity.

9.4 Results

The main objective of this initial analysis was to conduct a study of the spatio-temporal concentrations caused by free tours. For this purpose, the guided tours offered through the GuruWalk platform, between the 15th and 21st of July, 2024, were analysed. The analysed data include the number of free tours offered for each destination and, given that each offer includes several visits throughout the week and at different times, the number of groups offered each week has been calculated.

Notably, Cadiz stands out significantly with 47 free tours per week. This number not only places Cadiz at the top of the list but also suggests that the city has a robust tourist infrastructure and a high demand for guided tours. Cadiz, with its rich history and cultural attractions, seems to leverage these qualities to attract and retain tourists through a wide range of tours.

Next, Malaga ranks with 31 free tours per week. Malaga, known for its Mediterranean climate and its combination of history and modernity, seems to maintain an appropriate balance between the supply and demand of free tours. The presence of 31 tours per week indicates a strong but manageable influx of tourists seeking to explore the city through these services.

Donostia/San Sebastian and Palma also show notable figures, with 28 and 24 free tours per week respectively. Both cities are known for their coastal beauty and their cultural and gastronomic attractions. The number of tours in these cities suggests that they are well-established tourist destinations and that visitors actively seek structured ways to experience their offerings.

On the other hand, cities like Gijon, Alicante, and Almeria present a more modest offer, with 21, 15, and 12 tours per week respectively. These figures reflect cities with significant tourist potential but perhaps with a lower comparative influx or a lower dependence on free tours as a method of tourist exploration.

It is particularly interesting to observe that several cities, such as Calvia, Roquetas de Mar, Ribadeo, and Viveiro, do not offer free tours in the analysed period. These data may indicate a variety of factors: lower tourist influx, dependence on other types of tourism, or a less developed tourist infrastructure.

In terms of variability, there is a notable disparity in the number of free tours offered per week, from the 47 tours in Cadiz to the 0 in several other cities. This variability can be interpreted as a reflection of the diversity in tourist popularity and tourist infrastructure of Spanish sun and beach destinations.

In short, the distribution of free tours in the analysed Spanish cities reflects a wide range of tourist infrastructures and market demands. From the high offer in cities such as Cadiz to the absence of free tours in cities like Viveiro, these data offer us an interesting view of how sun and beach tourism is structured and distributed in Spain. The disparity in the numbers suggests that while some cities are highly oriented towards guided tourism, others may depend more on other types of attractions or have different tourist management models. It is important to underline that metropolises such as Cádiz, Málaga, Donostia/San Sebastián, and A Coruña are the epicentres of the guided tour offerings. These cities, due to their size and tourist appeal, present a high concentration of these types of services. However, in contrast, we find towns like Viveiro or Ribadeo, where the presence of guided tours is practically non-existent. Additionally, there are popular tourist destinations like Benidorm, Roquetas de Mar, Sitges, or Torremolinos where, surprisingly, the offering of guided tours is scarce. This analysis highlights the disparity in the distribution of these tourist services, opening an interesting field of study to understand the dynamics and trends of the sector.

One of the hypotheses we set out at the beginning of this research was the direct relationship between the volume of visitors and the number of free tours offered.

Figure 9.2 shows the destinations analysed in order of importance in terms of the number of visitors (in thousands) and the frequency of free tours in the same order. The number of free tours offered in the case study destinations ranges from between 0 visits (Roquetas de Mar, Ribadeo, Viveiro) to 47 (Cádiz). The relationship between the number of free visits offered and the total number of visitors to each destination presents an intriguing dynamic. When comparing these two variables, it is clear that destinations that offer more free tours do not necessarily coincide with those that receive more visitors. Therefore, this hypothesis is not confirmed.

Figure 9.3 shows the temporal concentration of tours analysed. They are based on the assumption that all tours offered by GuruWalk operate on the dates and times mentioned. The number of GuruWalk groups that operate at the times indicated on the x-axis is shown on the ordinate axis. The morning (9—12) is confirmed as the most popular time slot, followed by early afternoons (16–18), and late afternoons (18–20). In other words, the concentrations are in the early and late hours of the day, which is reasonable, given the high temperatures during the period analysed.

The distribution of free tours by time slot reveals interesting patterns about the tourist offers and tourist preferences.

It is observed that the morning slot (9–12) is the most popular for free tours. Cádiz leads with 24 tours, followed by Málaga and Donostia/San Sebastián with 11 tours each. This trend may be due to more pleasant temperatures and higher energy levels of tourists in the morning. In the midday slot (12–14), activity decreases considerably, probably due to lunchtime and the hot weather in some regions. Málaga stands out with 9 tours, but many cities do not offer tours during this time. In the early afternoon slot (14–16), very few tours are offered. Only Donostia/San Sebastián has a significant number (4 tours), which may indicate greater flexibility in its tourist offer. In the early evening slot (16–18), activity increases slightly. Palma and Gijón have 8 tours each, suggesting a preference for exploring after the

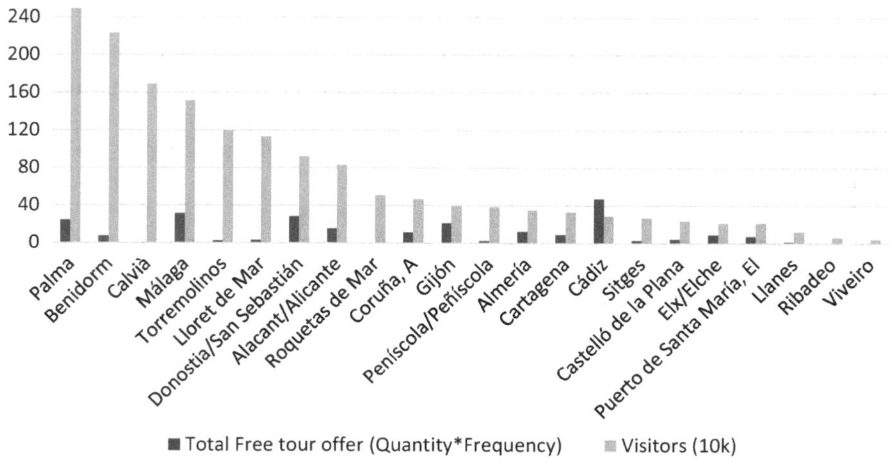

Fig. 9.2 Number of visitors and number of free tours offered

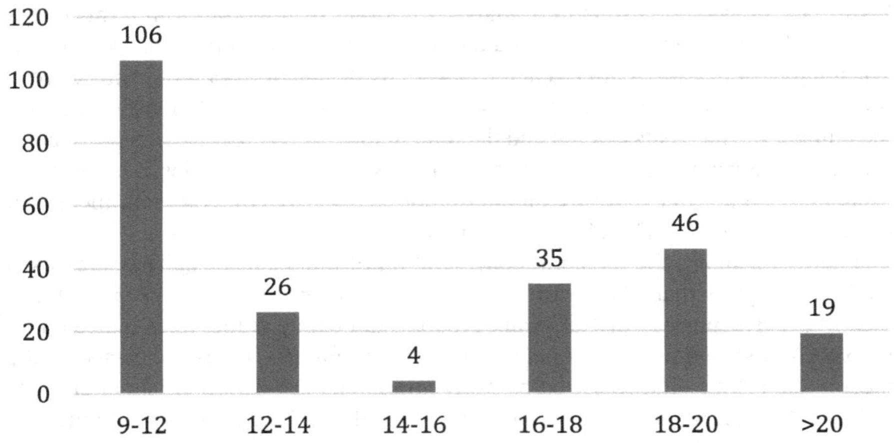

Fig. 9.3 Time frequency of free tours offered

siesta and before dinner. The late afternoon slot (18–20) is also popular, with Palma offering 8 tours and Cádiz 6 tours. Natural light and cooler temperatures may be attractive factors for tourists. The night slot (>20) experiences a decrease in the number of tours offered. The cities with the highest number of tours in this slot are Cádiz with 5 tours and Alicante with 4 tours.

Regarding the regulation of free tours in the analysed destinations, there is a direct relationship between the availability of free tours and the existence of regulation. Cities that have a larger offer of free tours have begun to develop regulations to control the groups of tourists that circulate through the city. This is the case in Alicante, Malaga, Palma, or Donostia/San Sebastián. These regulations limit the number of people per group, and the hours for the provision of guide service, and aim to limit the presence of groups and promote a situation that harmonises this presence and tourist activity with coexistence with neighbours.

Destinations such as San Sebastián have developed a decalogue aimed at tour guides to preserve the quality of experiences for both visitors and citizens and thus contribute to making Donostia a more sustainable and pleasant place. Among these recommendations, the limitation of the maximum size of the groups stands out, which has become mandatory under this regulation.

In addition, in Málaga, Palma, or San Sebastian, any tour guide company that wants to conduct guided tours in the city's public streets will have to carry out a procedure, which is a "Responsible Declaration" in which the company or the guide commits to comply with a series of conditions to carry out the activity, among which includes the commitment not to guide groups larger than 25 people. Guided tours in Alicante require prior registration at the Tourist Information Office, up to 2 h before the visit.

In any case, and for the regulations to be effective, it is important to monitor, measure their consequences, see the cases that arise, and analyze them with the sector. It is important to measure to continue improving.

9.5 Discussion and Conclusions

Despite the rapid rise of the collaborative economy and the role that the internet plays in tourist distribution, the literature review aligns with the statement by Rivera-García et al. (2023) attesting that such activity, although emerging in the tourism sector, has been minimally researched to date. Hence the originality of this work and the contribution to the literature on the subject.

The analysis of the data reveals a curious aspect of tourism: The availability of platform-mediated free tours does not directly correlate with the total number of visitors at each tourist destination. This essay aims to explore the factors contributing to this lack of correlation.

One significant factor is the exclusion of these tours from traditional tour packages. Platform-mediated free tours, despite their potential benefits, are often not incorporated into traditional tour packages. This exclusion might lead tourists to overlook these tours when planning their trips, thereby affecting the correlation between the availability of free tours and the total number of visitors. Another crucial factor lies in the varied tourist preferences. The tourism industry caters to a diverse range of preferences and interests. For instance, sun and beach destinations are particularly popular among traditional and family tourists. These tourists, seeking a peaceful family vacation, often opt for a second home or stay at the homes of relatives or friends. Their primary motivation is rest, leading them to engage minimally in other activities. They also tend to choose the same destination for several years (Noguera Tur et al., 2015). On the other hand, free tours attract those who value local insights and have limited time for exploration (Guruwalk, 2024). This variation in tourist preferences can contribute to the observed lack of correlation.

The length of stay also plays a role in this context. Free tours, with their efficiency in providing essential highlights, may be more appealing to visitors with limited time. Therefore, these tours are especially beneficial for short stays, further complicating the correlation with the total number of visitors (Guruwalk, 2024). The destination type and cultural attractions significantly influence the popularity of platform-mediated free tours. The type of destination and its cultural offerings can vary the appeal of free tours. This study aligns with the perspectives of various authors who assert that, despite extensive efforts by coastal destinations to reposition and reinvent themselves, the allure of sun and sand remains a fundamental aspect of tourism in these areas (Marin et al., 2021).

In this regard, the authors' prior research on the influence and impacts of free tours in cultural urban destinations found that mature destinations experience more significant impacts, including tourist overcrowding in city centres and increased social responses leading to specific regulations (Rivera-García et al., 2023). Conversely, destinations in the early stages of tourism development do not see significant impacts or regulatory concerns. Authorities in these areas often view free tours positively, associating them with attracting tourists and promoting them through their tourism institutions. However, the results of this study do not allow us to reach the same conclusions in the case of sun and beach destinations, confirming the theory that suggests the impact of platforms (in their case, accommodation) depends on the type of destination.

In conclusion, while the data indicate a lack of direct correlation between the availability of free tours and the total number of visitors, this phenomenon can be attributed to several complex and interrelated factors. Understanding these factors can provide valuable insights for tourism stakeholders to enhance the appeal and effectiveness of free tours.

The impact of free tours extends beyond the economy, encompassing significant social implications as well. On one hand, free tours can democratise access to cultural and educational experiences, enabling a broader audience to participate in tourism activities without financial barriers. This can enrich the cultural experience for both visitors and residents, fostering a greater understanding and appreciation of local history and culture. However, concerns also arise regarding how free tours may affect the quality of life for residents. The influx of large numbers of tourists can lead to congestion issues, increased local prices, and disruptions to the daily life of communities.

Just as smart cities have emerged to face management challenges, smart destinations have arisen to address their management challenges (Gretzel, 2018). These challenges undoubtedly include overtourism in certain spaces. As we have already indicated, overtourism refers to its negative impact on the quality of life perceived by residents and/or the quality of the experience perceived by visitors, as well as the fact that physical, ecological, social, economic, psychological, and/or political capacity thresholds are exceeded (Peeters et al., 2021).

Additionally, the lack of regulation in these tours can result in less sustainable and responsible practices, negatively impacting the local environment and urban infrastructure. Integrating sustainability into the platform-mediated free tour model presents a crucial challenge. The absence of a formal payment structure can hinder the implementation of sustainable and responsible practices. To mitigate these effects, free tour platforms need to adopt policies that promote sustainability, such as limiting group sizes, collaborating with local providers who adhere to sustainable practices, and educating tourists on responsible behaviour.

Careful management and appropriate regulation are fundamental to maximising the benefits and minimising the negative impacts, thereby ensuring balanced and sustainable tourism development. Since 2020, prompted by the COVID-19 pandemic, numerous countries have been adopting sustainable measures in their cities to create more habitable environments (Punzón & Pastor, 2020). Concurrently, the global tourism sector's growth has intensified concerns about over-tourism, which prioritises metrics such as visitor numbers and expenditure, often advocated by Destination Management Organisations (DMOs) (García & Ruiz, 2022). These organisations are traditionally viewed as pivotal to destination growth, judged by metrics like visitor arrivals and spending, once synonymous with success (Morgan et al., 2012). However, DMOs now face a dichotomy: Despite continuing to use these metrics, they are increasingly inadequate for accurate performance measurement (Dredge, 2016). DMOs need to employ legislative and management tools during the planning and management phases to ensure equitable distribution of tourism benefits and the implementation of sustainable practices that support resource regeneration. The market for sustainable tourism and ecotourism presents unique commercialisation challenges compared to standard mass tourism products. DMOs are crucial in balancing diverse interests to foster sustainable tourism destinations. They also spearhead campaigns to raise awareness of climate change risks and mitigate the tourism industry's environmental impact (García & Ruiz, 2022). Additionally, DMOs support endogenous sustainability, adaptive management, and social learning strategies through non-linear and integrative approaches. Although promoting responsible quality tourism might reduce visitor numbers, it is vital for long-term sustainability. The primary challenge for destination marketing is to unite all individual partners and pool resources to develop an integrated marketing mix and delivery system.

To summarise, while free tours offer flexibility and spontaneity, their popularity and impact on sustainability are influenced by various factors beyond the total visitor count. It's essential for destinations to manage these tours effectively to ensure they contribute positively to the local economy, community, and environment. Addressing the challenges of over-tourism necessitates a multifaceted strategy, combining regulatory measures, strategic management, and effective marketing. By tackling both the symptoms and root causes of overtourism, destinations can foster more sustainable and enjoyable environments for residents and visitors alike. Integrating these approaches can mitigate tourism's adverse effects.

Even though the researchers maintained the required scientific, methodological, and ethical rigour, they acknowledged the study's limitations concerning the sample size. Only 22 destinations were empirically examined, and the specific selection of a single platform, GuruWalk, was made. Despite GuruWalk being the largest in terms of volume, it does not represent the total national offer in this field. Adjusting the results to other potential samples is not feasible due to the lack of similar studies.

References

Aguiló, E., Alegre, J., & Sard, M. (2005). The persistence of the sun and sand tourism model. *Tourism Management, 26*(2), 219–231. https://doi.org/10.1016/j.tourman.2003.11.004

Bigné, E., Sánchez, I., & Currás, R. (2007). El papel de la imagen del destino en la valoración y comportamiento postcompra del turista de sol y playa. *Papers de Turisme, 42*, 57–73.

Blázquez-Salom, M., Cladera, M., & Sard, M. (2021). Identifying the sustainability indicators of over-tourism and undertourism in Majorca. *Journal of Sustainable Tourism*. https://doi.org/10.1080/09669582.2021.1942478

Cheer, J. M., Milano, C., & Novelli, M. (2019). Tourism and community resilience in the Anthropocene: Accentuating temporal overtourism. *Journal of Sustainable Tourism, 27*(4), 554–572. https://doi.org/10.1080/09669582.2019.1578363

Cohen, S. A., & Hopkins, D. (2019). Autonomous vehicles and the future of urban tourism. *Annals of Tourism Research, 74*, 33–42.

de Waal, M., & Arets, M. (2022). From a sharing economy to a platform economy: Public values in shared mobility and gig work in the Netherlands. In *The Sharing Economy in Europe* (pp. 241–261). https://doi.org/10.1007/978-3-030-86897-0.

Dredge, D. (2016). Are DMOs on a path to redundancy? *Tourism Recreation Research, 41*(3), 348–353.
Dredge, D., & Gyimóthy, S. (2015). The collaborative economy and tourism: Critical perspectives, questionable claims, and silenced voices. *Tourism Recreation Research, 40*(3), 286–302. https://doi.org/10.1080/02508281.2015.1086076
Femeniás Rosselló, L. B. (2019). *The role of beach attributes in sun-and-beach destination choice: An application to Spanish Domestic Tourism*. Master's Thesis, Universitat de les Illes Balears. UIBrepositori. https://dspace.uib.es/xmlui/handle/11201/154676
García, J. R., & Ruiz, R. P. (2022). Free walking tours. In *Encyclopedia of tourism management and marketing*. Edward Elgar. https://doi.org/10.4337/9781800377486.free.walking.tours
Gretzel, U. (2018). From smart destinations to smart tourism regions. *Investigaciones Regionales-Journal of Regional Research, 42*, 171–184.
Guruwalk. (2024). *GuruWalk: Los mejores guías de free tours del mundo están aquí*. https://www.guruwalk.com/es
Gutiérrez-Duarte, M., & Roldán-Martínez, A. (2020). Economía sumergida e intrusismo al amparo del turismo colaborativo: El caso de los free tours. *InDret, 2*, 139–170. https://doi.org/10.31009/indret.2020.i2.04
INE. (2024). *Encuesta de ocupación hotelera. Viajeros y pernoctaciones por puntos turísticos*. https://www.ine.es/jaxiT3/Tabla.htm?t=2078&L=0
Insch, A. (2020). The challenges of over-tourism facing New Zealand: Risks and responses. *Journal of Destination Marketing & Management, 15*, 100378. https://doi.org/10.1016/j.jdmm.2019.100378
Kenney, M., & Zysman, J. (2016). The rise of the platform economy. *Issues in Science and Technology, 32*(3), 61.
Khakzad, S. (2018). Promoting coastal communities through cultural tourism: The case of fishing communities in Brunswick County, North Carolina. *Journal of Heritage Tourism, 13*(5), 455–471. https://doi.org/10.1080/1743873X.2017.1391272
Koerts, D. (2017, March). Amsterdam: Interpreting the city in "free" walking tours. In *5th International Research Forum on Guided Tours* (pp. 112–123).
Leal Londoño, M. D. P., & Font Medina, X. (2018). Turismo y economía colaborativa: El caso de los recorridos gratuitos a pie en Barcelona. *Cuadernos de Turismo, 41*. https://doi.org/10.6018/turismo.41.32705
Lithgow, D., Martínez, M. L., Gallego-Fernández, J. B., Silva, R., & Ramírez-Vargas, D. L. (2019). Exploring the co-occurrence between coastal squeeze and coastal tourism in a changing climate and its consequences. *Tourism Management, 74*, 43–54. https://doi.org/10.1016/j.tourman.2019.02.005
Marin, J., Grijalvo, M., & Mundet, L. (2021). Can a mature sun & beach tourist destination change its image among tourists?: The case study of Lloret de Mar. *Tourism (Zagreb, Croatia), 69*(4), 527–542. https://doi.org/10.37741/t.69.4.4
Martín, J. M. M., Martínez, J. M. G., & Fernández, J. A. S. (2018). An analysis of the factors behind the citizen's attitude of rejection towards tourism in a context of overtourism and economic dependence on this activity. *Sustainability, 10*(8), 2851. https://doi.org/10.3390/su10082851
Morales-Pérez, S., Garay, L., & Wilson, J. (2020). Airbnb's contribution to socio-spatial inequalities and geographies of resistance in Barcelona. *Tourism Geographies*, 1–24. https://doi.org/10.1080/14616688.2020.1795712
Morgan, N., Hastings, E., & Pritchard, A. (2012). Developing a new DMO marketing evaluation framework: The case of Visit Wales. *Journal of Vacation Marketing, 18*(1), 73–89.
Namberger, P., Jackisch, S., Schmude, J., & Karl, M. (2019). Overcrowding, overtourism and local level disturbance: How much can Munich handle? *Tourism Planning and Development*, 1–21. https://doi.org/10.1080/21568316.2019.1595706
Navalón-García, R., & Mínguez, C. (2021). Tourist guides and free tours: A controversial relationship. *Tourist Studies, 21*(3), 486–506. https://doi.org/10.1177/14687976211016073

Nilsson, J. H. (2020). Conceptualizing and contextualizing overtourism: The dynamics of accelerating urban tourism. *International Journal of Tourism Cities, 6*(4), 657–671. https://doi.org/10.1108/IJTC-08-2019-0117

Nilsson, J. H., & Zillinger, M. (2020). Free guided tours: Storytelling as a means of glocalizing urban places. *Scandinavian Journal of Hospitality and Tourism, 20*(3), 286–301. https://doi.org/10.1080/15022250.2020.1772866

Noguera Tur, F., Ferrandis Martínez, A., & Madrid Liñeiro, V. (2015). Comportamiento comercial y hábitos de consumo de los turistas en un destino maduro de sol y playa: El caso de Cullera. *Investigaciones Turísticas, 10*, 231. https://doi.org/10.14198/INTURI2015.10.10

Oskam, J., & Boswijk, A. (2016). Airbnb: The future of networked hospitality business. *Journal of Tourism Futures*. https://doi.org/10.1108/JTF-11-2015-0048

Pasquinelli, C., & Trunfio, M. (2020). Reframing urban overtourism through the Smart-City lens. *Cities, 102*, 102729. https://doi.org/10.1016/j.cities.2020.102729

Pastor, R., & Rivera-García, J. (2020). Airbnb y la intermediación turística. ≙ Competición o coopetición? Percepción de los agentes de viajes en España. *Revista Empresa y Humanismo, 23*, 107–132.

Peeters, P., Gössling, S., Klijs, J., Milano, C., Novelli, M., Dijkmans, C., & Postma, A. (2021). *Research for TRAN Committee-Overtourism: Impact and possible policy responses*. Available at: http://bit.ly/2srgoyg

Prebensen, N., Skallerud, K., & Chen, J. S. (2010). Tourist motivation with sun and sand destinations: Satisfaction and the WOM-effect. *Journal of Travel & Tourism Marketing, 27*(8), 858–873. https://doi.org/10.1080/10548408.2010.527253

Punzón, J. G., & Pastor, R. (2020). How effective are the COVID-19 fiscal-support and restarting-tourism policies taken by the top 3 European destinations? *Journal of Tourismology, 6*(2), 241–248.

Rátz, T. (2016). 'Be global, go local' – innovation and creativity in the development of alternative guiding services in Budapest. *Journal of Tourism and Cultural Change, 15*, 476–489. https://doi.org/10.1080/14766825.2016.1189558

Richards, S., Brown, L., & Dilettuso, A. (2020). The Airbnb phenomenon: The resident's perspective. *International Journal of Tourism Cities, 6*(1), 8–26. https://doi.org/10.1108/IJTC-06-2019-0084

Rivera-García, J., Fernández-Villarán, A., & Pastor-Ruiz, R. (2023). Examining the impact of the platform economy on Spain's cultural destinations through the lens of free tours. *International Journal of Tourism Cities, 9*(4), 861–874.

Smith, M. K., Sziva, I. P., & Olt, G. (2019). Overtourism and resident resistance in Budapest. *Tourism Planning and Development, 16*(4), 376–392.

Srnicek, N. (2017). *Platform capitalism*. Polity Press.

Stokols, D. (1972). A social-psychological model of human crowding phenomena. *Journal of the American Institute of Planners, 38*(2), 72–83.

UNWTO. (2019a). UNWTO World Tourism Barometer and Statistical Annex, January 2019, *17*(1). https://doi.org/10.18111/wtobarometereng

UNWTO. (2019b, January). *"Overtourism"? Understanding and managing urban tourism growth beyond perceptions. Volume 2: Case studies. Executive summary.* Madrid: UNWTO.

Widtfeldt Meged, J., & Zillinger, M. (2018). Disruptive network innovation in free guided tours. *Scandinavian Journal of Hospitality and Tourism, 18*(3), 303–318. https://doi.org/10.1080/15022250.2018.1497317

Chapter 10
National Plans of Well Living (WLNP) and their Influence on the Ecuadorian Cultural Sector

Carlos Alberto Buitrón Mendizábal

Abstract Over the last decade, Ecuador has adopted strategic planning as a tool for state development, emphasizing territorial, institutional, and economic organization. This shift allowed the government to centralize its functions through institutions, fostering some degree of sectoral organization. However, these planning models have also created challenges that remain unresolved. Historically, Ecuador lacked a tradition of long-term planning. This changed during former President Rafael Correa's administration, which introduced comprehensive government plans. These plans established a state policy promoting integrated economic, social, political, civic, and cultural development. In the cultural sector, planning was a new and unfamiliar process for both the government and stakeholders. This made implementation complex and yielded limited results, affecting the sector's operations and long-term development. While these efforts marked progress by integrating cultural development into national strategies, they also revealed the inadequacy of existing models in addressing the unique needs of the cultural sector. Ecuador's experience underscores the challenges of applying broad planning frameworks to specific sectors and highlights the need for more adaptable and inclusive approaches. The cultural sector's case demonstrates how centralized planning, without sufficient customization, can limit sustainable development and long-term growth.

10.1 Introduction: Planning in Ecuador—National Development Plan 2007–2009

Prior to 2007, Ecuadorian governments did not consider the cultural sector strategic for national economic or social development. Consequently, culture was excluded from government plans, and cultural activities throughout the country's republican history largely depended on the interest of individual administrations. This lack of

C. A. Buitrón Mendizábal (✉)
MaCKLAB–uio, University of Deusto, Bilbao, Spain

L. Ronda et al. (eds.), *Leisure and Human Development*, Human Well-Being Research and Policy Making, https://doi.org/10.1007/978-3-031-90778-4_10

planning resulted in a small number of sporadic cultural activities, carried out without structure or consistency (SENPLADES, 2013).

In 2007, the government of the Citizen Revolution (Revolución Ciudadana—RC), led by economist Rafael Correa, assumed the presidency and adopted a new approach to culture by incorporating it into the government's plans. This marked a significant shift from the way previous administrations and the population had viewed the cultural sector. Under the new planning model, culture and its historically marginalized social actors were recognized as strategic elements for the development of a sustainable economy, aimed at contributing to the productive growth of the country.

The plans were structured in three phases and corresponded to each of the government periods. The first plan was called National Development Plan 2007–2009; and the subsequent plans were called National Plan for Good Living, 2009–2013 (PNBV 2009–2013), and National Plan for Good Living 2013–2017 (PNBV 2013–2017). Those plans sought to establish a new economic and social model focused on human welfare, respecting the environment and the social market economy. The focus of the plans prioritized the quality of life of the population and especially of the most vulnerable sectors, their economic growth and the conservation of the environment in the medium and long term (Sylva, 2013).

For their preparation, exhaustive diagnoses were carried out across different sectors, including the cultural sector. These diagnoses served as a foundation to identify the country's main problems and needs. The data collected informed the development of public policies, the design of actions, and the strategies necessary to meet the goals set in the first plan. It was revealed that the sectors of education, health, and justice operated in isolation, highlighting the challenges and limitations faced by the cultural sector. Additionally, the findings demonstrated a lack of knowledge and appreciation for the country's diverse cultures and expressions, an insufficient institutional framework for the cultural sector, and limited participation by social actors in shaping cultural policies, all of which hindered the sector's growth and development.

The diagnosis of the cultural sector revealed serious issues related to the fragmentation of cultures at the national, local, and regional levels. There was limited appreciation for cultural expressions and manifestations due to limited knowledge about them. Furthermore, the recognition of the work done by artists and cultural producers across all fields was insufficient, as they lacked the basic conditions necessary to perform their work. As a result, culture was undervalued, and cultural activities were not integrated into social and economic life, hindering the development of the cultural market and industries in the country.

This situation had a negative impact on Ecuador's tangible and intangible heritage and its preservation, declaring it an emergency. The diagnosis of the cultural sector also highlighted the need for the government to establish an institutional framework to organize and promote the participation of civil society, which had been marginalized due to prevailing social inequality. This inequality limited interactions between different cultures and worldviews (SENPLADES, 2007).

Historically, culture was regarded as an unnecessary expense because it did not generate profit and was viewed as unproductive and superfluous. Furthermore, more pressing issues in sectors such as health, education, defence, and security were prioritized (Cabrero & Pérez de la Torre, 2013). However, despite the significant shortages across the country, the cultural sector occasionally received small-scale economic allocations or subsidies. These were limited to specific activities and constrained the sector to operate based on the profitability it could generate for the government. García et al. (1987) warn about the role of the cultural sector for the state as follows:

Artists and intellectuals maintain a position of distance and distrust towards politics and planning. They see attempts to plan or organize culture as a threat to creative freedom and compare this action to the way authoritarian regimes have acted, in many cases trying to control art and culture. García et al. (1987) identified that the same thing happened with politicians who considered that societies have more pressing and urgent problems in priority areas, contrary to what may be the cultural sector, so it is necessary that the demands of small or unrepresentative sectors, such as culture, be addressed from the private or associative sphere, although in their discourse they always promote the need for their own culture and the support of the State (García et al., 1987).

The National Development Plan (NDP) (outlined as a cultural horizon what they called "Buen Vivir" (Good Living), which was aimed at rescuing national identity, diverse identities, and multiculturalism, also seeking the shared well-being of the entire population through a change in the cultural management model, planned for the medium and long term, participatory, deconcentrated and decentralized, taking into account the poorest population groups considered historically marginalized and opposed to the hegemonic foreign culture.

Rather than being a challenge for the State and its components, during its construction and implementation, the NDP was strongly opposed and rejected by some economic power groups, officials of government institutions belonging to various political parties that had direct institutional control over all sectors and levels of the State, and part of civil society. This was not only due to the planning model that was to be implemented but was reinforced by the campaign against the public sector that the private sector had started years before, which had the effect of rendering the public sector useless for the country's development (Sader & Gentil, 2003).

Nevertheless, the objective of the PND was to make the cultural sector profitable and productive by giving it an institutional framework and including various social and economic actors as producers and consumers of culture, thus creating and consolidating a cultural model that integrates various segments of the population with their respective identities as representative elements. It also sought to promote a model of cultural management that seeks to generate economic returns to progressively leave dependence on the State.

These changes that they wanted to generate strengthened the resistance of several actors, especially cultural and political actors who persisted in the romantic idea of freedom of culture, so it should be kept away from the mundane (market, productivity, service, or money) in order not to tarnish creativity. This generated the idea that the government should be solely responsible for managing and financing the cultural sector, although there were also patrons and collectors in a very small number belonging to the Ecuadorian economic elite who sought to maintain the purity of culture, continue with state funding, and maintain their privileges and the status this gave them.

The innovative aspect of the NDP, in addition to including culture in the planning model, was to incorporate it into the country's economic development axis, to ensure that the sector leaves behind the clientelist, paternalistic, and unprofitable model and becomes a sector that generates funds that contribute to the national economy and social development (SENPLADES, 2007).

For García et al. (1987, p.28) there are six forms of government related to culture: *"Liberal patronage, paternalistic traditionalism, populist statism, neoconservative privatization, cultural democratization and participatory democracy"*. The PND was identified to a greater extent with populist statism and to some extent with cultural democratization, merging them on the basis of the needs presented by the sector and especially by the government, which was the manager of planning and direct beneficiary of all the actions carried out, its main capital being political gain. To achieve the latter, the government, through its discourse, brought together those marginalized and forgotten by society and, with this in mind, proposed the rescue of national values and the national being that would be achieved through cultural development.

The State became the manager and therefore the protagonist of the cultural sector, and as in traditional populism, the mythicized figure of the leader was positioned and explicitly visible, always omnipresent in all the actions implemented, since he was the thinker and ideologist of all these actions. In this sense García et al. (1987) state that in populist state-centered systems, the idea of the nation is embodied in the State rather than in the people. While the people are referenced as the beneficiaries of government actions and are called upon to support them, they are not effectively recoginzed as the source and justification of those action.

Thus, the State sought to subordinate all popular initiatives to the so-called national interests set by the government, while any attempt at independent organization was disqualified (García et al., 1987). The government, which was responsible for the construction and development of actions in the cultural field, sought to make its image profitable by being recognized as the first to promote specific actions for the cultural sector with the support of various groups in the country's 24 provinces, and its actions were recognized and legitimized by popular vote (SENPLADES, 2007).

The functional structure of the NDP had 12 objectives and 8 general strategies that combined the social, economic, cultural, and political dimensions, whose principles were contemplated in the Constitution of the Republic created in 2008. The 12 objectives were based on 118 policies, 600 strategies, and 94 goals for which the central government and its entire bureaucratic apparatus were directly responsible. Politically, the PND antagonized the development model imposed by the International Monetary Fund (IMF) and the World Bank (WB) and attempted to create an alternative scenario to that of the social sectors from the vision of the so-called new left in Latin America, which was part of the process of construction of the new social development model.

The plan attacked what it considered to be the evils that had afflicted the nations of the region in the 1980s and 1990s, which were: free market, neoliberalism, commercial openness, and excessive exploitation of natural resources (SENPLADES, 2009). It also sought to break with the Washington Consensus and all the stabilizing policies that caused weakness of the institutional system, in addition to the deep economic and social crisis affecting Ecuador (SENPLADES, 2007).

Economically, the first NDP was aimed at changing production processes, so the government identified the Selective Industrialization by Import Substitution (ISI-S) as the way to promote the development of industry and production in the country. On the other hand, interculturality was configured as the basis of the construction process of the new Ecuadorian identity, which through a strong national cultural industry, creates and defends identity values, attacking the cultural alienation that had led to the excessive consumption of external and hegemonic cultural products, especially by the young population. To achieve this, the plan established as an objective of the cultural sector: "To affirm the national identity and strengthen diverse identities and interculturality" (SENPLADES, 2007), p. 293). To recover the lost identity and give relevance to what was marginalized and made invisible by the State and the white mestizo power groups that controlled the productive, industrial, and cultural sectors in Ecuador (Harnecker, 2011).

An important aspect was the proposal of a work distribution policy so that citizens could enjoy the other dimensions of human development such as liberating leisure—autotelic, which was contemplated among the principles of the planning model, and which had never before been considered in the country or at least explicitly proposed as it was in the NDP. Public policies sought to consolidate the model of distribution of work and leisure time. The purpose of these changes was to improve the quality of life of the population, consolidate the productive model by making it more efficient, and protect the environment by reducing consumption and developing sustainable productive alternatives (SENPLADES, 2009).

With these elements, all citizens could feel welcomed, represented, and protected by the State, however, as the government was the one who established how it should be, what it should have, which were the main elements and actions of culture, it resulted in a loss of autonomy of the sector which was subject to what was governmentally established and in a certain way to what was approved as culture, since the government had positioned itself as its promoter, rescuing national values and as the intervener of all cultural actions. The PND identifies another form of control where the State is responsible for guaranteeing the protection of the rights of society, ensuring the conditions for culture to exist by rescuing and extolling the national traits that had been devalued, which promoted the consumption of external cultural products that were against the national a situation that was attributed to foreign adversaries García et al., 1987).

Operationally, all proposals or actions that were in line with the government's line were accommodated, even if they were not included in the Plan, thus constituting a multifunctional model between populist statism and the apparent democratization of culture (or rather expansion of cultural activities) that ensured that this sector would develop and be functional to its interests. The model was replicated in Latin America and other countries that also worked for the rescue and exaltation of cultural values and identity, transforming culture into a tool with which the policies and actions of promotion and ideological consolidation of the governments considered progressive leftists in the region were strengthened.

The actions aimed at transforming the cultural sector contradicted its foundational principles, as government control hindered the effective reorganization, decentralization, and democratization of culture. Although these changes were intended to improve the sector's functioning, they ultimately failed to achieve the expected outcomes.

The achievements of the PND were considered to be the institutionalization of the cultural sector, the creation and application of laws and actions that gave it shape and order, and the consolidation of plurinationality, all aimed at combating the external threats that affected the development of culture in order to make it an active part of the productive sector. However, the real scope of the first plan was limited to a few actions that, although decisive, did not have an impact on a large scale and did not consolidate its development in the medium and long term.

10.2 First National Development Plan for Well Living (I PNBV) 2009–2013

During the 2009–2013 government period, the discourse centred on the social market economy, redistribution and generation of wealth, equitable social development, respect for the ecology, and the collaborative economy. These principles underpinned the concept of Good Living, and actions were initiated that impacted the cultural, economic, and social sectors. The National Plan for Good Living proposed meeting fundamental needs, achieving a dignified quality of life and death, fostering love and being loved, and encouraging the healthy flourishing of all in peace and harmony with nature, alongside the indefinite continuation of human cultures.

Good Living also emphasizes having free time for contemplation and emancipation. It seeks to expand and enhance the freedoms, opportunities, capacities, and potentialities of individuals. These must flourish universally and individually, enabling achievements without domination over oneself or others. This concept is seen as a desirable societal goal across territories and diverse collective identities. It calls for reconstructing the public sphere to foster mutual recognition and value for each other, acknowledging diversity while affirming equality, reciprocity, and the shared pursuit of self-realization and a collective social future (SENPLADES, 2009).

As outlined in the NDP, policies and strategies to promote entrepreneurship acted as catalysts for the cultural sector through public investment. The First National Plan for Good Living (PNBV) incorporated entrepreneurship into the broader transformation and diversification of the economy, aiming to consolidate a new national model. This included transforming the productive matrix to reduce reliance on extractivism as a primary economic driver while upholding the principle of respect for nature. Renewable resources were prioritized, with sectors such as culture, tourism, technology, knowledge, and innovation forming key pillars of development:

> "This new productive matrix prioritises the production of food for a nutritious, culturally and ecologically appropriate basic food basket. It includes a dynamic, flexible and eco-efficient industrial development, linked to local needs and potentialities derived from bio-knowledge and scientific and technological innovations. It relates to energy sovereignty and clean energies; the protection and enhancement of biodiversity and cultural diversity as a basis for alternative activities to extractivism—among them ecotourism and biomedicine—and the rescue and innovation of technologies that favour production processes in which work acquires value, maximises the yield of resources, and minimises impacts and effects on the environment" (SENPLADES, 2009, 339).

To achieve the objectives outlined in the First PNBV, the government increased the budget allocation for culture between 2007 and 2009, as shown in Fig. 10.1:

Due to substantial differences among the fields within the cultural sector, the allocated amounts varied. For example, publishing, literature, and cinema—due to their higher production and consumption capacities—received greater allocations compared to fields such as visual and plastic arts, theatre, and dance, which, owing to reduced public engagement, achieved less development and benefits.

In the First National Plan for Good Living (I PNBV), the policies of the cultural sector were substantially beneficial. They promoted sectoral development, institutional consolidation, encouragement of cultural enterprises, and the strengthening of interculturality and plurinationality. Marginalized peoples and societies were also included in the NDP. However, the economic model failed to achieve the desired transformative impact, which contrasted with the achievements in building Ecuadorian cultural identity.

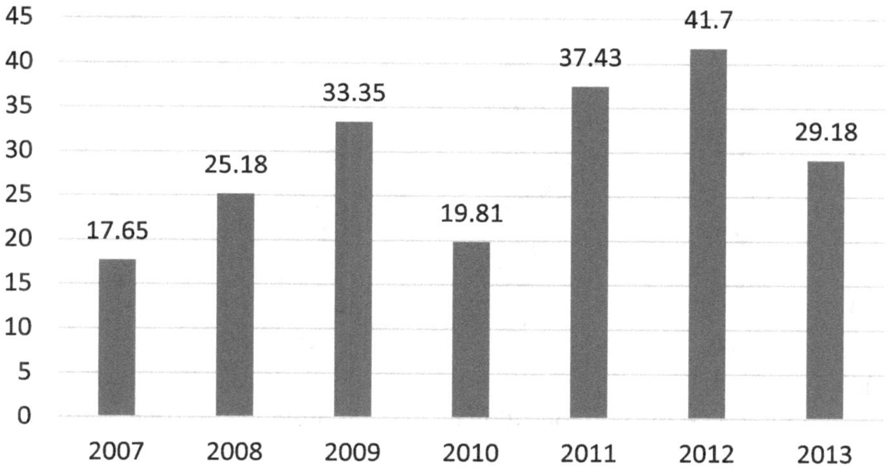

Fig. 10.1 Evolution of budget allocations of the Ministry of Culture and Heritage, Ecuador 2007–2013 (millions of dollars). Source: Ministry of Culture and Heritage, Ecuador (2013)

In the I PNBV, an evaluation of the PND achievements identified unresolved needs, such as limiting excessive natural resource exploitation and developmentalism. Cultural aspects that were insufficiently addressed included a lack of education and training for planners, inexperience among institutional managers, political interference, and insufficient integration of culture with ecology, economy, and education. Objectives and goals were generated to address these shortcomings. The plan aimed to strengthen the cultural sector not through the free market but by applying the principles of Good Living, seeking to build a humanist model prioritizing human development over capital accumulation. It also promoted Latin American unity while maintaining other elements of human development.

The I PNBV had to address disparities between sectors: Publishing and cinema achieved significant development, and music exhibited incipient but commercially profitable growth. In contrast, the visual, performing, and non-industrial literary arts were underrepresented in the First Plan due to their inability to present unified proposals as a sector (PNBV 2009–2013) (SENPLADES, 2009).

According to Ministry of Finance figures, the budget allocated to culture grew by 17% between 2009 and 2010, as illustrated in Fig. 10.2:

Another significant aspect of the I PNBV was the application of policies from other sectors to the cultural sphere, such as work redistribution. This policy allowed citizens to engage in other dimensions of human development and had a medium-term positive impact on the cultural sector. Redistributing work aimed to achieve employability for all, ensuring equitable access to free time. This approach improved

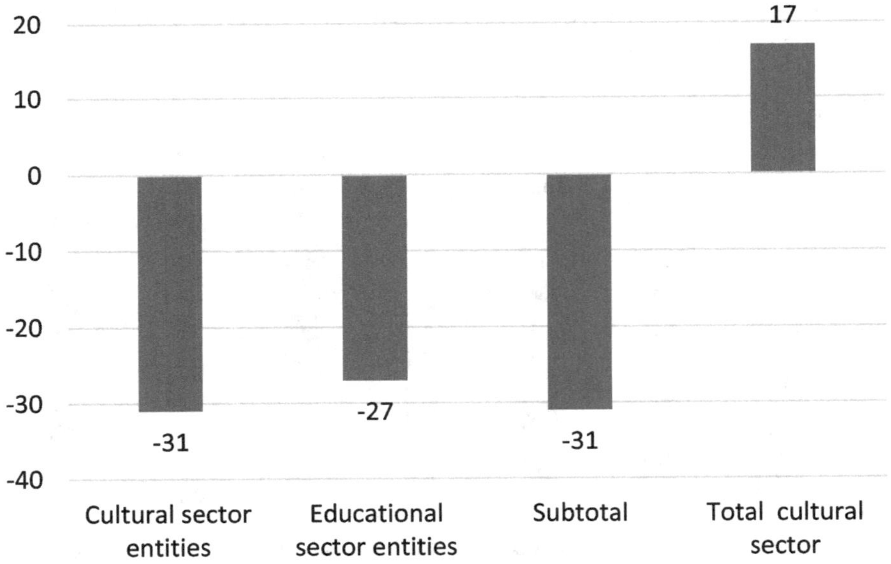

Fig. 10.2 State funding to cultural and educational entities, Ecuador 2009–2010 (number of entities). Source: El Telégrafo (2013)

cultural production and consumption, aligning with a human development model recognizing the balance of work and leisure.

The structure of the I PNBV mirrored the PND, with 12 objectives, 2 of which related directly to the cultural sector:

> "Objective number 7: To build and strengthen public, intercultural and common meeting spaces.
>
> Objective number 8: To affirm and strengthen national identity, diverse identities, plurinationality, and interculturality" (SENPLADES, 2009).

It was also important to recognize the non-instrumental use of time as one of the main actions that gave meaning to the use of public space and free time, factors that became part of the personal growth and health of the population. The need expressed by the government to have areas for cultural activities was proposed as public, healthy, happy, safe, and supportive spaces, which would promote in the population the appreciation of the non-instrumental use of time to develop cultural, physical, and recreational activities in order to improve their quality of life (SENPLADES, 2009).

One of the actions concerning the space for cultural activities of the I PNBV was to deconcentrate cultural institutions in the larger urban centres, since this concentration limited the access of smaller populations to cultural products and services, which in turn reduced cultural supply and consumption in the country. To solve this problem, infrastructure was created in different provinces to promote cultural production and the consumption of cultural services and products, which meant the de-privatization and de-commercialization of public space and its services.

The achievements of the I PNBV were the recognition of other identities, economic and social sectors including sexual diversities that had been made invisible and that from these actions was decreasing, for this moment the opening of the cultural sector was not a problem, however, the use of free time for their enjoyment and use in activities related to the cultural sector had a different reality, mainly due to the perception of culture as a classist element limited to the higher deciles of the population, while the lower deciles had limited and in some cases no access to cultural activities, so that a large part of the country's population was not used to participating in this type of practice.

On the other hand, the curriculum of the Ecuadorian educational system did not include cultural activities. Figure 10.3 shows that the consumption of the last decile is higher than the consumption of the first five (29.03% vs. 23.63%).

While free and democratic access to cultural spaces and the creation of cultural development networks in Ecuador was positive, the results of their implementation were not, despite the relationship created between cultural consumption, use of leisure time and use of cultural facilities, since cultural spaces and facilities were to be managed, preserved, and financed by the State itself.

Another of the policies of the I PNBV was to persist in the idea of transforming culture as part of economic-productive development, for which entrepreneurship was configured as a spearhead for strengthening the sector. However, there was a contradiction between the way in which the cultural sector functioned depending on the government and the capacity to strengthen the private, associative, and

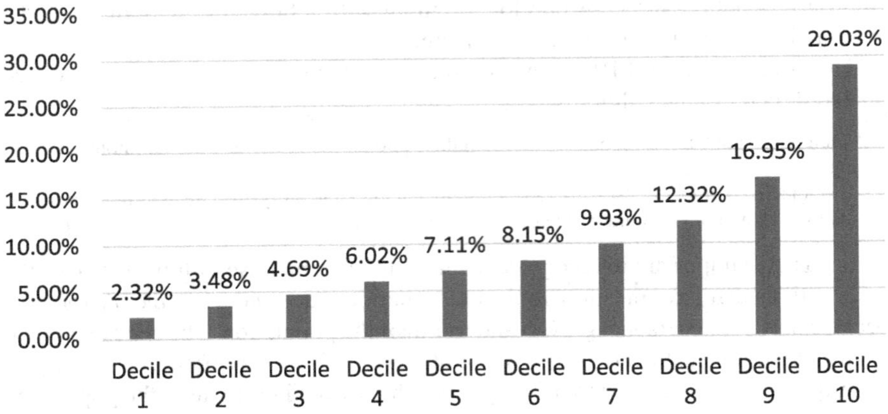

Fig. 10.3 Percentage of cultural consumption by deciles, Ecuador, 2012. Source: INEC (2012)

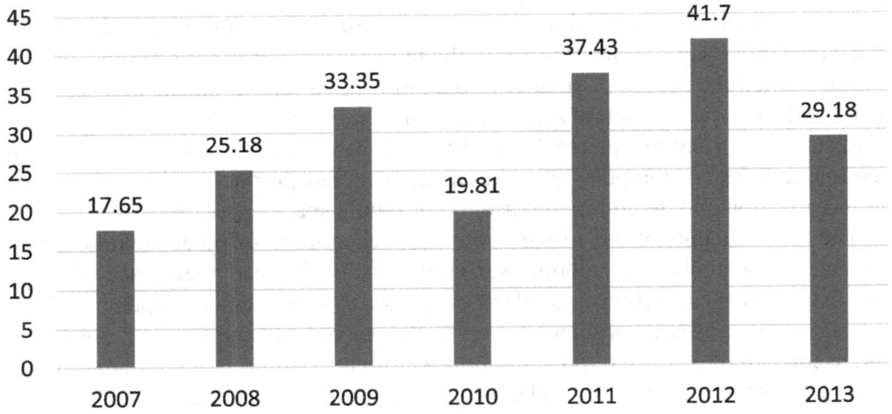

Fig. 10.4 Evolution of budget allocation of the Ministry of Culture and Heritage, Ecuador 2007–2013 (millions of dollars). Source: Ministry of Culture and Heritage (2013)

community sector for the development of free market enterprises and the cultural industry in the medium and long term.

The cultural sector, having the State as its sole financier, consolidated its dependence on the disbursement of funds, as can be seen in Fig. 10.4:

This reliance was also reflected in the contribution of cultural activities to GDP (Fig. 10.5):

Despite these limitations, the I PNBV implemented policies that supported institutional consolidation, productive development, and social inclusion while fostering interculturality and plurinationality. However, the economic model underpinning the plan remained underdeveloped.

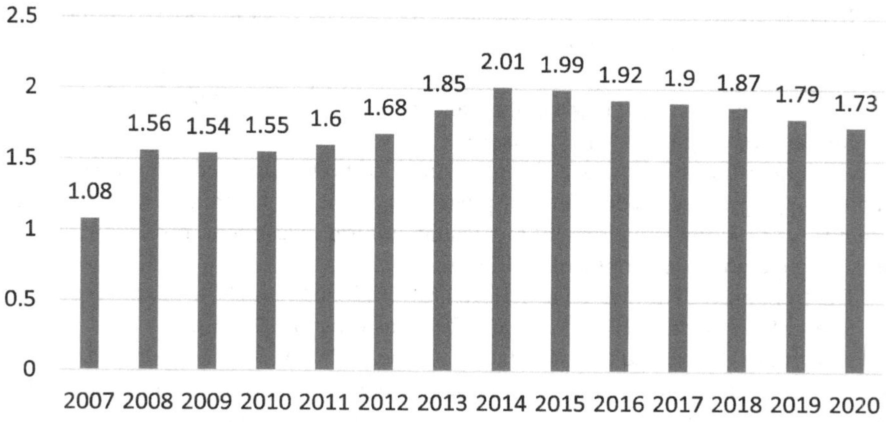

Fig. 10.5 Contribution of cultural activities to GDP, Ecuador 2007–2020 (percentage of GDP). Source: Ministry of Culture and Heritage (2013)

10.3 Second National Plan for Well Living (II) 2013–2017: Action, Management, and Operation in the Cultural Sector

During the last 4 years of the government (2013–2017), the Second National Plan for Good Living (II PNBV) was executed. This plan aimed to implement the policies and actions proposed as a continuation of what had been initiated in the PND and the I PNBV, addressing unresolved issues and consolidating achievements from the previous plans. To achieve this, the government adopted a more aggressive political discourse, as it was the first time in the history of the republic that a single government had won three consecutive elections. Maintaining popularity was seen as essential for advancing the country's transformation.

One of the key actions of the II PNBV was to promote cultural enterprises more aggressively. These were considered part of the strategic and indispensable sectors for wealth generation. This approach integrated culture into various fields, making it an integral part of the country's development strategy. This initiative was not unique to Ecuador but aligned with policies of the United Nations and its Office for Culture and Education (UNESCO), which facilitated funding from international organizations.

The implementation and operation of the II PNBV projected the achievement of its goals by 2030, based on four axes:

1. Closing inequality gaps.
2. Development of technology, innovation, and knowledge.
3. Environmental sustainability.
4. Expansion of the productive matrix and strategic sectors.

To meet these goals, various economic sectors had to collaborate. Culture was expected to contribute to improving the population's quality of life, as advocated by the UN, UNESCO, and the United Nations Development Programme (UNDP). These organizations recognized culture and cultural freedom as critical components of human development. The Ecuadorian government incorporated the Human Development Index (HDI) and the percentage of GDP allocated to culture as key indicators of progress in the cultural sphere. It was anticipated that by improving the country's economic situation and increasing cultural investment, both the HDI and overall population development would improve.

The trend of GDP allocated to culture grew until 2014, as shown in the Fig. 10.6:

Similarly, Ecuador's HDI grew until 2015, as illustrated in Fig. 10.7:

To achieve the second and fourth axes of the II PNBV—focused on technological development, innovation, knowledge, and the expansion of the productive matrix—the government prioritized substituting industrial products and transferring knowledge from industrialized countries to Ecuador. According to a diagnosis conducted for the II PNBV, 72% of exportable products were primary goods with low added value, and 44% of national production consisted of low-value products and services (SENPLADES, 2013).

This lack of value-added production and exports highlighted the need for educational reform. To address this, the government granted unprecedented numbers of scholarships for students to study in developed countries. Upon their return, these students were expected to apply their expertise to strategic areas.

However, implementing these proposed actions posed challenges due to the lack of experienced technical teams with sufficient knowledge to lead the processes at national, provincial, and local levels. This gap caused misunderstandings between the government and the cultural sector, with both struggling to align their goals. Consequently, the government primarily acted as an employer and fund provider.

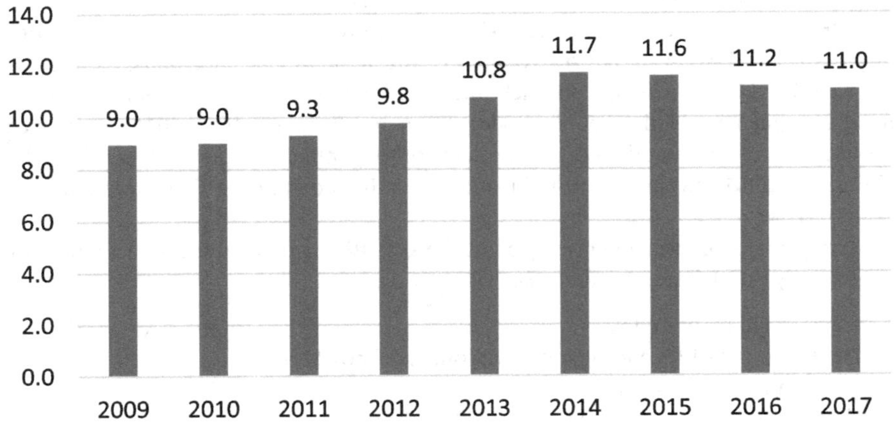

Fig. 10.6 Percentage of GDP allocated to culture, Ecuador 2009–2017. Source: Ministry of Culture and Heritage, Ecuador (2020)

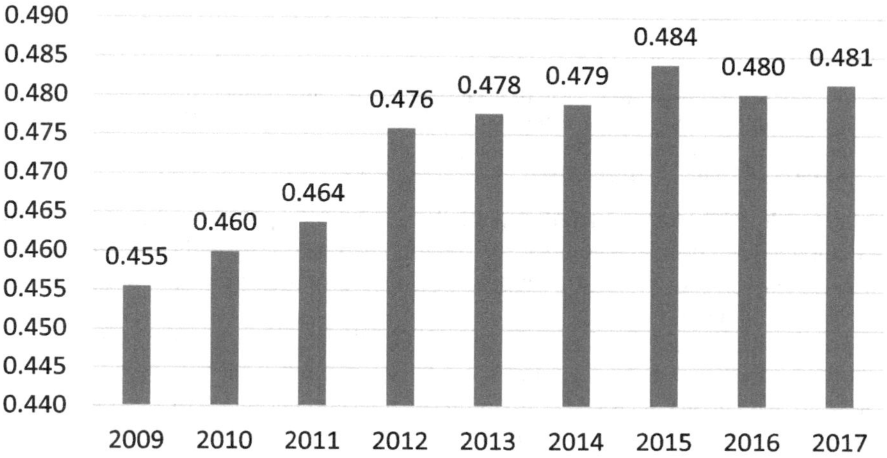

Fig. 10.7 Human Development Index (HDI), Ecuador 2009–2017. Source: Expansión (2017)

Table 10.1 Percentage of people according to academic training in charge of cultural management, Ecuador 2015

Academic background	Performing arts	Cinema	Design	Editorial	Phonographic
Administration	3.64%	7.14%	12.29%	22.92%	6.25%
Social Sciences	26.36%	2.86%	4.44%	19.44%	12.50%
Medicine	3.64%	0.00%	25.26%	5.56%	4.46%
Tourism	1.82%	0.00%	1.71%	0.00%	4.46%
Music	0.91%	4.29%	0.00%	0.00%	25.00%
Engineering	7.27%	7.14%	9.90%	6.25%	8.04%
Design	1.82%	7.14%	28.67%	2.78%	0.89%
Communication	7.27%	37.14%	3.75%	15.28%	15.18%
Arts	35.45%	30.00%	7.17%	4.86%	15.18%
Not Graduated	11.82%	4.29%	6.83%	22.92%	8.04%
Total	100%	100%	100%	100%	100%

Source: Guerrero et al. (2021)

Table 10.1 illustrates the academic backgrounds of those in charge of cultural management (Guerrero et al., 2021):

The II PNBV also sought to guarantee the right to work, with the State acting as the employer of last resort. This ensured vulnerable populations had access to employment. Policies aimed to promote decent jobs, particularly for excluded groups, and foster youth employment under conditions that enhanced their skills and knowledge (SENPLADES, 2013).

The role of the cultural industry shifted from being important to being necessary. Cultural industries, considered essential for the survival of the sector, were integrated into state planning, similar to models in Mexico, Colombia, Chile, and

Argentina. A definition of cultural and creative industries was introduced in the Organic Law of Culture (LOC):

> Cultural and creative industry shall be understood as the national productive sectors aimed at the production, distribution, circulation, exchange, access, and consumption of cultural and creative goods and services aimed at generating symbolic and economic value (Ley Orgánica de Cultura, 2016, p. 26).

The cultural industry included publishing, phonographic, multimedia, design and applied arts, film, and audio-visual sectors. Among these, audio-visual production emerged as the primary exportable cultural product, while the other sectors experienced fluctuations (Fig. 10.8).

This vision of culture from the government's planning generated resistance among the members of the cultural sector since it went against the principles and forms to which this sector was historically accustomed and also ran the risk of affecting access to public funds from the government because it was always a recipient and not a generator of funds. The cultural sector's lack of associative capacity did not allow it to rethink and/or improve the processes that the government had implemented, making it a non-propositional counterpart, but always resistant to the economic development model of the cultural sector: "The creation of a cultural industry would inevitably lead to the undermining of independent work, that is, the subordination of the practice of artistic creation to commercial needs." Cultural producers were not unaware of the importance of the economic dimension, and therefore urged the strengthening of the economic sustainability of cultural enterprises through government policies that address the market dimension necessary for cultural development (Guerrero et al., 2021).

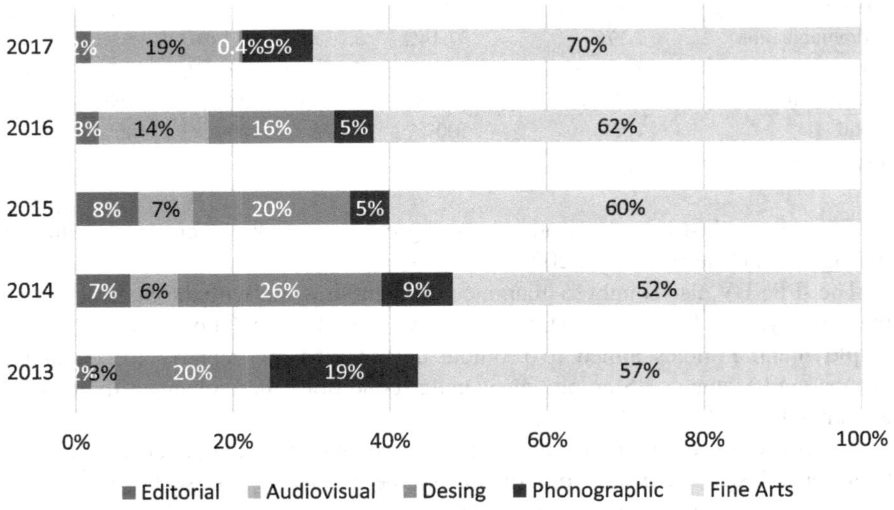

Fig. 10.8 Percentage of exports of the cultural sector, Ecuador 2013–2017. Source: Central Bank of Ecuador

On the other hand, an idea of cultural products and services as a superfluous element of entertainment and not of self-sustaining development had been positioned in the Ecuadorian social imaginary, and despite the changes and progress achieved with these plans, the conception was still maintained that in some cases, due to their costs, they were aimed at people with greater purchasing power or that they should be free and freely accessible to less favoured sectors, and for the cultural sector to survive in the country, which has frequently been subject to significant economic variations, it needs these governmental funds.

At times when the state budget allowed it, cultural programmes and festivals were created, implementing the mechanism of budget allocation through competitive funds to support the development of the sector's activities, executed by the Ministry of Culture through its various agencies.

Figure 10.9 shows the sectors to which the competitive funds were allocated.

Between the years 2015–2017 the cultural sector was affected when Ecuador enters into economic recession due to a severe natural disaster that affected several provinces of the country and by a significant reduction in oil prices (product on which the Ecuadorian economy is based) with which the amounts allocated to culture decreased as well as the production of the public, private, and associative sector. However, during this period the consumption of imported cultural products did not decrease because it was in the hands of multinational companies, this caused an increase in the entry of foreign products into the country with the potential to change its cultural perception. The following figure shows the growth trend in the number of cultural enterprises (Fig. 10.10):

However, despite the apparent growth in the number of cultural enterprises, the growth of cultural production was reduced, as seen in Fig. 10.11:

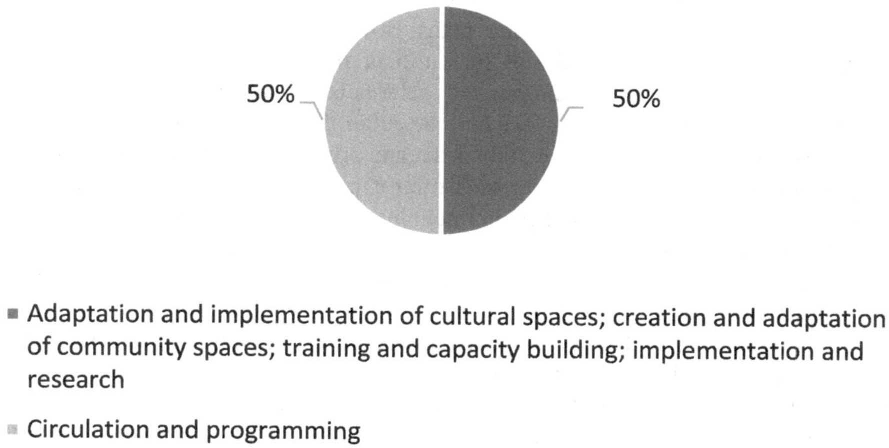

Fig. 10.9 Modality of competitive funds (%). Source: Information System of the MC and P. Fondos de Fomento Cultural

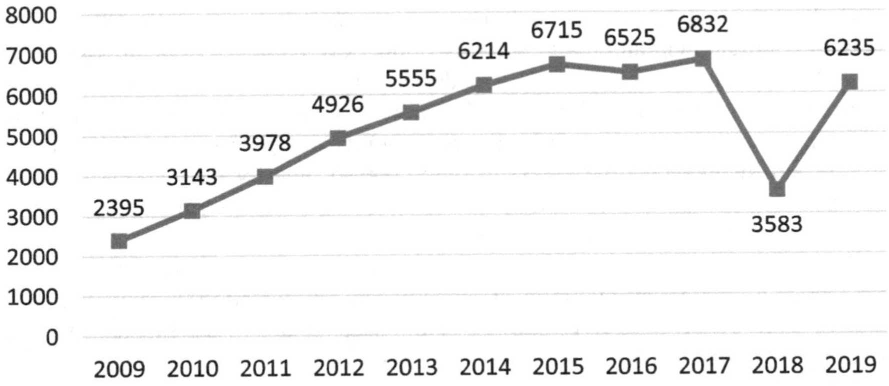

Fig. 10.10 Trend in the number of cultural enterprises, Ecuador 2009–2019. Source: INEC

10.4 Conclusions

The planning models implemented in Ecuador focused on economic development and performance, excluding crucial sectors in comprehensive planning, such as the cultural sector, which was relegated to the background because it was considered allegorical and unproductive, remaining limited to the country's economic growth.

In Ecuador, the absence of state policies and laws on cultural matters resulted in a lack of funding for programmes and actions to foster its institutionalism, management, promotion, and operation, generating an inefficient and unstable structure of incipient growth and development, thereby perpetuating the cultural sector's dependence on the State (Sánchez-Parga, 1989).

Starting in 2007, the implementation of national government plans marked a turning point by identifying culture as a key sector for economic and social development and incorporating it into national plans. However, the lack of planning experience and the sector's non-existent institutional framework limited the model's scope, resulting in poor execution and paternalistic state interventionism that affected both the plans' performance and the cultural sector in general.

Although the national plans brought order and organization to the cultural sector, they also served as a mechanism for state control, positioning the government as the axis of cultural development and government institutions as the only entities responsible for its development, execution, control, and promotion. This relegated the private and associative sectors to the role of external beneficiaries, excluding them from participation in the productive model.

Despite including cultural enterprises and recognizing culture as necessary for sustainable economic development, the planning model did not have a major impact because its structure hindered the development and profitability of the sector.

For the plans to promote cultural enterprises, a specific cultural model interacting with other sectors unrelated to cultural activity was required. That is to say, the state should not be solely responsible for cultural development. State planning

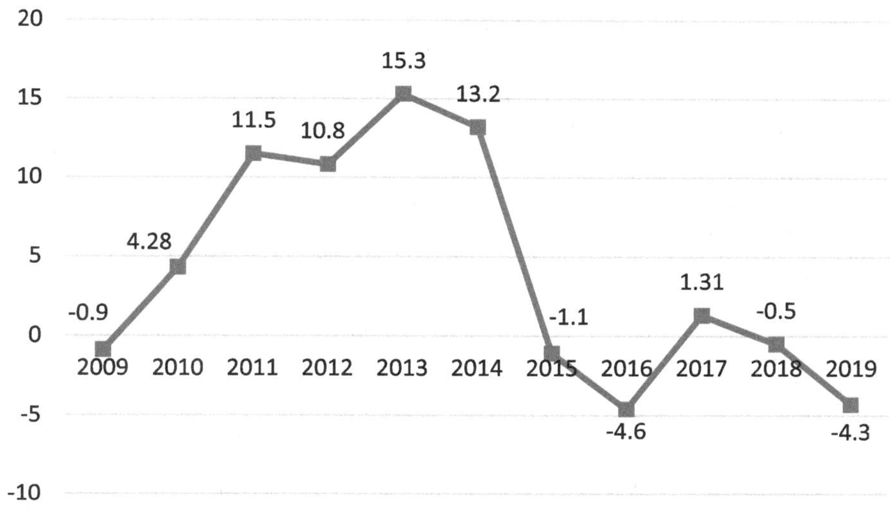

Fig. 10.11 Growth rate of cultural production, Ecuador 2008–2020. Source: Ministry of Culture and Heritage (2022)

models should integrate the sector with the productive apparatus, the educational system, and civil society, not only through plans, policies, and laws, but also through actions that consolidate the participation of all sectors involved in culture (Guerrero, 2021).

It is essential that Ecuador's future governments understand the importance of culture, not only in terms of identity, history, heritage, education, and social aspects, but also as an economic foundation for sustainable development, forming part of the country's non-extractive productive matrix. To this end, they should promote the depoliticization of the sector, generate reforms in the cultural law to strengthen its link with the productive and service sectors, optimize public, private, and associative cultural institutions, develop educational strategies to promote cultural consumption, encourage the creation of cultural enterprises focused on promotion and distribution rather than on production, eliminate tariffs and taxes on products related to cultural production, create public policies based on state planning models that promote the development of cultural enterprises, and encourage free trade of cultural products and services to consolidate the cultural market in Ecuador.

References

Asamblea Nacional República del Ecuador. Ley Orgánica de Cultura. Registro Oficial Suplemento 913. Quito, 30 de diciembre de 2016. Fecha de suscripción: 2016-12-2 Fecha de publicación: 2016-12-30 Número de registro: Año IV - N° 913 Sexto Suplemento.

Banco Central del Ecuador. (1987). *La planificación en el Ecuador* (1st ed., Vol. 27). Quito, Ecuador: Departamento Editorial Banco Central del Ecuador.

Cabrero, F., & Pérez de la Torre, A. (Eds.). (2013). *Hacia un diálogo de saberes para el buen vivir y ejercicio de los derechos culturales: Selección de ponencias*. FLACSO.
Económica, J. N. (1978, December). Planificación del desarrollo. *Revista de la CEPAL, 6*, 60.
Ecuador, B. C. (1987). La planificación en el Ecuador. In B. C. Ecuador (Ed.), *La planificación en el Ecuador* (Vol. 27, 1st ed., pp. 1–53). Departamento Editorial Banco Central del Ecuador.
García, N., Bonfil, G., Brunner, J., Franco, J., Landi, O., & Miceli, S. (1987). *Políticas culturales en América Latina* (2nd ed.). Editorial Grijalbo.
Guerrero, G., Bravo, A., & Vinueza, L. (2021). *Entre el proceso creativo y la industria: Una aproximación a la economía de la cultura en el Ecuador*. EdiPUCE.
Harnecker, M. (2011). Ecuador. Una nueva izquierda en busca de la vida en plenitud. Quito, Pichincha, Ecuador: Abya Yala.
Leiva, J. (2012). *Pensamiento y práctica de la planificación en América Latina* (Vol. 75). CEPAL.
República del Ecuador. (2009). *Plan Nacional de Desarrollo Plan Nacional para el Buen Vivir 2009–2013: Construyendo un Estado Plurinacional e Intercultural*. Secretaría Nacional de Planificación y Desarrollo – SENPLADES.
República del Ecuador. (2013). *Plan Nacional para el Buen Vivir 2013–2017: Construyendo un Estado Plurinacional e Intercultural*. Secretaría Nacional de Planificación y Desarrollo – SENPLADES.
Sader, E., & Gentil, P. (2003). La trama del neoliberalismo: mercado, crisis y exclusión social. En La trama del neoliberalismo: mercado, crisis y exclusión social (pág. 30). Buenos Aires: CLACSO.
Sánchez-Parga, J. (1989). Cultura, sociedad y estado. *Ecuador Debate, 18*, 14–15.
SENPLADES. (2007). Plan Nacional de Desarrollo 2007-2010. Gobierno Nacional de la República del Ecuador. Obtenido de. https://www.planificacion.gob.ec/wp-content/uploads/downloads/2013/09/Plan-Nacional-Desarrollo-2007-2010.pdf.
Sylva, E. (2013). Las políticas culturales y el buen vivir. In F. Cabrero (Ed.), *I Congreso Ecuatoriano de Gestión Cultural: Hacia un diálogo de saberes para el buen vivir y el ejercicio de los derechos culturales* (pp. 1–12). FLACSO.

Chapter 11
Restorative Leisure in Citizen Participation: An Alternative for the Promotion of Social Demands

Santiago Forero-Lloreda, Johanna E. Zarate, and Camilo A. Angulo

Abstract Restorative leisure is an analytical framework designed to recognise popular festive activisms that promote social rights arising from the autonomy and distinctiveness of vulnerable human groups. This recognition has been achieved through the management and implementation of living laboratories of creation. These laboratories, as situated actions, provide spaces, time, and resources for diverse forms of participant communication. As a result, various cultural manifestations of leisure have been identified, reflecting the claims of Latin American communities. These manifestations showcase, through their subjectivity and resilience, diverse forms of empowerment. Through participatory observation and the characterisation of discursive expressions, graphic and audio-visual tools have been developed. These tools contribute to social transformation by amplifying the voices and representations of the individuals involved.

11.1 Emergence of Restorative Leisure

Restorative leisure has emerged as an analytical category within social research in Latin America, particularly in Colombia, between 2018 and 2023 (Forero & Lazcano, 2022). It is methodologically grounded in a qualitative approach, employing situated interventions within the framework of an exploratory inquiry. The primary aim of this inquiry has been to recognise restorative practices and experiences that contribute to the rebuilding of the social fabric in communities systematically subjected to violations (Forero, 2023).

These practices and experiences are rooted in the territorial, popular, and ancestral knowledge embedded in the cultural traditions of the human groups involved in

S. Forero-Lloreda (✉) · J. E. Zarate · C. A. Angulo
Universidad Jorge Tadeo Lozano, Bogotá, Colombia
e-mail: santiago.lloreda@utadeo.edu.co; johanna.zarate@utadeo.edu.co; camilo.angulo@utadeo.edu.co

L. Ronda et al. (eds.), *Leisure and Human Development*, Human Well-Being Research and Policy Making, https://doi.org/10.1007/978-3-031-90778-4_11

the restorative leisure characterisation study. The most effective method for identifying the specificities of this social phenomenon is the systematisation of experiences (Mejía, 2012).

In this publication, the study group, research approach, and structure will be presented, alongside the results underpinning the concept of restorative leisure. The focus is on the community of young people from the Muisca indigenous cabildo in Suba, a locality northwest of Bogotá D.C., the capital of Colombia (Forero & Lazcano, 2024).

11.1.1 Context and Background to the Emergence of Restorative Leisure

Colombia is a country whose history has been shaped by various forms of structural violence, including discrimination, exclusion, racism, and inequality—all of which stem from the processes of colonisation. These colonial processes, deeply embedded in the structure of the State, have perpetuated modes of governance that obstruct meaningful and transformative social change. This situation has exacerbated socio-economic disparities, particularly among the nation's most vulnerable populations (Quiceno, 2016).

Over more than two centuries since the establishment of the Republic, during which Colombia nominally declared its independence, the most autochthonous populations with deeper ancestral roots have remained marginalised—both geographically and ideologically. This marginalisation reflects an imbalance between citizens whose human development is largely oriented by Western ideologies of life and those whose cultural frameworks stem from the cosmogony of native peoples. The disparity in access to fundamental rights continues to grow (Escobar, 2017).

The persistent tensions and invisible barriers created by these dynamics hinder access to various forms of social and human welfare. These barriers are further compounded by the fact that welfare models are neither generalisable nor adaptable to the diverse communities inhabiting Colombia's national territory. On one hand, such models primarily benefit "mestizo" society, which aligns more closely with Western doctrines and life purposes. On the other hand, they neglect indigenous populations whose spiritual, political, and social systems are deeply rooted in the cosmogony of *Abya Yala*—a term used by the tribes of Panama and Colombia to describe the Latin American territory.

In this context, a new dimension of knowledge has begun to emerge, shedding light on an unprecedented category within leisure studies. While forms of leisure have been extensively characterised within Western thought, there has been comparatively little recognition of leisure as it relates to the identity and idiosyncrasies of precolonial communities that still exist today, albeit under conditions of cultural and geographic exclusion (Forero, 2023).

The most significant connection this research establishes with contemporary leisure studies lies in two key insights. First, it recognises ancestral practices and experiences within the Latin American context that use time to foster wellbeing. Second, it demonstrates that leisure, when understood from this perspective, can serve as a means to achieve social rights in unconventional ways. This is particularly relevant when public policies fail to adequately support populations that neither identify with nor benefit from such policies. Consequently, this emerging analytical category has been termed *restorative leisure* (Forero, 2023).

11.1.2 Systematisation of Experiences in Restorative Leisure

The systematisation of experiences has been a methodology widely used in research associated with Latin American decolonial studies. For this reason, some of the most vibrant inquiries in this region have identified rich objects of study in the consolidation of academic fields. These inquiries clarify and propose alternatives that contrast with Western thought and, in general, support the claims of the most forgotten and marginalised communities in the region (Mejía, 2012).

Through interventions called *living laboratories* of creation (Fig. 11.1), researchers engage for significant periods through participant observation (Restrepo, 2016). These laboratories establish favourable environments for integrative coexistence, fostering practices and experiences intrinsic to the social phenomena rooted in the identity of the communities. They also emphasise collaborative and cooperative interaction, recognise festivity as a driver of social change, and encourage intergenerational encounters that balance tradition with the future. Researchers, therefore, act as mediators between the aims of the inquiry and the voice and action of the

Fig. 11.1 Live creation laboratory presentation: "Go ahead, paint without compromise"

communities. They collaborate with participants to determine the study's objectives, recognition and analysis categories, methodologies, and relevant findings (Forero & Lazcano, 2024).

For the present intervention, three key areas of recognition were established: (a) alternative ways of achieving social rights, given that the Colombian State does not provide for them; (b) the meaning of festivity in restorative processes within vulnerable communities; and (c) the characterisation of a new leisure sphere that complements—from their perspective—others rooted in Western thought (Richter & Cuenca, 2018).

Education, health, coexistence, participation, and work—viewed from an ancestral perspective—were central to the recognition process guiding this research. As these dimensions are consubstantial to human dignity, they were identified as the driving force behind the community's festive practices, which promote cooperative ethics. This approach diverges from the competitiveness, progress, or development emphasised in classical Western ideology, instead fostering a notion of human flourishing centred on the protection and care of life (Nussbaum, 2012).

These aspects draw attention to a situated notion of Latin American leisure, where time is organised and used differently from the compartmentalised allocation of work, study, rest, free time, and fun common in Western contexts (Gomes, 2017). The study reveals that ancestral practices of overlapping times and activities do not necessarily follow chronological distinctions in daily routines. Instead, festivity emerges as a driver of social change, advancing learning, healing, environmental adaptation, and other social processes.

The development of the systematisation of experiences, agreed upon by the researchers and the Muisca youth community, fostered an intercultural relationship. Its central objective was to demonstrate how time is used for restoring basic social rights and how the joy associated with certain festive practices acts as a catalyst for social transformation.

For this study, the concepts of subjectivity and resilience serve as synthetic translations that unify the community around actions supporting their vindicatory ideology. These concepts operate as categories of recognition in the systematisation process, helping to understand the potential of restorative leisure as a tool for social transformation.

The process of systematising experiences relies on words, arguments, ideas, images, and life stories recorded in audio-visual and material media, providing qualitative evidence of what resilient and restorative subjectivity entails for the community. As will be detailed in the methodological development and the step-by-step evolution of the laboratory, the research team sought to uncover the origins of the circumstances motivating the community. They explored how critical aspects of their discomfort are transformed into activism through the plastic expression of their artistic works, from ideation to materialisation.

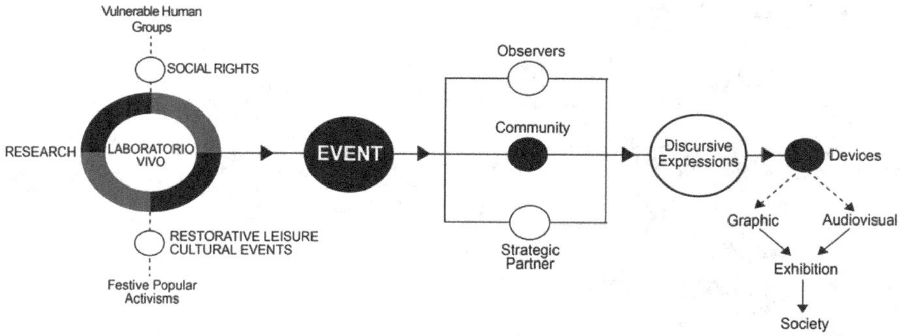

Fig. 11.2 Replicable model living creation laboratory (*laboratorio vivo*): "Go ahead, paint without compromise"

11.2 Live Creation Laboratory: "Go Ahead, Paint Without Compromise"

It is pertinent to mention that living laboratories of creation have been consolidated in various contexts as platforms for open innovation. Intervention and action are driven by a shared motivation among participants, providing a space for ideation, simulation, and prototyping of new ideas that emerge through imagination as a precursor to transforming realities (Bravo, 2019). By leveraging the possibilities of language as a psychological tool of a higher order—and in this case employing subjectivity and resilience—it has been possible to determine how these two human capacities are linked to the social demands of the community. These connections are reflected in the final works, both through the verbal descriptions provided by the young Muisca and in the aesthetic content of their creations.

Given the exploratory nature of this research, which examines the experimental dimension of the social phenomenon defined by the role of festivity in social transformations within vulnerable communities—as a manifestation of leisure with restorative purposes—it was agreed with the youth of the Muisca indigenous cabildo to implement a living laboratory of creation. This laboratory's participatory dynamics followed four phases, resulting in a replicable model (Fig. 11.2) for future interventions.

11.2.1 Conceptualisation of Restorative Leisure

The conceptualisation of restorative leisure emerged through dialogic engagement with the Muisca youth, focusing on their interpretation and use of time to sustain and prioritise their ways of being and inhabiting their territory. In this first stage of the laboratory, and in alignment with a systematisation that values the voices of the

Fig. 11.3 Living laboratory of creation: "Voices of the community involved"

community, an autonomous characterisation of restorative leisure was developed (Fig. 11.3).

The results show that Muisca youth associated leisure and restorative practices with the following concepts derived from their cosmogony:

- Associated with leisure: freedom, autonomy, pleasure, doodling, parkour, *bihote* (party), guard, inspiration, music, spending time, self-awareness, free time.
- Associated with restorative: create, freedom, weave, language, denounce, phoenix, resurgence, new opportunities, recover what was lost, memory lifeline, return to order, recreational activities, healing.
- Associated with resilient and restorative subjectivity (Fig. 11.4): making political decisions, public spaces for training, popular pedagogy, collective lands, memory and tradition, care of wetlands.

11.2.2 Construction of a Claim Manifesto

In reflecting their concerns as citizens of native communities (Fig. 11.5) and their desire to preserve Muisca cosmogony, the youth created a manifesto asserting their rights.

During this second stage of the laboratory, and consistent with a systematisation that surveys the primary motivators of indigenous activism, the following key points were included in the manifesto:

- The precedent was set: "Forgetfulness of primary heritage in favour of privileging Western culture".

Fig. 11.4 Living laboratory of creation: "Resilient and restorative subjectivity"

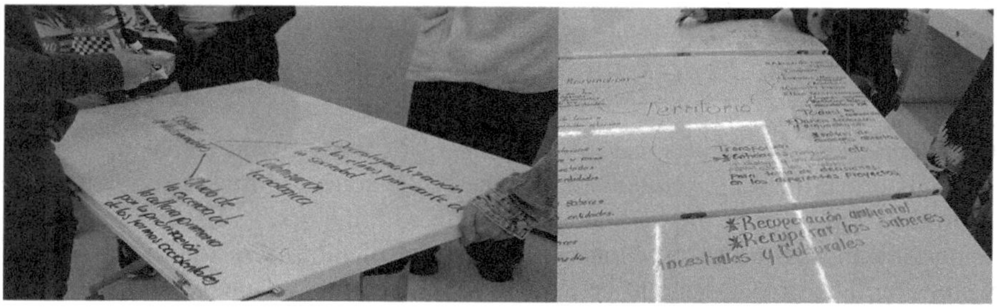

Fig. 11.5 Living laboratory of creation: "Concerns as citizens belonging to native communities"

- It was argued that: "It is necessary to avoid stigmatizing ethnic groups within Western society."
- It was mentioned that: "Technological colonization has co-opted identity and created monetary oppression."
- It was agreed that: "The lack of freedom and leisure expression affects mental and emotional health, compromising self-awareness and cultural identity."
- It was stated that: "The territory represents the union between habitat and body. It drives the struggle to recover the essence of the word through language, memory, education, and family."
- It was said that: "Freedom is limited by money and status, leading to forced displacement, inadequate education, and poor quality of life".
- It was agreed that: "The territory is the origin of environmental recovery and acts as a regulator to mitigate the destruction of fauna and flora caused by uncontrolled urbanization."

Fig. 11.6 Living laboratory of creation "Representations and narratives"

11.2.3 Graphic Representation and Creation of Artistic Works

Graphic representation was used as a means of expression and activism, drawing from historical memory, symbolism, and the visual signs of Muisca tradition.

In the third stage of the laboratory, aligning with the first two stages, the representations and narratives associated with the use of time in restorative processes were externalised, and the topics central to Muisca community activism were established (Fig. 11.6). Following this groundwork, the research team facilitated the creative processes associated with the artistic expression of the youth.

11.2.4 Exhibition of Creative Works

The artistic works produced during this process were employed as mechanisms of denunciation and activism, reflecting the social and human rights issues relevant to the community's identity and aspirations for human flourishing.

In the fourth and final stage of the laboratory, the complete cycle of the process culminated in a public exhibition of the creative works (Fig. 11.7). This exhibition provided tangible evidence of the diverse conceptions of leisure time, its purposes, and the native approaches to managing fundamental rights that matter to the community.

Finally, as a methodological approach for future interventions aimed at recognising other expressions of restorative leisure, the configuration of a replicable

Fig. 11.7 Public exhibition of creative works

laboratory model is proposed. This laboratory model can be implemented using a participatory and adaptive approach, allowing different communities to contextualise and customise the process. The approach includes providing detailed guidelines for the conceptualisation of restorative leisure, facilitating workshops for the construction of claim manifestos, and offering resources for the graphic representation and creation of artistic works.

Additionally, a platform can be established for the exhibition of these works as mechanisms for denunciation and activism, ensuring that each community can express its concerns and aspirations in a manner that is authentic and relevant to its cosmogony and cultural context. Currently, an autonomous research project is being developed on the platform of the Observatory in Design and Creation at Jorge Tadeo Lozano University in Bogotá, Colombia, to further this purpose.

11.3 Articulating the Methodological Process with the Intervention

As mentioned, for restorative leisure, resilient and restorative subjectivity establishes its scope by systematising experiences carried out throughout the living laboratory of creation in its four phases.

Through the audio-visual materials used in the research, the occurrence of these concepts is recognised through the recording of the voices and actions of the young participants in the laboratory: "Go ahead, Paint without Compromise", from which relevant information was obtained to clarify the restorative capacity of leisure in ancestral practices that claim access to fundamental rights embodied in artistic works. Initially, the *dialectic systematisation* (Mejía, 2012) operated on the recovery of the community's memory through semi-structured surveys recorded in a micro-documentary created for this purpose. Similarly, and with the same type of systematisation, phases I and II of the living laboratory of creation "Go ahead, Paint without Compromise" were carried out. In the first phase, the most relevant ideas regarding the concepts of leisure and restoration were systematised. In the second, the most powerful arguments supporting the creation of the vindicatory manifesto were classified. In the third and fourth phases, the methodology of systematisation as *a look of knowledge over practice* (Mejía, 2012) was applied to the sketching process and the final configuration of artistic works, respectively.

11.3.1 Dialectical Systematisation

Dialectical systematisation, through its methodological approach, establishes that interaction mediated by dialogue allows for an understanding of the circumstances of the members of the studied community. It uses conversation and the exchange of ideas through an exercise of inquiry and response that addresses the evolution of a specific activity. As this activity takes shape in tangible evidence, it becomes possible to identify arguments that bring out motivations, aspirations, and reasons that justify the decisions made by the community (Mejía, 2012).

The analysis of the narratives and artistic expressions of the participants through dialectical systematisation allows for understanding the strategies employed by the community to preserve its identity and reclaim its place in society. As a recording substrate, the resulting micro-documentary—the product of this collaborative process—(Fig. 11.8) becomes a moving testimony of the resilience and creativity of the indigenous people, inviting critical reflection on power relations and the construction of collective memory.

The documentary outlines important narratives that, extracted from the participants' life stories through semi-structured interviews, place the environment, work associated with the identification and appropriation of the territory, the discovery of traditional medicines through native plants, the use of coca leaves and tobacco to honour the spirits, and the practice of dances and rituals to maintain collective

Fig. 11.8 Image of the micro-documentary, living laboratory of creation: "Go ahead, paint without compromise"

cohesion and reinforce their cosmogony at the centre of the argumentative interest. This reveals the complexities of the Indigenous experience in the urban context, which, despite being marked by migration, violence, and discrimination, maintains a relationship of balance and reciprocity with the land, others, and the community.

As this research delves into the experience of the living laboratory, exploring how art becomes an instrument of memory, empowerment, and social transformation, it becomes evident through the constructed graphics, collective creation of urban murals, and orality, how a vibrant narrative is woven that resists invisibilisation and celebrates the cultural richness of native peoples.

Dialectical Systematisation Results

As a result of the dialectical systematisation (Mejía, 2012), and informed by the semi-structured interviews that sought to clarify the resilient and restorative subjectivity in the narratives of the Muisca youth group, the following vindicatory ideas were noted:

- The need to establish respect for Muisca ways of life associated with the preservation and care of the territory.
- The importance of cultivating the customs and rituals created by their ancestors in terms of understanding and comprehending the role of nature as a source of inspiration and coexistence between animals, plants, things, and people.
- The preservation of the Muisca language, clothing, attire, music, and values that generate an identity for the community.
- Ancestral education and curative medicines as forms of human development consubstantial to their beliefs, as well as graphic representations, modes of interaction, and associations (*mingas*) for the welfare of their fellow human beings.

Beyond a concern for individual growth, their sense of community and collaboration stands out.

11.3.2 Systematisation as a Look of Knowledge Over Practice

Systematisation as a look of knowledge over practice, through its methodological approach, establishes that, in the materialisation of actions, it is possible to perceive the emergence of adaptive knowledge developed from generation to generation that sustains the evolutionary process of communities with common socio-demographic characteristics, producing identity and cultural roots related to the organisation of the different social processes that represent them (Mejía, 2012).

From the living laboratory of creation, there is a great interest in understanding the graphic representation and creation of artistic works as a device that can use restorative leisure, enabling a community to elaborate a social process of reparation after having been silenced for various reasons. This process allows the community to recover, to some extent, its historical memory, symbology, and visual signs, which in this particular case correspond to elements of the Muisca tradition in Colombia.

The expressions cultivated through the community's knowledge, their plastic means of expression, and their methods of management and communication made it possible to visually narrate—to a foreign audience—stories about their understanding of spatial-temporal relationships, without using words, through a visual discourse that referred to the existence of natural, mythical, and fantastic worlds (Fig. 11.9). These impressions materialised during the laboratory through drawings by the participants, charged with the transcendence of a collective visual memory and an interpretation of realities (Buitrago, 2019).

Connecting with studies on the visual discourse of ancestral Latin American civilisations such as the Olmec, Maya, Xochilcas, and Aztecs, we can highlight multiple figures that represent concepts traditionally captured in paintings, sculptures, or textiles, referred to as glyphs by semioticians, sociologists, and anthropologists. These serve as keys to the past, which allow for the articulation of traces of pre-Columbian practices with urban traces of their contemporary representatives, recognising an aesthetic identity through formal configurations. These configurations, apparently based on both material and immaterial understandings of animal referents, invite us to explore the boundaries of traditional Western knowledge and begin to coexist with past, present, and even future realities (Restrepo, 2016).

During the development of the laboratory, three compositions stood out from a more complex construction of glyphs, allowing us to highlight the interconnected visual connections found in the community's social dynamics. The interpretation of these connections focused on data visualisation and social representations, understood from the "Circles of Wisdom" concept developed by researcher Manuel Lima

Fig. 11.9 Living laboratory of creation. Sketches drawn from natural, mythical, and fantastic worlds

(2017). This visual perspective transcends disciplinary boundaries and explores intertwined information from both the past and present in a social fabric (Figs. 11.10 and 11.11).

This accumulation of human knowledge throughout history presents unique insights into the cyclical nature of data acquisition, which intertwines and evolves over time. From the interpretation of Lima's (2017) approaches, the representation of circles has been used throughout history as a visual method of constructing knowledge and culture in societies (Fig. 11.12). These representations can be seen in ancient star maps, modern network diagrams, and community claims, capturing the very essence of ideas and information as fundamental elements of identity, expression, and reparative experiences in the social fabric.

Each of these wisdom circles is a manifesto in itself, with a unique combination of colours, shapes, and lines that embody the concepts and connections uniting civilisations in timeless ways. By structuring and organising knowledge in innovative ways, these circles become blank canvases upon which communities can

Fig. 11.10 Living laboratory of creation: drawings reflecting pre-Columbian practices with urban traces

Fig. 11.11 Living laboratory of creation: interwoven information of past and present in a social fabric

Fig. 11.12 Living laboratory of creation: circles of wisdom

express their own narratives, assert their identity, and demonstrate their agency in human history.

Results of Systematisation as a Look of Knowledge Over Practice

The primary function of this systematisation process (Mejía, 2012) is to recognise, in the situated action and graphic expression of the community, the translations they make of their narratives using their glyphs. Through abstract or figurative representations, and through the explanations provided by the Muisca youth during each step of the process, it became clear how geometric, humanoid, phytomorph, or anthropomorphic representations describe the integration and consubstantiality of humans with animals and the earth in a cosmogony that privileges equality between humans and non-humans.

The sun, moon, and colours, in an abstract way, represent rituals and the times in which they occur, seeking to generate mythical interconnections. This aspect is crucial, from the perspective of leisure, to note the unconventional relationship the community has with time through festivity, as compared to the Western concept of time. The *jolgorio* (popular party) is tied to agricultural cycles and the stages of maturity, during which young people, as part of their formative growth, acquire responsibilities towards the collective and the preservation of their customs and identity.

The above is compiled from phase three of the laboratory, where the purpose was the recovery of initial expressions. In phase four, corresponding to the public exhibition of the finalised works, the systematisation focused on recognising the works as a whole and clarifying the community's vindicatory messages, both through the narrative explanation of the works and their aesthetic perception.

In summary, the activism embodied in the final artistic works aims not only to send a message—through pictorial expression—that explains the complexities of the Muisca cosmogony in relation to their ways of life, but also to demand respect in order to preserve them. Furthermore, these works express what is important to them in terms of the formative process of their individuals, contrasting values with Western cultures, and their expectations regarding their survival. As seen in the different works, the integration of nature's beings with mythical representations enacts a reality where the spiritual and earthly realms are not separated. The confluence of musical instruments, elements of the earth, and animals explains the rituals that honour life. Bright colours highlight the dreamlike and imaginative aspects, representing a reality made possible through the use of coca leaf and tobacco.

11.4 Discussion and Final Conclusions

It is important to highlight the emerging theoretical heritage of Restorative Leisure from the communities' own practices and experiences (Forero, 2023). Through this experimental way of producing knowledge, it is essential to validate ancestral knowledge as an alternative that equates the structure of information and data traditionally obtained through purely Western methodological perspectives (Tuhiwai, 2012).

The so-called Systematisation of Experiences of Latin American origin turns out to be a mode of collaborative interaction that seeks to create agreements between researchers and working communities (Mejía, 2012). This methodological approach, central to the research, seeks to find mechanisms for joint work that, agreed upon by all actors involved, prioritise the cosmogony of the Muisca youth, primarily recognising their social construction of reality. This includes integrating the spiritual dimension with the social processes they engage in, around their ways of being in the world, thereby clarifying their particular diversity as an indigenous people.

The framework for the meeting, referred to in the research as the Living Laboratory of Creation: "Go ahead, paint without compromise", served as a catalyst for situated action. From this, it was possible to concentrate the collaborative work around the transformations of the Muisca youth. For the research, finding a mechanism for the ideation and materialisation of the vindicatory ideology of these young people was fundamental. By associating the time of creation with the community's own rituals, a common objective emerged in the sketches and works made. These works manifest the youth's desire to achieve fundamental rights, offering an original and unprecedented way of addressing their discomfort and inequities (Forero & Lazcano, 2024).

Finally, as a conclusion for the research on Restorative Leisure (Forero, 2023), it is valuable to establish this concept as an analytical category of social research, constructed from the knowledge and idiosyncrasy of the communities. This is especially important when these communities demonstrate that, in their use of available time, community demands form the pillar of their motivations. Moreover, through their cultural practices and experiences, they achieve materialisations for their welfare that go beyond those provided by public policies meant to care for them.

References

Bravo, E. (2019). Revisión sistemática del concepto de laboratorios vivos. *Dimensión Empresarial, 18*(1), 78–104. https://doi.org/10.15665/dem.v18i(1).2018

Buitrago, O. (2019). *El poder didáctico de las historias*. Alfahomega.

De Lima, M. (2017). *Book of circles: Visualizing spheres of knowledge*. Princeton Architectural Press.

Escobar, A. (2017). *Autonomía y diseño: La realización de lo comunal* (1st ed.). Tinta Limón.

Forero, A. (2023). *El ocio restaurativo en la reparación colectiva: Una aproximación emergente desde los laboratorios vivos de creación* [Unpublished doctoral thesis]. Universidad de Deusto.
Forero, A., & Lazcano, I. (2022). Aplicaciones, extensiones y transformaciones del ocio serio en actividades restaurativas: Casos urbanos y rurales en Colombia. In A. Madariaga & M. Rodrigo (Dirs.), *Ocio saludable y construcción de ciudadanía* (pp. 68–79). Aranzadi.
Forero, A., & Lazcano, I. (2024). El ocio restaurativo: Un modelo práctico de intervención y creación situada para la construcción de derechos sociales. In A. De Juanas, F. García, H. Hossein, & H. Hossein (Coords.), *Juventud y autorregulación del tiempo: Intervención socioeducativa para el bienestar integral* (pp. 277–291). Dykinson.
Gomes, C. (2017). Leisure in Latin America: A conceptual analysis. In K. Spracklen et al. (Eds.), *The Palgrave handbook of leisure theory* (pp. 71–83). Palgrave Macmillan. https://doi.org/10.1057/978-1-137-56479-5
Mejía, M. (2012). Sistematización: Una forma de investigar las prácticas y de producción de saberes y conocimientos. *Viceministerio de Educación Alternativa y Especial.*
Nussbaum, M. (2012). *Crear capacidades: Propuesta para el desarrollo humano*. Paidós.
Quiceno, N. (2016). *Vivir sabroso: Luchas y movimientos afroatrateños, en Bojayá, Chocó Colombia*. Universidad del Rosario. https://doi.org/10.12804/th9789587387506
Restrepo, E. (2016). *Etnografía: Alcances, técnicas y éticas*. Envión Editores & Pontificia Universidad Javeriana.
Richter, F., & Cuenca, J. (2018). Huertos de ocio y vida comunitaria: La agricultura urbana como experiencia de participación ciudadana. In A. Madariaga & A. Ponce de León (Eds.), *Ocio y participación social en entornos comunitarios* (pp. 189–214). Universidad de la Rioja.
Tuhiwai, L. (2012). Caminando sobre terreno resbaladizo: La investigación de los pueblos nativos en la era de la incertidumbre. In N. Deniz & Y. Lincoln (Coords.), *El campo de la investigación cualitativa: Manual de investigación cualitativa* (Vol. 1, pp. 190–230). Gedisa.